"Craig Hall has written a book for the bedside table of every entrepreneur, for it shows how dreams come true, through work, community, and faith in the process of life. I strongly recommend women entrepreneurs read this book. These inspiring and instructive stories will expose them to the enduring greatness of their own dreams and offer invaluable guidance to help make those dreams a reality."

—Shina Richardson,
founder of TDA, Inc., and member
of Social Venture Network

"Hall's book clears away the noise around entrepreneurship without losing the excitement. His book both teaches and inspires."

—Dr. Stephen Spinelli, Jr.,
Director, Arthur M. Blank Center
for Entrepreneurship, Babson
College, and a founder of Jiffy Lube
International, Inc.

"THE RESPONSIBLE ENTREPRENEUR is both thought provoking and compelling. It profiles inspiring, real people who have made a difference—people who contributed not just for money, but to also enrich the lives of others."

—Roger Staubach,
Hall of Fame quarterback for the
Dallas Cowboys and Chairman and
CEO of The Staubach Company

"This book is full of poignant insights. My highlighter ran out of ink not a third of the way through."

—W. Michael Cox,
Senior Vice President and Chief
Economist, Federal Reserve Bank
of Dallas; co-author (with Richard
Alm) *Myths of Rich and Poor*

THE
RESPONSIBLE
ENTREPRENEUR

How To
Make
Money
and
Make a Difference

By
Craig Hall

CAREER
PRESS
Franklin Lakes, NJ

THE RESPONSIBLE ENTREPRENEUR
Edited by Dianna Walsh and Mike Lewis
Typeset by Eileen Munson
Cover design by DesignConcept
Printed in the U.S.A. by Book-mart Press

To order this title, please call toll-free 1-800-CAREER-1 (NJ and Canada: 201-848-0310) to order using VISA or MasterCard, or for further information on books from Career Press.

The Career Press, Inc., 3 Tice Road, PO Box 687,
Franklin Lakes, NJ 07417
www.careerpress.com

Library of Congress Cataloging-in-Publication Data

Hall, Craig, 1950-
    The responsible entrepreneur : how to make money and make a difference / by Craig Hall.
        p. cm.
    Includes index.
    ISBN 1-56414-581-6
        1. Entrepreneurship. 2. Social responsibility of business. I. Title.

HB615 .H2334 2001
658.4'08—dc21

                                        2001035877

To Kathy,
my partner
and
best friend

— ✦ —

Acknowledgments

This book was truly a team effort. I required a lot of guidance from those mentioned here and others. Thanks so much to all involved.

Those Friends Written About in the Book

Special thanks go to the real friends whose stories I've written about in this book, with the hope and belief that their stories help explain the concept of being a responsible entrepreneur and inspire others to do the same. They are, in order from the book: Steve Mariotti, Gerry Hargitai, Doraja Eberle, Albert C. Black, Jr., Katharine Wittmann, Bernard Rapoport, Kenny Blatt, Adrian Draghici, Petra Groiss, Fahim Tobur, Ambassador Richard Schifter, Trevor Cornwell, Don Braun, Cheryl Newman, Viktor Lantos, Tamas Perlaki, Patrick Brandt, and Rabbi Arthur Schneier. Many, many thanks for your time, effort, help, and commitment to this project.

Research and Background

This book started with what I found to be the difficulties in the transition from Communism to free markets in Central and Eastern Europe. In addition to my own business experiences and working for the Southeastern European Cooperative Initiative, I also attended school and received a graduate degree from the Diplomatic Academy in Vienna, specializing my efforts on subjects concerning Central and Eastern Europe. Werner Neudeck, my advisor and economics professor, and too many other great professors to list, were very helpful in bringing this region into focus. Additionally, I interviewed more than 100 businesspeople (mostly from Austria) who did business in and knew Central and Eastern Europe well. One who stands out for giving me a lot of time and help is the Chairman of Bank Austria, Gerhard Randa. Others generous with their time and help include George Jaksity, Herbert Stepic, John Leake, Witold Szymanski, and my partner Gavin Susman.

Writing, Editing, and Publication

Thanks also to the great team of so many that helped in the actual writing and preparation of this book, which evolved during three years. After the first year-and-a-half there was an entire manuscript prepared with the research, collaboration, and writing assistance of Cheryl Newman, who is now president of Skytech Europe in Budapest. Cheryl stayed with the project and went on to be key in the revised current book even though her Skytech activities have consumed her time. Sally Stephenson, who helped edit and write my last book, also helped extensively on this project. She is excellent at editing, writing, generally bringing out "my voice," and making things readable and fast moving. Mark Blocher has been instrumental in research, editing, writing, and encouraging me through the whole process of the three years. Monica Goldman, Jennifer Smith, and Becky Neuenschwander, all assistants of mine, helped in the typing of numerous drafts. Becky also worked very hard with Mark in the editing. Melinda Jayson did a detailed review and edit. Patricia Meadows, Gary Brewster, Joe Mathewson, Charley Wise, Ambassador Richard Sklar, Ambassador Richard Shifter, Ambassador Jim Rosapepe and Sheilah Kast Rosapepe, Ambassador Joe Presel, Harvey Lee, Diane Lynne, Trevor Cornwell, Gerry Hargitai, Carole Cohen, Tony Gumbiner, Paul Goriup, Mark Alley, Fahim Tobur, Doraja Eberle, Katharine Wittmann, Vebi Velije, and my son-in-law Michael Hahsler, among others, read, commented, and helped me revise where needed. I am particularly thankful to Harvey Lee and Ambassador Joe Presel, who both really critiqued my early manuscript in a constructive way that urged changes that ultimately led to a clearer focus, and to Dedi Leahy for her thoughtful comments.

As the book is now moving quickly into production, I have chosen to go with a very entrepreneurial and exciting publisher, Career Press, owned and run by Ron Fry. Working with Ron and associate publisher Anne Brooks and the rest of the Career Press team is great. I knew when I met Ron and Anne that they were the right choice for this book.

Last, but far from least, my deepest thanks to Kathy, who despite her pressing ambassadorial duties and very limited time gave me continual encouragement and reviewed the book several times and to our children, Melissa, Brijetta, Kristina, David, and Jennifer for their constant support.

CONTENTS

FOREWORD

During the past 23 years, the citizens of South Dakota have blessed me with the opportunity to serve in the United States Senate and House of Representatives. As such, I have been able to observe and to participate in the development of a broad array of public policies. In my view, the best of these policies have consistently been those that provide a mechanism to encourage and empower Americans to not only achieve personal success, but also to help others. At our best, we create an environment wherein, as the late President Kennedy said, "a rising tide lifts all boats."

In developing our cities, protecting our environment, training and retraining our work force, and educating our youth, to list a few examples, responsible Americans, encouraged by good public policy, have made and will continue to make a positive difference in our quality of life. At the same time, not all parts of our society have participated in or benefited from this approach. The American Dream remains outside their experience. I hope not for long. I share Craig Hall's view that part of the answer to our nation's challenges is to encourage responsible entrepreneurship. Real hope and opportunity for individuals to start or expand a business or otherwise take risk has made a positive difference in the past and can continue to do so.

Support for responsible entrepreneurism has value beyond our national borders. During my visits to former Communist countries, I have seen the positive influence of new democratic freedom and economic competition. At the same time, I have seen that many challenges lie ahead. Encouraging overseas the hope and opportunity that so many of us in America experience gives support not only to these transitioning countries, but also to our own interest in having international partners committed to democratic principles and free trade. In our increasingly interdependent world, America, as the sole world superpower, must be a responsible leader.

The American Dream, and the responsibilities this dream imposes on those lucky enough to experience it, is a story worth telling the world and retelling ourselves. We have made mistakes, to be sure, but we also have the great advantage that much of America has grown up with an almost innate sense of hope and opportunity.

Craig Hall lived the American dream, but he didn't fully understand the dream until fate and his brilliant ambassador wife combined to place him in Austria in 1997. For nearly four years, he traveled from the Ambassador's residence in Vienna through Central and Eastern Europe. There he met the entrepreneurs who are working to bring economic and political freedom to nations once hidden behind the Iron Curtain.

The Responsible Entrepreneur is, in part, his remarkable account of those travels. His introduction to more than a dozen unique entrepreneurs in Europe and America are illustrative of "responsible entrepreneurship"— the ability to "do good and do well" at the same time.

Part biography, part "how-to" guide, and part eyewitness account of history in the making, *The Responsible Entrepreneur* is a wonderful and invaluable tool for anyone who wants to make money—and make a difference.

—Senator Tom Daschle, Majority Leader

INTRODUCTION

In 1997 and 1998, almost 10 years after the fall of the Berlin Wall, it seemed to me that there would be great opportunities for entrepreneurs in Central and Eastern Europe. After an extensive look into the countries near Austria, I found to my surprise a huge difference in mindset between what I had been used to in America and what existed in these emerging democracies and transitioning free markets. Where I was used to hope and opportunity, the people in these countries were used to despair and abuse of the system.

Over time I decided to write a book directed at Central and Eastern Europeans to share the benefits of the American system and to tout the American Dream. As I completed drafts of that manuscript, I realized that segments of American society, primarily low-income pockets in major urban areas, had mind-set problems very similar to the population of Central and Eastern Europe. Though they were born in the United States, these people had been left out of the American Dream.

I began to realize that entrepreneurship, even in America, has been a dynamic and changing concept. Negative myths about entrepreneurs in the United States are not as pervasive as they are in Central and Eastern Europe, but they still exist. Over a three-year period, my thoughts evolved to broaden this book to include what I believe is an emerging trend in America and throughout the world: responsible entrepreneurism. This is a philosophy of starting business or other ventures, taking risks and doing things that are creative and different but not with the selfish, shallow view that one side has to lose for the other side to win. Indeed the message that this book sends is that entrepreneurs can and should be a vital part of improving the world. Entrepreneurs can and should work with each other to expand the pie so that both sides win. And when responsible entrepreneurs are celebrated for their important contributions, hopefully others will follow in their footsteps. The possibilities are endless.

PART ONE

AN ENTREPRENEUR'S

JOURNEY

Chapter 1

WE'RE NOT ALL
"J. R. EWING" –
10 MYTHS ABOUT ENTREPRENEURS

Not long after my family arrived in Vienna, I was shaving within earshot of the kids, who were watching television. I grinned when I heard the familiar cadence of the theme song from *Dallas* and joined them just in time to see the Dallas skyline and hear Larry Hagman, as the rapacious J. R. Ewing, say, "Guten Tag, meine Frau." I had never given much thought to the important role the United States plays in Europe, but it didn't take long to find out that bits and pieces of our culture, for better or worse, are everywhere. These old reruns of the selfish, greedy, underhanded J. R. dubbed in German are indicative of what shapes certain myths of entrepreneurs throughout the world.

Sadly, these myths or stereotypes about entrepreneurs exist in both America and Europe. This is especially true in low-income neighborhoods that have been excluded from the ideals of the American Dream and in former Communist countries striving to become free markets. There, entrepreneurs are seen as part of the problem rather than potentially important contributors of needed solutions. Admittedly, entrepreneurs are not easy to understand, but it is worthwhile to try to understand them because they make a positive difference in the world. With more broad-based understanding and support, entrepreneurs could contribute to the greater good on a more widespread basis. So let's bust these myths right now.

6 Myths About Entrepreneurs in Business
Myth #1: Entrepreneurs Only Care About Making Money!

Many people think entrepreneurs do what they do strictly for the money, and that taking risks is all about the entrepreneur's personal reward. While fear of poverty or use of money as a scorecard may have some relevance—and there are, of course, some entrepreneurs focused primarily on financial profits—generally, money is not the ultimate motivator for the majority of entrepreneurs.

Like most for-profit business entrepreneurs I know, including Albert Black, Gerry Hargitai, Bernard Rapoport, Katharine Wittmann, and the other "for-profit" entrepreneurs highlighted in this book, the money is really secondary to other goals. Money plays a role, but not the one you might expect. For example, Bernie Rapoport talks about an experience that puts his financial views into perspective. He explains that he was once frustrated with having spent the time to try on a suit without knowing how much it cost. He liked the suit, but, when the salesman told him it was on sale "for only $750," Bernie told him, "That's ridiculous, I don't pay more than $300 for suits." Bernie says that he would rather pay $300 and give the $450 left over to someone who needs it. Clearly, while Bernie believes his businesses should make money, it is not because he wants more material things for himself.

Overall, many entrepreneurs are like Bernie Rapoport—sometimes to a fault. Many successful entrepreneurs do not lead lavish lifestyles that reflect their financial success. Their motives are often more about ego and emotion. For most entrepreneurs, money is just a way to keep score. Money is also a way to do bigger and more exciting deals. The thrill of challenge, the motivation of a new idea, and the risks involved have far more power to motivate the entrepreneurial spirit than money.

Myth #2: Winning Means Somebody Else Is Losing!

For years, I have heard people speak of success in business as being "on the backs of others," suggesting that if an entrepreneur is winning, somebody else must be losing. This attitude makes it seem like the only possible outcome of a business deal is to have one side win and the other side lose. The resulting bottom line is zero. This is sometimes referred to as the "zero-sum game."

According to this theory, if one neighbor has three rabbits and another neighbor has two rabbits and they each want to have four, someone is going to end up with four in the end and someone is going to end up with only one. But entrepreneurs think differently. An entrepreneurial approach to this situation might be a quick check of who has male versus female rabbits. Negotiating an ability to mate one neighbor's female rabbit with another neighbor's male rabbit could easily end up with additional baby rabbits for everybody. Entrepreneurs are creative, expansionary thinkers. Rather than accepting a zero-sum result, and, contrary to the myth that an entrepreneur's success comes at the expense of others, entrepreneurs often try to figure out ways that both sides can win.

For virtually every entrepreneur in this book, winning is not accomplished in a vacuum where the sole objective is to achieve. Winning is a function of practical solutions to help people on the other side of negotiations so that they in turn will support the entrepreneur's plans and agendas. Albert Black gets more productivity and effort out of his employees because he isn't just asking them to work harder for money alone. Instead, he is providing them with education, profit sharing, and more importantly, respect and support to help them better their lives. Because of Albert's attitude, people want to work at his company, and they work extra hard to be their best. It is a win-win relationship—the kind that most entrepreneurs work for.

Myth #3: Nice Guys Finish Last!

Throughout my childhood, I constantly heard that "nice guys finish last." The popular thinking was that to succeed, one must be tough, selfish, and ready to do whatever it takes to beat the other side. Somehow, I always sensed that was not correct. While certainly it is fair to say that there are entrepreneurs who are not nice guys, it is by no means a requirement for success. To the contrary, many entrepreneurs who are nice, decent people build better relationships and, in turn, accomplish great things for that very reason.

The entrepreneurs in this book are nice people who are not finishing last. Albert Black helps his employees get educations. Doraja Eberle takes the time to listen to people's needs and remembers them as individuals. Busy insurance company owner Bernie Rapoport takes time out to personally teach low-income children how to read. Gerry

Hargitai is always available to come to give a speech or help others. These are all busy entrepreneurs who value being nice to other people as a real priority. They have succeeded not by being mean spirited or unfair, but by being good people.

Myth #4: If You Can Get Away with It, It's Okay!

We all know the business philosophy that says, "If everybody's doing it, I can do it too." I used to hear that phrase a lot in America in the 1980s, and now I hear it in Central and Eastern Europe. Around the world, bribery and technically illegal "shortcuts" are commonplace. Still, it's a big mistake to think that just because everyone else is doing something wrong, that taking the same shortcuts is the way to entrepreneurial success.

In the 1970s and '80s in Dallas, there were a number of business practices in real estate and in the savings and loan (S&L) industry that "everybody was doing" that were very profitable. For example, people who owned savings and loans and were also in the real estate business would loan money to one another on a more favorable basis than normal without proper underwriting standards. In other words, one real estate guy's S&L would make a loan to another real estate guy on a piece of land that was not worth as much as the loan in return for the other S&L making a similarly improper loan the other way. For years it seemed like the right thing to do and regulators turned their heads.

But then in the 1980s, regulators clamped down on savings and loans because of big losses and looked for people to blame. Many people I knew who were perceived by the community to be fine, upstanding citizens, found themselves being examined for violating legal lending technicalities. A large number of these people, including lawyers and political leaders, ended up in jail.

I can already see in the formerly Communist countries of Central and Eastern Europe that governments are changing informal rules and clamping down on corruption. People who engage in bribery or in making privatization deals by paying off government officials look like winners at the moment but, in time, they may end up under a punishing microscope. Not one of the entrepreneurs you'll meet in this book has rationalized his or her way to the top. Honesty pays the greatest long-term dividends.

Myth #5: The Greater the Risk, the Greater the Reward!

This myth is often passed on to young entrepreneurs as economic gospel. The theoretical relationship between risk and reward is coincidental at best, and then only in certain situations. Risk is a relative concept. All else being equal, real risks are modified by knowledge, experience, hard work, passion, and unforeseen circumstances. Equally important in considering risks, perception of risks is often different from reality. What one person considers high risk might be from another's perspective a sure thing. Who then can say what's a great risk or a great reward?

In my career, I have often done things others perceived to be very risky. Many of the properties my company bought were in terrible physical and financial condition and often were in default on debts. But I saw opportunity where others only saw problems. Risk is a concept that is totally dependent upon perception. Applying knowledge to any investment can change the risk profile. My company was one of the few in the United States that would take on problem properties. We were frequently sought out by owners to provide management expertise on properties that were not for sale. We had extra knowledge from past experience and, therefore, the risks associated with these properties often seemed insignificant to us, while others viewed them as overwhelming. Don't let anyone judge your reward by the size of a perceived risk.

Myth #6: As an Entrepreneur, You Can Get Rich Quick!

We've all heard of those dotcom millionaires. In the Internet/technology world, it sure seemed like people got rich overnight. But always remember that things often seem easier than they are. For every story of someone who got rich quick, there are three or four who failed and many others still struggling to succeed.

Sanjiv Sidhu, the founder and largest shareholder of i2 Technologies, is a friend of mine who appears to many people like someone who got rich quick. When i2 Technologies went public, his stock on paper was worth around $700 million. Since then it has gone up and his net worth is in the billions. That makes it look like he simply made a huge amount of money without much time or effort. But the truth is Sanjiv was an engineer who left a high-paying, secure job at Texas

Instruments to start i2 Technologies. He then spent many years working seven days a week with very little income and no assurance of success. He was fortunate that after years of hard work and sacrifice it all paid off, but his was hardly an overnight success.

This is very often the case. As described further in Chapter 15, the reality is that during the early years most entrepreneurs struggle to survive. It was years and years before I ever had any real financial success. Albert Black, Kenny Blatt, Bernard Rapoport, Gerry Hargitai, and all the other for-profit entrepreneurs in this book tell the same story.

The fact is, if you're going to become an entrepreneur and think you can make a quick killing, the more likely it is that you'll be killed quickly!

4 Myths About All Entrepreneurs

Myth #7: A Good Business Plan Is the Entrepreneur's Critical Roadmap to Success!

Venture capitalists often make business plans the key criteria in deciding whether or not to fund new companies. Business educators often talk about business plans like they are the Holy Bible of business success. The theory is that the better and more complete the business plan, the better the business will go. This is a myth.

While having an idea or a goal is critical, believing that you can create a structured business plan that will endure time or place is simply naïve. In the real world, it rarely happens. In Chapter 6, you'll see how Doraja Eberle committed to move 900 tons of food from Germany to Sarajevo before she had any real plan. First she thought she'd use trucks running 24 hours a day with lots of drivers sharing shifts. But, the fact is, that idea failed. She abandoned that plan and out of necessity tried using a train. Her situation is typical of a real entrepreneur's approach. Successful entrepreneurs know when to use creative problem solving rather than theoretical business plans.

Business plans can be useful initial tools, but they should be used only as guidelines. Trial and error, luck, creativity, flexibility, and adapting to unforeseeable developments ultimately are what make an entrepreneurial venture succeed.

Myth #8: You Can Be Taught to Be an Entrepreneur!

With all due respect to Harvard, Bill Gates quit school. Entrepreneurs are the least likely to fit in or finish graduate levels of formal education at great establishment schools. To say, "I can teach someone to be an entrepreneur," is an oxymoron. The entrepreneur is born in spirit and attitude, not out of a textbook. If you don't have it in you, no matter how many courses and degrees you get in entrepreneurship, you still won't feel comfortable taking the risks required of an entrepreneur. As Bernie Rapoport told me, "You can't teach someone to be an entrepreneur any more than you can teach him or her to become a great piano player or a great artist. You can teach the techniques of painting or piano playing, but only people who have the real skill for greatness can become a concert pianist or accomplished artist."

That said, I do believe in entrepreneurship education. Many great business teachers have helped their students explore entrepreneurial skills and opportunities, thus helping them discover the hidden entrepreneur within. When these students understand what entrepreneurism is really all about, some are inspired to take the leap into fields where they can be assertive, innovative, and creative—where their innate sense of entrepreneurism can be best utilized.

Myth #9: Entrepreneurs Must Start Young!

Many people believe that because entrepreneurs must be creative, innovative, insightful, and assertive risk takers, they must also be young. Don't buy it. When Ambassador Richard Schifter was turned down to be Undersecretary of State because, at age 72, he was considered to be "too old," he went on to serve on the National Security Council! There he started a whole new Southeastern European regional initiative. At age 76, he was working long intense days, outpacing individuals half his age with his energy and vitality.

Schifter is not an unusual case. Ray Kroc started McDonald's at age 52. Bernard Rapoport bought a new insurance company at age 83. Katharine Wittmann was 50 when she started her long fight for return of the family dairy. No more excuses—you're never too old.

Myth #10: Entrepreneurs Can Be Found Only in Business!

The stereotype of the entrepreneur is one who is the founder and owner of the for-profit business. But Webster's dictionary defines an entrepreneur as "a person who organizes and manages an enterprise, especially a business, usually with considerable initiative." No mention of the words "for profit" here. Even more broadly, my friend and entrepreneur expert Steve Mariotti tells me that the Center for Entrepreneur Leadership at Babson College defines entrepreneurs as "people who pursue resources not presently in their control and who have a vision of wanting." Steve believes, as I do, that being an entrepreneur has to do with mind-set: Entrepreneurs think differently from other people.

Entrepreneurs are risk takers, creators, innovators, and people who start things. They are people who dare to make their dream come true. Entrepreneurship is a way of acting out thoughts, and while often out of the mainstream, entrepreneurs are vital to the common progress and welfare of society. While entrepreneurs exist in business, they are also active in most other walks of life. In nonprofits, in education, in religion, and yes, even in government, we can discover entrepreneurs who are mavericks, creators, risk takers, and leaders who are making things happen.

Chapter 2

A Texas-Sized Fork in the Road – Rediscovering the Entrepreneur in Me

Sometimes, going far away helps us see things in closer definition and gives new perspective to things that we thought we already knew. My recent stay in Vienna, Austria, while my wife served out her tenure as U.S. ambassador has given me a new definition and new perspective on the world of entrepreneurship that I thought I knew so well. To understand how my view has changed, let me take you back to where I started.

I Was the Class Clown and a 90-Pound Weakling

I grew up a part of America's vast middle class. My mother was a Catholic from modest means. She was among the first group of women ever to enlist in the Navy, and she later became an art teacher. My father was from a Jewish family that had a thriving business that depended on imports from Germany. When my father was young, shortly before World War II, his family was wealthy and he was scheduled to attend Harvard University. But instead, Dad was drafted to fight for the Allies. By the end of the war, because the imports from Germany had been cut off, his family was flat broke.

My parents married after the end of the war while Dad was still in the service. He attended college briefly but soon left to work and support his new family. My recollections of my childhood are far from happy ones. I remember waking up in the hospital after having seizures when

I was two years old. The diagnosis was epilepsy. By age four or five, my seizures were fewer and more controlled by the drug Phenobarbital, which was prescribed for me until age 13. But the drug, a depressant, had a profound effect on my childhood and caused me to be deficient in every respect. It slowed me mentally, physically, and, indirectly, emotionally. By most objective views, I would have been the least likely to succeed as an adult at almost anything. While my older brother succeeded in school and sports and made my parents proud, I was a problem child. Throughout those years, I was barely able to pass from grade to grade. The consummate class clown, I was desperate for recognition and success.

In an effort to succeed at something, I tried athletics. The first day of football practice, I suited up with the other prospective team members and began doing drills. We all lined up to run and tackle a dummy that was held up by two chains. I ran as hard as I could, jumped up and barely hit the dummy. Hitting it much too high, burdened by heavy pads and gear, when I came down from this big jump I landed wrong and broke my ankle in several places. So much for football. It was clear this would not be my path to the spotlight.

Later in high school, I decided to try baseball. In all fairness, the coach did tell me to wear a mask when I played catcher. Stubborn and independent, I paid no attention to the advice. If you can believe it, the first day of practice, I was blinded by the sun and took a hard ball in the face, which severely broke my nose. Athletics were not to be my thing.

Thinking back, I now see that I never accepted my circumstances as a child. I wanted to change the hand that life had thus far dealt me. Even with medical obstacles in my way, I had a vision that if I worked hard I could do more, be better, and achieve anything. That outlook has always kept me going.

None of this basic ambition came as a result of being pushed by my family or any one person around me. Like many Americans, I simply believed in the American Dream. I did not realize any of this at the time, but I now see that the unique American environment greatly influenced me. While I was not a happy child, I still knew that in America, with hard work, I could succeed at almost anything.

Greenrivers Anyone?

I was only 10 years old when I started my first business, with 47 cents saved from returning empty bottles to a drugstore. One day that neighborhood drugstore had a large "Going Out of Business" sign displayed in its front window. I trudged in to express my disappointment to the owner, Mr. Shures. Our ensuing man-to-man talk helped me recognize that what I took to be an economic disaster was really a great opportunity.

The drugstore had a unique soda fountain drink called "Greenrivers." It was a sweet, green drink made with special syrup and carbonated water. Knowing that I was one of his best customers for Greenrivers drinks, Mr. Shures asked me if I was interested in buying his remaining syrup. I jumped at the opportunity. The problem was, I only had that 47 cents. When I described my financial situation, he suggested a price of 50 cents. I could quickly make up the difference by finding and returning some more bottles. We immediately shook hands on the deal. I ran around looking for bottles, and then went home to scoop up my change, anxious to become the proud owner of four bottles of gooey Greenrivers syrup.

I was now well on my way to starting a unique twist on the proverbial lemonade stand. Day after day, I went to my corner with a borrowed CO_2 cartridge and my Greenrivers syrup. At a nickel a glass, I truly made a killing. My investment of 50 cents grew to more than $37. Even at age 10 though, I could sense a serious business problem developing: My inventory of Greenrivers syrup was running out! I quickly realized that I had made a critical mistake. While I had bought the entire inventory that Mr. Shures had to sell, I did not have the formula or ability to make more syrup. I ran down to the drugstore hoping to find Mr. Shures and a remedy to the situation. Instead, I found the store closed and empty. Less than five days later, my Greenrivers sales company suffered a similar demise. I ended up grossing more than 100 times my money, but, sadly, with the end of the inventory, it was also the end of the Greenrivers stand.

It was not, however, the end of my youthful ventures in business. Greenrivers had sparked my interest in becoming an entrepreneur, and, for the next eight years, I worked at many jobs, saving all the money I could, with the general belief this would give me flexibility later in life. I washed pots and pans at a local restaurant for 75 cents an hour. I worked as a busboy at another restaurant. I was a night watchman in a large county barn, which was used to store road maintenance trucks. In the summer, I worked on a road crew shoveling gravel. I worked at a Goodyear tire store changing and plugging leaks in tires. I did not know what I would invest my earnings in, but my goal was clear: I wanted to make it something meaningful.

Looking back, I realize savings and investment are ideas that are not foreign to most American kids, not when I was a child and not today. In America, most of us grow up with positive feelings of individual empowerment to try things, start businesses, and spread our wings. It was not until much later that I realized my early entrepreneurial activities were not the type of thing all young Americans felt they could or should do. I have also learned this is very different in many other parts of the world. And, certainly in our country, some parts of our society and some neighborhoods are still left out of the American Dream.

H & B Coffee Services, and More

After the inventory demise of my Greenrivers business, I continued my entrepreneurial efforts interspersed by working at "real jobs." I always worked long hours at lots of jobs and saved my money to invest in the next idea.

At one point, I started a lawn-mowing business. This actually became a big success, but I'll explain more on that later. Another time, I delivered newspapers. I did many things that lots of children do, but I like to think I did them with a greater passion and aggressiveness. My determination was to make something of myself and eventually prove to those who put me down that they were wrong.

When I was 15, John Brownell, a friend of my older brother, and I were talking one day about a business idea that John had but couldn't get off the ground. John was 20 years old at the time and in college. He had read about a coffee service business where you could invest in small machines that would warm up water and then combine it with little packets of coffee, soup, tea, or hot chocolate so that the consumer could quickly get the hot drink of his choice. The idea was to place the machines for free in doctors' and dentists' offices and then sell them the packets of coffee and other items at a markup. John had invested $600 in the business venture and bought some machines but had failed to place any of them. He simply didn't have the time or initiative to make it happen.

We negotiated a partnership. We called the venture H & B Coffee Services. We used his machines and equipment, and I did the work, though at times because I was too young to drive he took me to meetings. The split that we negotiated was two-thirds to me for doing the work and one-third to John for having the initial $600 for machines and supplies. He also retained ownership of the machines because our partnership merely borrowed them. This was the first of many win-win relationships to come.

The venture worked well. It actually continued as a success for a couple of years. John was thrilled. He got more than his $600 back plus he had his machines to resell at the end of the business. It was good for me, but, after a couple of years, new machines made ours obsolete. I was off to other more exciting new ventures. By age 17, with all of these efforts, I had saved slightly more than $4,000.

Becoming "The Youngest Landlord" and Growing a Real Business

In my early teenage years, when business would come up in conversations with my uncle, he would tell me, "Business is a dirty game." Teachers in school would say, "Nice guys finish last in business," and, "You can't do well and do good." All of this affected me, but in reverse. I simply did not believe a businessperson could not be a good guy and succeed. While business was not my long-term goal, I was determined to prove that all of these people were wrong.

In 1967, while I was a high school senior in Ann Arbor, Michigan, University of Michigan tenants were fighting with the local landlords about everything from maintenance to the amount of rent. A "rent strike" started in which the local Tenant Union encouraged the students to withhold their rent. To most people this would not have been a time to invest, but to me it was exactly the right time. Over a 10-month period, I spent several days each week driving around with Bernice Schneider in her uncomfortable old car looking for any buildings I could afford with $4,000 as a down payment. Bernice was a kind, frail, older lady who had been a less-than-super successful real estate agent for many years. She was my first real estate teacher. She was also the only real estate broker willing to give me—a 17-year-old wanting to buy a building—the time of day.

On October 10, 1968, I bought 427 Hamilton Place in Ann Arbor, Michigan. I quickly found myself in the middle of the tenant-landlord rent strike. At age 18, I had taken the entire $4,000 I had saved from age 10 and used every penny as the down payment on a $27,250 purchase. I still owed the legal fees for the closing. This was planned as a one-time only real estate investment. Time, ambition, and circumstances eventually led to a real business. In 1968, it never crossed my mind that real estate or business in general would be my lifelong career.

As the proud new owner of this very rundown, old rooming house with eight rental rooms, a common kitchen and bathroom, a four-bedroom apartment on the ground floor, and a basement, I thought I could do the maintenance, treat everyone fairly, collect reasonable rent, and make a fair profit. Boy, was I ever wrong. Student tenants resented my being so young. They were constantly starting rent strikes. Also, having a variety of foreign students in my rooms made part of my job more like being a United Nations peacekeeper. The wide variety of odors from the kitchen was the source of many disagreements. Cleaning the shared kitchen and bathroom was one of my least pleasant daily tasks. This was hardly anyone's idea of the glory entrepreneurs are supposed to enjoy, but it is a fair representation of the real world of new businesses.

My ideal that if you are being a good guy the tenants will pay promptly did not immediately prove true. Indeed the whole idea of making money also proved to be an illusion. But I stayed with it. To pay for the losses my rooming house had (you read it right, losses), and to have a very modest personal living standard as a university freshman, I had to work a full-time job at a hospital moving heavy equipment. For the first two-and-a-half years of my expanding business, I was a university student and worked a 40-hour-a-week job. Finally, unable to do it all myself, I dropped out of the University of Michigan between my junior and senior year. Ironically, one of my professors, who tried to talk me into staying in school, a few short years later brought me back as a frequent guest lecturer in graduate level business classes on real estate.

For my first few years in business, I was the sole management company employee, maintenance person, cleaning person, investor relations person, and general jack-of-all-trades. I wasn't very good at all of these roles. My maintenance abilities were horrible. Often I would have to convince tenants that being too cold or too hot was more in their minds and that they ought to just be happy with the situation they were in; that is, I could not fix it and could not afford a real mechanic. Generally, my gift for making friends resulted in the tenants not staying mad at me. Ultimately, I always ended up scraping the money together to get things fixed. Soon, I had the overwhelming desire to expand my business.

From the second building on, I raised the needed down payment money for new purchases from individual investors who became my limited partners in partnerships I controlled and ran. Investment amounts were initially at $200 per investor, then in ever-growing sums as the properties we purchased grew in size and complexity. By the 1980s, individual investor amounts were averaging $150,000. But, whether the partnerships were sold in increments of $200 or $150,000, the concept was still the same. We were selling our ability to take a property that wasn't making money and turn it into a profitable investment over time. Sweetening the deal were the tax benefits investors got at that time for this type of real estate investment. Over 18 years, my companies raised more than $1 billion in private partnership equity for real estate limited partnerships.

Early Survival Requires Hard Work, Faith, and Being a Little Crazy

In the early years, in addition to working my full-time outside job, I took on property management from others while also running the partnership properties. This allowed me to make ends meet and grow the business. Desperate for cash flow, my property management company was known for its willingness to take on anything. Sometimes we would get what seemed to be the worst properties in the world. But we had some good clients, such as a bank that had a run-down, foreclosed property in a bad neighborhood. We also managed properties for the U.S. Department of Housing and Urban Development (HUD). HUD even gave us letters of commendation for collecting rent. Other management companies did not aggressively try to collect rent because their employees were fearful for their personal safety given the tenant profile.

Not all of my clients were of the high caliber of banks and HUD. One of our largest clients in the early years owned a property that everyone said was owned and, previously before us, managed by the Mafia. When we got the property management contract, the people who hired us neglected to tell their relatives and friends who were on site running the property that they were being replaced by us. I remember going in to take over the property and being lifted up by a very big guy in a dingy hallway. He pushed me against the wall, pulled a gun and said, "Until Rudy tells me, nobody is coming in here and taking over this property." Fortunately, Rudy confirmed by phone that I was okay, whereupon the guy put his gun away and shook my hand with a friendly, "Welcome." That was a truly strange experience, but it was just the first of what would be several working for Rudy and his partner Sam. In those situations, I learned to expect that their employees might just pull out a gun to stimulate conversation. In hindsight, when I think about the things that I did to ensure the business survived, even I am amazed.

After Survival Come Quantum Leaps

After the first six or seven years of growing but not achieving any real cash flow or profit, things finally started to improve. In the winter of 1974, we put together a partnership raising $1,100,000 from limited partner investors as the down payment for the $10,000,000 purchase of Woodcrest Villa, a 432-apartment unit property. In December 1974, we held our company Christmas party for the then 43 Hall Management employees at the Woodcrest Villa's clubhouse, which had an incredible indoor-outdoor swimming pool. Swimming outside while the snow was coming down at our company party made me feel like things could just never get better. Life was great!

In early 1975, I took an even bigger step. For most entrepreneurs, starting a business is often about struggle and survival. That can go on for a number of years. Then there are these quantum leaps. Sometimes things occur that can change your circumstances dramatically. The change can be financial, but it also can be in status, respect, or your approach to business. The point is, one day you're struggling, surviving, and just getting by, and, the next day, things just seem different and better.

In 1981, we opened regional offices in Dallas, Phoenix, and Atlanta. In 1983, we moved our headquarters to Dallas. I became part of the established entrepreneurial real estate community of Texas. Throughout my career, my company has owned, including properties sold, about 100,000 apartments. At one point in the mid-1980s, we owned 72,000 apartments and were then the second-largest apartment owner in the world. In partnership with others, I bought the Dallas Cowboy football team. My companies also diversified into other types of real estate and non-real estate businesses. At age 35, I was controlling $4 billion in assets and my net worth was close to $300,000,000. I was also on lots of civic boards, giving away a substantial amount of money to charity, and generally leading a prosperous and seemingly perfect life as an entrepreneur. But things don't always stay smooth, and, for me, this was just a calm before the storm that would change my life.

A "Can Do" Attitude: Taking the Bad with the Good

Aggressiveness and thinking big are innate characteristics of most Texans. This perpetual optimism, sometimes known as a "can do" attitude, is contagious. It was part of my impetus for moving my real estate company from Michigan to Texas. Texas was a growth market, and it seemed to most Texans, even recent transplants like me, that we couldn't have a serious downturn in real estate because of the strength of the area's overall economy. We expanded aggressively, becoming the largest apartment owner in Texas and the Southwest at the top of the boom.

On September 15, 1985, I was on top of the world, cruising along at 35,000 feet, sitting in the comfortable seats of the Dallas Cowboys chartered jet on the way to Detroit to play the Lions. Tex Schramm, president and general manager of the Cowboys, was across the aisle from me. Tom Landry, the legendary coach, was sitting behind me. I suppose this was just another game for most of the people on the plane. But for me it was a homecoming of sorts. In addition to being here for the game, I was hosting a business brunch for investors. I was on a winning streak and so were the Cowboys. No one, especially me, thought the Cowboys would lose that weekend. That weekend in Detroit was prophetic of things to come: No one had expected Dallas to lose the game, and probably no one expected that Hall Financial Group's winning streak would turn stone cold.

While the supply of residential and commercial real estate continued its aggressive expansion, demand began to plummet. The oil and gas industry had begun to falter in 1982 and continued to do so for the next two years. In 1985, many people thought the market had bottomed out, but 1986 was devastating. During the first six months of 1986, oil prices fell from $20 to $10 a barrel. While good for the East Coast, this was bad for Texas. Job loss in the oil industry was more severe than anyone could have predicted. A lot of the resulting unemployment was structural and permanent, and for the first time in recent Texas history, people were moving out of the state to find jobs.

One day there had been way too much money chasing deals, and the next morning the well dried up. Lenders were having their own problems with bad real estate and oil and gas loans on the books. The arrogance of the 1970s oil boom came back to haunt us: "Texas" was suddenly a dirty word in the money centers of New York and around the world.

In the last half of the 1980s, people I had come to know and respect, Texas movers and shakers like the Hunt brothers, Clint Murchison, from whom we had purchased the Dallas Cowboys, former Texas Governor John Connally, and many others were making headlines by filing Chapter 7 bankruptcy. Chapter 7 bankruptcy is especially heartbreaking because it requires a liquidation of assets, as opposed to Chapter 11, which allows for reorganization. I counted my blessings that I wasn't there with them, and proceeded to put my nose to the grindstone. I had my own share of debt to deal with. Yes, I controlled $4 billion in assets, but those assets also carried about $3.7 billion in debt. As I would learn, high leverage—that is, owing too much—can be dangerous.

In 1986, private limited partnership sponsors like Hall Financial Group were being hit with a double whammy: the poor economy coupled with new tax laws that would devastate the industry. In 1985, Hall Financial Group was the largest limited partnership private placement sponsor in the world and had purchased close to $1 billion dollars of property. We raised $320 million in equity that year, but almost all of it was to be paid to us in installments over the next six years. Those investors were counting on tax laws that allowed losses from their investments as tax deductions. The Tax Reform Act of 1986 changed all that. Deductions for these investments were not going to be allowed any more. These investors had just had the rug pulled out from underneath them by the U.S. Congress. Worse yet, for the first time in history, the tax law change would be retroactive.

Even in the United States, the government can and sometimes does make big mistakes. It hurts a lot to be on the wrong side of a mess like this, but it's part of the reality of being an entrepreneur. We can never control all the important variables around us. Government decisions, whether you're in the United States or in Central or Eastern Europe, have an enormous, uncontrollable impact on business. Entrepreneurs are always affected, for better or worse, by events beyond our control. The best we can do is control what we can, stay flexible, and respond as needed to changes around us.

So, in 1986 the rules had changed, and the Texas economy began to crumble even further. Virtually all of the Texas limited partnership private placement companies similar to Hall Financial Group began to fall into Chapter 7 bankruptcy and ultimately complete liquidation. But we kept holding on.

It's never been a sin to go broke in Texas. There's often been a fine line between being fabulously wealthy and flat busted. It's all part of the wildcatter heritage and philosophy of the state: To make it big, you often must risk everything. And the tables can turn, oh so quickly. They did so for me on December 10, 1985. I was walking through the hallways of the Hall Financial Group building checking in on various projects. I was in a great mood after having just completed a stock transaction with First Federal of Michigan that would net $12 million in profit. As I walked into the finance department, Don Braun, then our assistant treasurer, said he was just on his way to see me. "We've got a problem," Don said. The November revisions of our budget were in, and the deficits were larger than anticipated. The properties needed another $11 million immediately and, by the end of the year, they would need another $40 million. In other words, Hall Financial Group needed to raise $11 million, pronto, which meant I was going to have to write another big personal check. There went the First Federal profits. Fortunately, I had the money but, for the first time, I began to seriously worry about what the future would bring.

Why hadn't we realized our problem earlier and done something to remedy the situation? In a word, leverage. Large-scale real estate business is highly leveraged, meaning mortgaged. The risk in high mortgage amounts in real estate is that rental income can decline when a market softens, but expenses such as advertising and the costs from move-outs and move-ins, which are more frequent in a soft market, rise. At the same time, interest payments remain constant or even rise. With our annual rent revenue of more than $300 million a year, even an unexpected decline of 5 percent could cause a shortfall of $15 million. The declines that occurred in 1986 were as much as 15 percent. We didn't know it then, but it wasn't going to get any better for the rest of the decade.

Though I wasn't legally required to do it, ultimately, I put more than $175 million back into the properties to try to save them. In most cases, we could have just let them go back to the lenders, but more than a billion dollars in investor money was at stake. I felt responsible for that money and those people, so, from 1986 until 1989, I liquidated virtually all of my non-real estate holdings and used every penny to support the partnerships and my limited partners.

On January 15, 1986, we disclosed the bad news to our 10,000 investors, and, though I had anticipated there would be news coverage, I had no idea what big news it would be. The wire services and broadcast news picked up a story that ran in *The Dallas Morning News*. Suddenly headlines everywhere were heralding, "Craig Hall Covering $40 Million in Real Estate Losses; Some Partnerships May Go Bankrupt."

Bankruptcy was a dirty word to me then. I thought it meant failure. I thought it meant giving up. It would be downright embarrassing. In Texas in 1986, though, bankruptcy meant, if anything, the opposite. Carefully structured, it could be the right business decision, a way to protect properties from creditors, to restructure, and to stay in the game. We would file bankruptcy only as a last resort, but we had to consider it as an option, and I had told that to my investors. The news stories were technically accurate, though overblown.

We remained in the headlines over the next several days, which was devastating to our salespeople, who were still trying to sell our limited partnerships. Then on February 3, 1986, *The Wall Street Journal* ran the next bombshell headline: "Hall Financial's Loan Problems Could Hit Savings and Loans." Pitting us against the S&Ls in an adversarial role was no help to our ongoing negotiations. From there the problems began to snowball. February 4, 1986, was one of the worst days of my life. I was negotiating with Drexel Burnham Lambert on a $50-million debenture for a related company to raise funds for expansion. During recent months, the people we'd been dealing with at Drexel had been positive about the deal, but now told us that because of the negative press, they couldn't sell it. That same day, Continental Insurance called us and said they were canceling our utility bonds because they no longer had confidence we could pay the utilities on our properties, again because of the press. If other bonding companies followed suit, we would have to come up with an average of $60,000 to $70,000 in deposits for each of our 243 properties—more than $15 million we didn't have!

Then, Bankers Trust called and told us it had decided against extending our $100 million line of credit and wanted immediate payment, which was impossible. One of our large investors stopped paying capital installments on 10 investment units. Tenants in our office buildings called, wondering what would happen to their leases if we went bankrupt. The bad news just kept growing.

Two days later, examiners from the Dallas Federal Home Loan Bank began knocking on the doors of Resource Savings Association and Hall Savings Association, two savings and loans that I owned. They wanted to make sure we weren't looting the institutions to save our business. Banks were walking away from financing arrangements for new acquisitions, and some of our lenders were demanding full payment of our loans when in normal times they would have been renewed. It was worse than a nightmare because I couldn't just wake up. This was reality.

In those days, I would say, if you took a private poll, most people would have agreed that our fate was all but sealed. To the average newspaper reader, all of our hard work to come to an agreement with our lenders was a waste of time. One analyst said in a newspaper story that we were "merely rearranging the deck chairs on the *Titanic*." But despite every obstacle, we just kept on keeping on and solved one challenge after another. One by one, we took each issue head on.

By the end of 1986, my personal net worth was down $100 million and still falling from a high of almost $300 million just a year earlier. Worst of all, I had very little cash. Still I felt victorious, having simply survived 1986. While disappointed and surprised at the difficulties, I realized that the savings and loan disaster was a new problem area. It was hard for people to cope with the challenge. I was frustrated but not bitter. In time, I would be tested further.

In business in the United States, like everywhere around the world, often events occur that we cannot control and that affect our very survival. In retrospect, I realize the keys for me were to take each day one at a time, never, never giving up, and to believe in the long term. At the time, I also was blessed with an outpouring of support from investors and others who knew me and offered their encouragement. This made a great difference. I didn't think about it then, but I know now that I believed in the spirit of the American Dream. Perseverance, hard work, honesty, and the belief in the idea that good eventually triumphs over evil all kept me going. It seemed at times like an awful void with no escape, but I held to my vision of long-term justice and success.

Learning Not to Take Freedom for Granted

It's easy to take freedom for granted. For years I didn't realize how fortunate I was to have been born an American. It took my time in Vienna, traveling to other parts of the world, and a lot of reflection for me to realize how blessed most Americans are.

My life as an entrepreneur, at best, would have been very different in any other country. Anywhere else, it may have been nearly impossible to earn and save $4,000 by selling Greenrivers drinks, washing pots and pans, and doing every other odd job I could find before I was 18 years old. Few countries in the world would encourage an 18-year-old to openly own property and become a landlord, let alone over the next 18 years acquire as many as 72,000 apartments. With no family history or background in the real estate business, and without family financial support, I was fortunate enough to start, literally from nothing, and build a huge business. I am grateful to say that I have lived the American Dream.

Despite my current appreciation and perspective, I must admit that the United States system is not perfect. My personal experience bears this out, though my overwhelming view remains that, on balance, we Americans are blessed with a great system. My financial problems that started in late 1985 and continued into the early 1990s tested my self-confidence and fundamental beliefs in many ways. The U.S. government took over many of our lenders. Some of the individuals in new positions of power, after taking over the lenders' loan rights, acted contrary to the private sector's normal business interests. For a while life seemed anything but fair.

Some overzealous government lawyers filed a lawsuit in April 1992 that effectively resulted in my filing a Chapter 11 reorganization under bankruptcy laws, in part because I simply could not afford the legal fees to fight the army of government lawyers. By trying to save my investors through voluntarily putting in $175 million of personal funds, I had drastically weakened my financial position. No other creditor could or would have pushed me into Chapter 11 because it was not in their financial interest. I was paying everyone as much as possible and fully disclosing everything. But the government lawyers filing the lawsuit were not motivated by the government's best interest. Politically, a lawsuit showed "action," so they proceeded.

It was a painful and difficult time. I was frustrated and depressed, but I didn't give up. Ultimately we settled all matters with the government and successfully reorganized and came out of Chapter 11. But to this day, thinking about those difficult times is very hard for me.

Our American system is a reflection of the diverse group of pioneers who founded our great country. It is also a reflection of the rule of law coupled with a general openness that is essential to our system. Most importantly, it is a product of what we as U.S. citizens do everyday to protect our freedoms. While the system's not perfect, I am deeply grateful and proud to be an American.

At the heart and soul of this system are freedom and responsibility. Freedom encourages a 10-year-old to start a business, however small, and grow up to become a successful entrepreneur. Freedom allows people to fail as I did in 1992. Freedom encourages people who fail to start again and rise and succeed, as I have been fortunate enough to do. Freedom is a major catalyst for entrepreneurs.

But along with this freedom comes responsibility. In retrospect, the hard times I experienced while under what I felt was unfair scrutiny reinforced the reality that in the short run "life isn't always fair." Rather than complain or look to others, it is our responsibility to make our systems of government better. The big picture is what counts, and for that to be good we need real freedom. To ensure that freedom continues, we must take a stand and work to change things that are wrong. We cannot expect simply to be the recipients of freedom and government protections without being responsible for stopping unfair or unjust actions.

I am not alone in having taken our freedoms for granted. This almost casual attitude toward freedom is integral to the American Dream. As believers in the American Dream, sharing a common belief that individuals can make a difference, we just assume we have the freedom to act.

This shared dream also encompasses a belief in our financial system and in opportunity. We are taught from an early age that people can go from rags to riches. Again, while America is far from perfect, it remains a land of opportunity. Stories abound about immigrants arriving with three or four dollars in their pockets and becoming millionaires.

When I was growing up in Ann Arbor, Michigan, my interests were anything but business. I had no desire to be involved in what I saw as a boring, uncreative field. Money was also of no real interest to me, certainly not a motivation to "sell out" and do something other than what I wanted to do. Despite those feelings, the American Dream and the opportunity to both prove and improve myself were instilled deeply in my psyche by the culture that surrounded me. As an American, I knew that through our financial system I could find opportunity and prove myself if I took action. For better or worse, the best way to keep score in this system has always been through making money. Despite my ambivalence about money, my disinterest in what I perceived to be traditional business, and my many other interests and activities, I still became a businessman. Along the way, though, I also have learned how creative and fun it is to be an entrepreneur.

Entrepreneurs: From the Midwest to the Wild West

Popular attitudes toward entrepreneurs differ somewhat between Central and Eastern European countries just as they do in the United States between various regions. In Michigan, when I was growing up, if you were not an auto industry executive, you simply could not be a high-level member of society. All of the more important social functions were oriented to the auto companies and the senior management of those companies. Also, because Michigan has the largest labor union membership in the United States, small entrepreneurial businesses were often regarded, at best, with suspicion.

The experience of not being terribly well received as an entrepreneur in my home state made my visits to other areas of the country like Atlanta or Dallas something of a revelation. I saw how attitudes can shape experiences, and this became a major impetus for moving. In 1983, when I moved 90 employees and their families in my company from Detroit, Michigan, to Dallas, Texas, it was partly because the location was better for my business and partly because I wanted to be in an area where I would be respected for being an entrepreneur.

After the move to Dallas, I realized that what I thought would be a major change was even more important than I had originally thought. Dallas valued entrepreneurs in the same way that Detroit valued auto executives. Dallas is, after all, the Wild West where entrepreneurs share some heritage with oil and gas wildcatters. Risk, individualism, freedom, and reward for effort are at the heart of the Dallas business and social environment. That's what makes Dallas a breeding ground for new businesses. My American experience has taught me that entrepreneurship flourishes where it is encouraged. This can and should happen in Central and Eastern Europe and neighborhoods of the United States that have been left out of the American Dream.

Rebuilding Is Easier with Knowledge, Experience, and Luck

After 1992, I committed myself to make a lot of money as quickly as possible. For maybe the first and only time in my life, the financial bottom line was critical to me. The company management had worked hard to survive; now we turned to making money in real estate.

We had very little capital but we used what we had to our best advantage. We developed subdivisions on land we already owned and bought and sold other parcels. We reworked our apartments using the turnaround techniques we had built our business on. We then sold a number of our improved apartments and used the money to take a big risk.

In 1994, we were the first investors in 10 years to buy office buildings and land in downtown Dallas, which had the highest downtown vacancy rate of any big city in the United States. We bought more than one million square feet of Class A office space at an average of $72 per square foot.

By 1997, we sold our downtown office buildings for a $50,000,000 profit. We had improved occupancy and rental rates. We had changed the lobbies, added parking, added art, and improved the management. But in large part we were very lucky in our timing.

We had a good base of knowledge, experience, and substantial assets to rebuild from, although they were heavily mortgaged. We worked hard and I think smart, but in the end it was a lot of luck that caused us to, in total, increase our net asset value by more than $200,000,000 between 1992 and 1997.

Starting Over—Again

When my wife, Kathryn Walt Hall, was first appointed U.S. Ambassador to Austria in 1997, my plan was to carry on with my U.S. business activities and expand my horizons by investing in Central and Eastern Europe. Entrepreneurship had been central to my life for as long as I could remember. By the time I was 35, my company had had more than 4,000 employees. Being the owner of the company, serving as its chairman and president, feeling in control of my business and my life was comfortable for me. It felt great to walk into our headquarters in Dallas and know that floors full of people worked for a company that I built. Yet I was ready for a change, and, like the rest of the family, I was excited to be moving to Austria.

To avoid even the appearance of a conflict of interest with Kathy's role, my investment interests would have to be outside Austrian borders. Austria's proximity to so many formerly Communist countries led me to explore what I thought would be significant business opportunities there. My plan was to open up satellite offices for my U.S. real estate business and develop office buildings in some of the new markets. I was convinced that the former Communist countries needed to catch up economically and would require modern office space to compete.

But this plan quickly evaporated. I learned that to develop an office building in some of these markets could take as many as 100 or more permits, each accompanied by a small bribe. I thought this was outrageous. People explained to me that this was merely a cost of doing business in Eastern Europe. To most people in the United States, bribes are unthinkable. Most markets usually require one or sometimes two permits. Between the bureaucracy and either overt or indirect graft, I simply had no interest in becoming a developer in Central and Eastern Europe. My initial view of business opportunities there was very negative as a result of witnessing the extraordinarily difficult transition the people in these countries were undergoing. Years of Communist-inspired entitlement mind-set had to be changed.

As an entrepreneur from a young age, I was used to being my own person. Even before I had heard the word entrepreneur, I knew that something in me was different. I enjoyed challenges, risks, pressure, and getting things done. For me, my early youthful activities were simply a natural manifestation of who I am. Like most Americans, I took my circumstances for granted.

Ironically, my journey into former Communist Europe helped me appreciate how fortunate Americans are in terms of our freedoms and entrepreneurial spirit. Over time, I also came to know entrepreneurs in Central and Eastern Europe and see them as a real hope. I couldn't help but compare the American entrepreneurs I know and the entrepreneurs in the former Communist countries that I was meeting. As I did, many interesting common traits became clear.

Despite the impediments to economic achievement in "left out" neighborhoods in the United States and the transitioning former Communist economies, some entrepreneurs have succeeded. Moreover, contrary to the myths about entrepreneurs being greedy, self-interested takers rather than givers, I found the opposite to be true. A number of encouraging traits are common among entrepreneurs from these very different worlds. Over and again, these traits disprove many of the myths about entrepreneurs.

Entrepreneurs: From the Wild West to the Wild East

The more I surveyed Central and Eastern Europe as a potential investor, and the more I learned about the region, the more concerned I became. Corruption; dishonesty; the negative, cynical mind-set of the people; and the absence of a fair and dependable playing field were evident everywhere I went. I knew that there was money to be made there, but ethical players in business and government were in short supply. Soon I realized that the problems I was identifying were a massive regional issue that should concern anyone contemplating investing there.

Despite these problems, young American entrepreneurs came to the region in great numbers after the fall of Communism. As pioneers in a new gold rush, most of them ended up leaving very disappointed as they learned free markets don't succeed overnight. Some stayed longer, like 35-year-old Gavin Susman. He brought the American Dream and lots of energy with him from the United States to Eastern Europe. Learning about Gavin's experiences was my first foray into the economics of the region. His work there is a quick illustration of how the Communist mindset has stifled business in general and entrepreneurship in particular.

Kathy and I had been in Vienna for less than a month when Gavin called me up out of the blue wanting to meet. He explained he was a friend of one of my closest friend's daughters, and told me he was an investor in various businesses in Central and Eastern Europe.

"So, Craig, what about you?" he asked me during our conversation. I gave him my regular answer at the time about exploring real estate opportunities, focusing on Kathy's needs, learning German, and developing my art collection. I think he sensed my restlessness, and we agreed to meet.

Gavin arrived at our first meeting dressed in old blue jeans and a T-shirt, a far cry from the rather formal, well-dressed Austrian businesspeople I'd been meeting since arriving in Vienna. Exuding confidence, Gavin clearly marched to the beat of his own drum in more than just fashion. At the time, I was still in a mild state of culture shock, missing business partners and friends, and so meeting Gavin was like taking a trip back to Dallas. Gavin is very animated, and his energy is infectious. His directness, though at times shocking, is generally refreshing.

Since we first met in 1997, Gavin and I became business partners in numerous ventures in Central and Eastern Europe. In one of our early conversations, Gavin discussed the severe decline in the Hungarian stock market, expressing dismay over his own losses. His description of Hungary's market sounded like a real opportunity to me. In late summer

1998, stock markets were collapsing the world over. The crash of first the Asian market and then the Russian market clobbered the emerging markets of Central and Eastern Europe. Hungary was collapsing even further than Gavin's original fear, but for different reasons than those affecting Asia and Russia. My view is that Hungary declined in part because of its own success. It was, and arguably remains, the most successful and liquid stock market of all the formerly Communist countries in Central and Eastern Europe. Therefore, stockholders who had unreachable money in the Russian market were forced to sell stocks on the Hungarian exchange when they needed cash, which drew the market down.

For me, all of this meant it was time to invest. I sensed that the market was lower than where the companies should have been valued based on their fundamentals. I asked Gavin to research and recommend stocks for my approval and manage the process, offering him a piece of the upside. We created a working relationship on a handshake and, with Gavin, I eventually made major investments in the market. Then Gavin and I invested with others in a private company owning nine brick factories in the Czech Republic. Later we also bought into a privatization management company in Poland, an export company in the Czech Republic, and a privatization company in Croatia that manages privatization vouchers for war victims.

This venture into European markets has been exciting—but not easy. A decade after Communism, these countries are still having difficulties transitioning to democracies and free markets. I think the best hope for the region comes from individuals like the successful entrepreneurs you'll meet in this book. People who are doing well *and* doing good.

Chapter 3

Entrepreneurs
Make the World
Go Around

Entrepreneurs, large and small, are a little bit like The Little Engine That Could. "I think I can, I think I can..." What drives entrepreneurs in the face of adversity? And more importantly, where would the world be without these passionate, persistent individuals?

On a global basis, entrepreneurs are making a positive difference. Unfortunately, because of the myths described in this book, the difference they make often is less than what it could be if entrepreneurs were better understood. Obstacles notwithstanding, many entrepreneurs persevere and continue to contribute positively to their communities. Entrepreneurs offer a unique hope for a better future in formerly Communist countries and in American neighborhoods left out of progress.

Doing well and doing good is a growing phenomenon. Believing in a fair, level playing field and working to expand the global pie of a better life for all is what I call Responsible Entrepreneurism. It's an idea that is spreading. It is an idea we all need to encourage.

Reflections from the Wild East

My nearly four years in Central and Eastern Europe gave me a new perspective on the American environment for entrepreneurs. I began to really understand what is vitally important about entrepreneurs. While entrepreneurs are overcoming the odds to succeed in other parts of the world, the American environment provides a unique support system.

It's no accident that the United States has been the birthplace of the highly entrepreneurial technology revolution and the "New Economy." But what sets the U.S. system apart and makes it so entrepreneurial? Why do entrepreneurs want to be in America? And, why are they so important to areas with great need for economic development?

It Is the Mind-Set That Matters

American concepts of success and private ownership are difficult for people in formerly Communist countries to understand and accept. Even though structures and institutions are being altered there, it is far more difficult to change a mind-set created through 45 years of Communist oppression and generations of totalitarian regimes. The reliance on central planning and the lack of ambition that follows do not disappear overnight. The capitalist system doesn't operate on a switch. We cannot simply say to an oppressed people, "You are free now, go and be capitalistic!" Sadly, many people in the formerly Communist areas of Central and Eastern Europe are fearful of showing success. They are afraid rather than proud of making a profit because of an atmosphere of skepticism and intense jealousy surrounding those who are successful.

While a great deal needs to be done in the areas of policy and institutional change, we should not underestimate the power of the mind-set and opinions of the people to compel them to either action or hopelessness. I am convinced that America's unique story of progress is based on the spirit of freedom of individual beliefs. This dream goes hand-in-glove with freedom and real, participatory democracy.

It takes a lot of hard work to preserve both America's freedom and entrepreneurial opportunities. There is no "free lunch" in America. Success is earned. Risks and even failure are part of the process. The American Dream is one of opportunity for all. But this beautiful concept comes with a price: We must all work to protect and achieve it. It is not about entitlement but individual empowerment. Communism represented the antithesis of individual empowerment by controlling the major decisions in the lives of its people. As one Eastern European entrepreneur told me, "Communism took everything from me but my name."

"Left Out" of the American Dream

My perspective on areas of the United States that are populated primarily by low-income African Americans, Hispanics, Caucasians and other ethnic groups has changed as a result of my experiences in Austria. While America for most people is a land of opportunity, there are some neighborhoods where people have been "left out." These people simply have not felt the hope for prosperity and success that most Americans experience. Whole neighborhoods have been left out of the American Dream. Racism is partially to blame, but the full answer is far more complex.

A mind-set of cynicism, negativity, and dependence exists in these areas similar to what I found in formerly Communist countries. These areas of America are places where people often lack access to information. Often innocent to such things as "reading the fine print," these people are taken advantage of and find themselves prey to high interest rates on car or home loans. Ironically people who can afford it the least are often overpaying for basic needs such as food and rent.

Some Things Are the Same—All Over the World

As I've learned since coming to Vienna, the concepts basic to successful entrepreneurship are by no means universally known. Young adults in the transition economies of Central and Eastern Europe spent their childhoods enduring the daily struggle for basic goods and services that characterized their controlled economies. As children they weren't encouraged by their circumstances to make their own money or build a business. As a result, today they often don't fully understand the concept of private enterprise. Children in America's inner cities often face similar struggles, as well as a daily struggle to get through the school day alive to face altogether different "entrepreneurs" on their neighborhood streets.

The state of entrepreneurial development and responsible thinking in these areas varies, but in all areas far more potential exists than is being realized. Economies like these must be developed in a way that benefits the population at large. Entrepreneurs running small and medium-sized companies are the engines of robust, dynamic economies. What is needed is to encourage positive entrepreneurial activity through education, role models, a positive attitude, and a commitment to entrepreneurship. History has proven that entrepreneurs who do well for themselves also do good for the greater community around them. Entrepreneurs make the world go around. Here's why.

Risk Takers Are Needed

Risk is a relative concept. I have often done things others perceived to be very risky, because I saw opportunities where others only saw problems. In the lowest income neighborhoods in the United States, children risk their lives in school where weapon searches have become standard practice. They risk their lives walking home on streets, which are the turf of gangs and drug dealers. These children have a well-defined sense of personal risk. How will it serve them later?

Risk takers are essential to transition from Communist, centrally planned economic systems to working free markets. An entrepreneur in a transition economy accepts more than the ordinary business risks. He or she may also face the uncertainty that comes with fragile and unpredictable governments, the risks of corruption, angering organized crime, and more.

One of the elements that is likely to drive entrepreneurial activities is the potential for enormous rewards. Entrepreneurs who venture into markets like Romania or Croatia may find even more opportunity than entrepreneurs in transition economies like Poland and Hungary, where far more competition already exists. With the right attitude and approach, the entrepreneur can accept the higher risk, knowing that there may be a significantly higher reward.

Innovators Are Needed

Those areas left out in the United States and transition economies have a desperate need for innovation. Under Communism, the government told people what to produce, what they would eat, and where they would be housed. Similarly, in many of the left-out American neighborhoods, a downtrodden, oppressed lifestyle controls the thought process of many people. This control stifles creativity and innovation.

Entrepreneurial innovation, prompted by encouragement, education, and financial support from many sides can take up the slack when governments stop making all the decisions. Over time, marketplace innovation improves production and quality and inevitably creates new products and ways of approaching problems.

Jobs Are Needed

As a result of taking risks and being creative, entrepreneurs are a dynamic force for creating and powering the economy. Left-out neighborhoods in the United States and transition economies need their economic engines stoked. They need jobs. They need businesses that want to grow. Because of the traditional lack of risk taking and creativity in formerly state-run economies, growth has been stifled and inefficiencies are rampant. Given the opportunity, entrepreneurs can be a driving force. In the United States, low-income neighborhoods may have benefited slightly from the abundant progress made during the entrepreneurial boom of the late 20th century, but far more is needed.

Entrepreneurs will not be satisfied with the status quo. They'll find new ways to approach problems. They'll create new products and services and then find creative ways to get them to the consumer, building new businesses along the way. In the process, they will create thousands of new jobs.

In the short term, the process may seem to be fraught with insurmountable and circular problems. A business needs customers for its products in order to make money. It can't make products if nobody will buy them. On the other hand, people need to have jobs in order to have the money to buy the products they want. It may at first be difficult for businesses to find customers for their products because their customer base has relatively little money. The exciting thing is that entrepreneurs don't give up. The process will be erratic, but each incremental step will lead to the next. Each small company that creates a product people buy will slowly expand and hire more people. Those new employees will have money to go out and buy other products, supporting yet more new businesses. This is true in the United States, it's true in the formerly Communist countries of Central and Eastern Europe, and it's true all over the world.

Stakeholders in Society Are Needed

Encouraging responsible entrepreneurs creates more stakeholders in society. The result is less crime and more social and economic stability. If enough people take the risks of business ownership, create jobs for those who want to work, and provide them with disposable income, then social and economic stability will evolve. Entrepreneurs have a true investment in their country's and their neighborhood's futures and are a critical component of their success.

Entrepreneurs in America's most challenged areas can be a powerful lobby for improving market conditions. They have a real need for streetlights that work, shoppers who feel safe, and secure financial transactions. They become serious stakeholders in creating and maintaining a thriving, positive community.

Entrepreneurs Who Do Well and Do Good Are Keys to Positive World Development

My journey into the world of foreign service and former Communist countries has led me to conclude that individuals who practice responsible entrepreneurism are critical to a more stable, democratic world. Working with my wife and in my other roles representing U.S. interests in parts of Europe has been exciting and gratifying. During our almost four years abroad, my thoughts evolved about the interplay between business and government in making people's lives better.

Hope, opportunity, and hard work are the best antidotes to poverty and crime. Encouraging individuals to discover the entrepreneurs within them can help solve the bigger problems. Responsible entrepreneurism, whether in a transitioning or mature free market, is a major force for a healthy democracy.

The Entrepreneur in All of Us

For many people, taking risks and being creative and adventurous in business, social services, or government are natural parts of human behavior. But we may not be aware that these traits are within us. The tendency to be entrepreneurial is not universal, but I think it is hidden in many people. The attitudes of a society, government, neighborhood, or even a family can encourage or discourage these entrepreneurial traits. Entrepreneurs can excel where public policies and culture encourage entrepreneurial growth. Entrepreneurs are stifled if a government or society fails to provide the structure and environment for success.

We in America are very fortunate. We have extraordinary freedoms and enjoy a sense of individual empowerment. Yet not every American participates fully in the free market society. While for most Americans hope and opportunity are a part of everyday life, all Americans don't feel the same sense of opportunity. We must continue working to resolve these problems in the United States so that no one is left out. However, despite these and other shortcomings, I believe that more opportunity and encouragement for individual risk taking and responsible entrepreneurism exist in the United States than in any other country.

When I was in my teens and having trouble in school, I held to an intuitive belief that with hard work my life would improve. As a teenager, my academic and athletic records suggested something other than success was in my future, yet, with each difficulty, my determination grew. This is part of a mind-set held by a majority of Americans but not by many people in other parts of the world. My youthful problems were not an anchor that dragged me down, but merely a challenge to overcome. Belief in the ability to overcome is part of the entrepreneurial spirit. I took these feelings for granted at the time, but today I feel blessed to have lived in a country that encourages this spirit in so many people.

The entrepreneurial spirit gave me the opportunity. That was the easy part. Hard work, taking risks, the willingness to "pay my dues," and a lot of luck determined my future. But the key was I never doubted that success was there for the taking. I only had to "go for it." So I did.

By living in Central and Eastern Europe, I have learned that this mind-set, held by so many Americans, is far from ubiquitous. Communism is gone, but positive spirit, strangled so long by the lack of free choice, has not yet recovered. That can and must be changed. The mind-set of hope and opportunity is the essence of the entrepreneur.

Throughout this book, you'll meet entrepreneurs I respect from the United States and Central and Eastern Europe. These are people who have "made it" in spite of great obstacles. They are young and old. They represent entrepreneurship in a number of different fields, including many you might not expect. The common thread is that they are proof of how entrepreneurs can "do well and do good." Through their actions they dispel the myths in Chapter 1. They are each changing the world for the better.

PART TWO

THE MYTHS STOP HERE

Chapter 4

TURNING ADVERSITY TO GOOD –
STEVE MARIOTTI

Steve Mariotti received an M.B.A. from the University of Michigan, Ann Arbor, and has studied at Harvard University, Stanford University, and Brooklyn College. His professional career began by serving as a Treasury Analyst for the Ford Motor Company's divisions in Venezuela, Mexico, the Caribbean, Argentina, Peru, Chile, South Africa and the Export Division.

Steve Mariotti

In 1982, Steve Mariotti made a significant career change and became a Special Education/Business Teacher in the New York City school system, choosing to teach in notorious neighborhoods such as the "Fort Apache" section of the South Bronx. It was here that Steve Mariotti developed the insight and inspiration to bring entrepreneurial education to low-income youth. This led to founding the National Foundation for Teaching Entrepreneurship (NFTE) in 1987. Since its founding, NFTE has become a major force in promoting and teaching entrepreneurial literacy and basic academic and business skills to economically disadvantaged young people both in the United States and abroad. To date NFTE has served over 35,000 young people and trained more than 1,500 teachers and youth workers in 42 States and 14 Countries.

Steve Mariotti has received numerous honors and awards for his work in the field of youth entrepreneurship, including: Best Economics Teacher in New York State, Mobil Oil Corporation Award (1988); National Award for Teaching Economics, The Joint Council of Economic Education (1988); Minority Business Enterprise Project (1989); Entrepreneur of the Year Award, *Inc. Magazine*, with Ernst & Young and Merrill Lynch (1992); and the Salvatori Prize for American Citizenship, The Heritage Foundation (1997).

Mr. Mariotti has co-authored 16 books, including *How to Start and Operate a Small Business*, with Tony Towle, and *Entrepreneurs in Profile*, with Jenny Rosenbaum. A more advanced version of *How to Start and Operate a Business*, was published by Times Books, a division of Random House, in 1996. Now in its second edition, this popular book, *A Young Entrepreneurs Guide to Starting and Running A Business*, has sold more than 65,000 copies.

— ✦ —

A Personal Imprint on Entrepreneurship

Steve Mariotti is a great entrepreneur, and his approach bears his own personal imprint. Steve is methodical and conscientious. He puts things together one piece on top of another. I am more impulsive and believe in acting on gut instincts. Neither approach is right or wrong. We both take actions based on unique life experiences. Only in hindsight have we realized the significance of how events motivated our entrepreneurial actions.

Steve and I share many beliefs about entrepreneurship, including that you always want to know your customer. In the mid-1970s in Belleville, Michigan, Steve Mariotti was one of my customers, living in one of the apartment complexes I owned. Neither of us had any idea that our paths would cross 25 years later on another continent.

Quantum Leaps—"You Have to Get into Trouble to Get Out of Trouble"

Unlike Steve Mariotti, my experience has taught me that jumping in and taking risks is the right approach to business. "You have to get into trouble to get out of trouble," I've often said, so many times now that I'm convinced it's an integral part of basic entrepreneurial culture. That's how progress is made. Sometimes taking what appears to be a crazy risk is necessary to make things happen.

Knob on the Lake, one of my first large real estate ventures, had great amenities and more than 1,000 apartments, but it was a financial disaster. In 1974, gasoline prices were very high, and Knob on the Lake's location was a commuter nightmare. It was on a major highway far from any major cities and employment centers. Seeing Knob on the Lake was an epiphany to me though. I knew that this was to be my next challenge.

Before moving my company's headquarters from Michigan to Dallas in 1983, each January I would take a one-week vacation away from the frigid Great Lakes winter. Just before boarding a plane at the Detroit airport to start my vacation in 1975, I called my senior managers and held a conference from a pay phone. I had just driven by Knob on the Lake, and I told them to start looking into it. "This will be our next property," I said. "We'll buy it as soon as I get back."

I ignored all of their practical questions such as "How do you know it's for sale?" and "How could we possibly do that? It's too big." I simply said, "It has to be for sale because it looks vacant. It may be a financial disaster, but we can turn it around."

The year 1975 became one of great intensity for me. Knob on the Lake had been built and developed by Frank Volk, Sr., who was then 79 years old. Frank was near financial collapse and behind on payments on multiple phases of the development. His real estate career had been fabulous, but he had taken on this huge project, rolling all of his capital into one venture. Unfortunately, it had bombed. Frank was facing personal bankruptcy and loss of other assets if, at a minimum, he couldn't find someone to pay his current bills and manage the property effectively.

Early in our relationship, I stressed to Frank that I owned large properties, was "a player," and was capable. I showed him the materials that we had used for a partnership offering for a property called

Woodcrest Villa. We had raised $1.1 million in that offering. Frank's deal would need $5 to $6 million just to bring everything current. The property was also losing $165,000 a month.

None of these facts deterred me. I knew that this was to be my deal, and I had a vision of what I could do. This was the largest apartment complex in Michigan and one of the largest in the United States, and it was in great trouble. I was excited! It was the ultimate challenge for a 24-year-old entrepreneur in the apartment business, and I wasn't going to be swayed by losing $165,000 per month, or by the $5 to $6 million in unpaid bills.

By the end of January 1975, I'd had a number of meetings with Frank. Although at one point there was another buyer in the pipeline, by February Frank Volk and I started negotiating in earnest. I convinced him that the only way for him to avoid personal bankruptcy and get any money out of the sale was to find someone he could trust. I was honest with him. I didn't have the money, but I did have energy and motivation, and I wouldn't betray him. Our final deal involved my taking over the property and closing on March 5, 1975. I paid his lawyers' legal fees of $23,000 and gave him a note, which I certainly wouldn't be good for if I couldn't work out the major problems at Knob on the Lake.

In hindsight, no one with any sense of practicality or grasp of reality would have done the things I did at age 24 to buy such a large and complex property. Even with all of the problems, this was a huge property, pushing the purchase price to approximately $25 million. We were trying to buy it with virtually no down payment, and I had not talked to any of the lenders. I knew that there were six mortgages, all in default, several hundred thousand dollars of unpaid creditors, and many disgruntled people beginning to file lawsuits against the property. Yet I had an absolute commitment to get in the middle of these problems and unravel them.

In the midst of the serious negotiations with the lenders and creditors, I was also working on the operations and marketing side of the property. After all, we were only 56 percent occupied, and, without a turnaround to generate more income, there would be no money to repay anyone.

When Life Hands You Lemons, Make Lemonade

Slowly, we made progress on management, streamlining, cutting costs, and improving the property for the residents. This was the era of unexpected oil shocks to the U.S. economy, so we were coping with the dual problems of high gasoline prices and the poor commuter location of the property. We couldn't make those problems go away no matter what we did, so we had to reposition the property through creative marketing.

We couldn't compete with properties closer to Ann Arbor, where the University of Michigan was, so we seized on a marketing concept promoting "Exurbia." We defined our market to include graduate students wanting more than normal university housing. In Exurbia, one somewhat long step from the university, people could get away from it all and live at a lake and golf course. Most potential renters couldn't afford the gas for long trips to get away, so our pitch was why not live in Exurbia every day? Steve Mariotti and thankfully many others thought it was a great idea and moved to what people had told me was a "lemon."

Exurbia was a great concept, but our repositioning would only work if we gave Knob on the Lake an appealing name. We literally needed to turn our "lemon" of a deal into a success or "lemonade." To remind us of the challenge, half jokingly in one of our brainstorming meetings, someone said, "Let's call the property 'The Lemon.'" I liked it, but others thought it was terrible. We settled on Lemontree. The "lemon" theme was developed throughout the project. Maintenance personnel were "Lemonaides" and jars of lemon drop candy were in the reception area. Lemontree became the first of many "trees" in our apartment forest and proved to be a thriving asset for us.

As the leasing results improved, we continued negotiations with the lenders and creditors, eventually reaching a different agreement with each party. There were more than 70 distinct creditors, and, because we had no money, each of them took one promise or another. It was a jigsaw puzzle in which each deal involved what we would do in the future if we could pull all the remaining pieces together. Avoiding bankruptcy was a delicate balance of numerous individual agreements held together long enough to raise some money and make all of them work.

Because the long-term economics of the deal were still uncertain, I knew that the way to raise money from investors was to market the tax benefits. I was extremely fortunate to find a sophisticated tax lawyer,

Arthur Klearstein, who changed my life. He suggested that we could take a front-end fee! We hadn't done that before. This time though, with his help, we wrote ourselves into the deal for $660,000 in fees. This was a common practice at the time, though as a young syndicator I had no idea. I worried about our ability to still raise the investor money. Ultimately, we raised the entire $3.3 million from 29 investors. For the first time in my life, I had a significant amount of real cash money. Frank Volk received *all* the monies we had promised him. All of the lenders and creditors got exactly what we had promised them.

My January 1975 entrepreneurial vision became reality. We had made a quantum leap by buying a property that was two-and-a-half times larger than anything we had owned previously. In fact, it was larger than everything else we owned put together. We also had raised far more money than ever before and done so in a very complicated, sophisticated transaction. In the process, I had met many people, some of whom have stayed in my life throughout the past 25-plus years. Others, who I thought had moved on, have recently come back. Steve Mariotti is one of those.

Salzburg—Years Later

In the summer of 1998, both Kathy and I gave speeches at the Young Presidents Organization (YPO) University in Salzburg, Austria. YPO is a multinational group of company presidents and CEOs younger than 50 years of age. I first joined while in my mid-20s and remained a member until recently turning 50. Kathy gave a keynote speech on European Union (EU) Expansion Plans and whether or not Turkey should become part of the EU. I gave a speech on the rise, fall, and rebirth of Craig Hall. As it turned out, it was a lot of fun, and my speech was well attended. YPOers love stories about people, and I'm always happy to share mine along with, hopefully, a few lessons learned. My stories include not just the good times, but, more importantly, how I learned from the difficult ones. For me, it was both an honor and a growth experience to speak at the Salzburg YPO University.

After my speech, I perused other parts of the education program, and I saw a topic on how to teach young children to be entrepreneurs. Then I saw the name Steve Mariotti, but didn't put it together instantly. I did feel I recognized the name, and the description of the class fascinated me.

Steve Mariotti was going to talk about how kids could be taught to set up businesses. I went and sat in the rear of the lecture hall.

The class had already started when I quietly entered the back. I saw an enthusiastic man talking to an audience that included the children he really wanted to reach and their parents. This was what YPO calls a "family university." It was a great experience for all. In this particular class, Steve was presenting a hands-on version of how and why entrepreneurial activity in a for-profit business makes good sense for children. It was fantastic to see Steve walk back and forth and get the audience involved with his natural, direct, exciting style.

Later that day, I saw Steve at lunch and we renewed our acquaintance, making the connection back to Lemontree. Steve is a really nice guy who wants to change the world with a quiet but strong ambition. Steve is the kind of guy who moves mountains with an idea and incredible persistence. He is passionate and on a mission to spread the ideas of entrepreneurship to youth, particularly those in less fortunate circumstances throughout the world. He is one of the world's leading experts on entrepreneurs, and his enthusiasm on the subject is contagious.

From Ann Arbor to the Toughest School in New York

Steve and I were both born in Ann Arbor, Michigan. He moved to Flint in his teens and attended high school there, but ended up back in Ann Arbor at the University of Michigan. Things have calmed down a bit in Ann Arbor from the more radical Vietnam protest days when I was a student and building my original business of rooming houses and apartments for university students. Steve and I both thrived in the liberal academic environment surrounded by good minds. This environment influenced the whole community. At that time, part of the atmosphere was an anti-business attitude that adversely affected opportunities for entrepreneurs.

Coincidentally, Steve and I share another early life experience. We both spent some time working as door-to-door salesmen. Door-to-door sales can be very profitable but are incredibly difficult. Ironically, I would say neither Steve nor I have the effervescent, charismatic personality that typifies the aggressive door-to-door sales types. I know for me, any success I had in that business was thanks to my tenacity and a desire to learn and succeed. I sold Cutco knives. I remember the worst part of my sales experience was the part of the sales pitch that we were taught to use to get in the door. We were told to carry a big stuffed animal that the company loaned us and say to the lady of the house she had won a prize, implying it was the stuffed animal. Only after our sales pitch inside the house were we to fess up that the real gift was aluminum foil worth probably 50 cents. It always bothered me, and, after a while, I simply quit using the approach the company pushed. I nevertheless became a very successful salesman.

Steve was an Avon cosmetics salesman during college. As he says, "Selling really helped me appreciate the process of business—the art of making money…of making the sale." I certainly understand that. Even today, albeit from a relatively mild-mannered, quiet approach, Steve's sales ability continues to be important in all of his current efforts. An important part of being an entrepreneur is knowing how to sell an idea.

After finishing college, Steve went on to get an MBA at the University of Michigan and then won a summer scholarship to study economics at the Institute for Humane Studies at Stanford. There, he was one of only 20 young economists who studied under F. A. Hayek, the Nobel Prize winner for economics in 1974. His intense study under Hayek gave Steve a solid grounding in free-market principles. Among other things, he recalls Hayek's belief that the free market offers the most effective way of identifying each of our strengths and how our competitive advantages can be developed. That, like every other building block in Steve's life, would ultimately lead to his great entrepreneurial efforts with the National Foundation for Teaching Entrepreneurship (NFTE).

While Steve was studying under Professor Hayek, who was then in his 90s, the professor had assigned topics to each of the 20 students for an oral report. Steve's report to the class was the first presentation. After Steve finished, the famous professor said to the other students that they had just heard a great report from a brilliant young economist. He said in time Steve likely would be recognized worldwide as a great economist. Steve was proud and he called his girlfriend, parents, and his brother that night to tell each of them how the great professor had proclaimed him to be the future for economics. The next day in class he held his chest out as he walked in and took his place to hear the next student report. At the end of student two, and later he would learn students three through 20, Professor Hayek would effusively comment about each presentation with similar positive reinforcement. Oh well, so much for becoming a full-time academic economist!

Steve went from his studies with Professor Hayek to Ford Motor Company. He spent two-and-a-half years with Ford working as a financial analyst in South Africa and Latin America Ford finances. One morning over coffee, Steve and I were talking about his Ford Motor days and many other earlier experiences, and he reflected on how proud he was of Ford and the small role he might have played in its adoption of the Sullivan Principle, which was basically a boycott of South Africa until Nelson Mandela was freed from prison. Political affairs of this type rarely reached corporate boardrooms, but thanks to Leon Sullivan, an activist who took on the issue, Ford and other companies jumped on board. Leon Sullivan went on to spend 15 years pushing efforts to free Mandela. He was credited by Nelson Mandela as being one of the key forces for his release from prison.

After two-and-a-half years of the corporate world, Steve decided to leave and become an entrepreneur. He moved to New York and opened an import/export firm, specializing in importing specialty items from small African businesses. He looked for niches where big companies were not importing or exporting and handled a wide range of products.

Steve's Life-Changing Experience

Steve, like virtually all entrepreneurs I know, is a very open person. He talks about himself with great ease in both a positive and negative light. Whether one-on-one or in small or large groups, he is self-effacing and very direct as he addresses situations and influences that have made a difference in his life.

One day, I was with Steve at two separate presentations. The first was before a class of new NFTE teachers, who were preparing to join the ranks of the already 1,500 certified NFTE teachers. The other class was part of a joint effort by three organizations: Goldman Sachs, the Center for Talented Youth, and NFTE. This effort targets 100 specially identified talented low-income minority individuals in New York. Steve was telling a group of "mentors" (young professionals in their 20s who had volunteered to help in the program) his experiences and background. In both presentations, you could hear a pin drop in the room as he enthusiastically spoke about the experiences he had that led him to found NFTE.

Steve explained that in 1981, while jogging on New York's Lower East Side, he was approached by a group of teenagers who demanded money. Steve didn't have money in his jogging suit, and they proceeded to beat him up. The experience was painful both physically and emotionally, and for years he continued to suffer flashbacks. Steve explained that as a way of working through this traumatic event, he got into teaching.

"I began a career as a special education teacher in New York's most difficult impoverished neighborhoods," he says. "My first year was almost as traumatic as the mugging."

Boys and Girls High was one of New York City's roughest schools. In one of Steve's classes, a student set fire to another student's coat. Steve was threatened and cursed. Radios blared in his classroom, spitballs were thrown, and any chance to get kids to pay attention was almost non-existent. In what was a typical ritual, Steve often had to throw some students out of his class in order to get or keep control.

Steve explained that his first year of teaching was horrible. He was in charge of the program for student retention, but he found himself throwing more and more children out of his class in order to keep any semblance of control. He started with 75 children and at the end of the year, the class was down to 15.

That year, 1982, he received an award as the best new teacher. The students loved him. They had a party in his honor and a banner read, "Good Luck Homeboy—Best New Teacher." Yet something clicked in him, and, instead of feeling like a success, he felt like a failure. He realized as he looked around that he had only a fraction of the children left from those who had started in his class.

He wanted to get to the bottom of things. He did not lightly accept the accolade of being the "best new teacher," but instead wanted to understand why he had to throw out 60 students to get 15 through. He started calling all of the children he had thrown out and invited them to a dinner.

About half of them showed up. At the dinner, he asked them why they had behaved so badly. One of them said, "Mr. Mariotti, you're boring." They said he had nothing to teach them. He asked if there ever was anything he taught that they liked. One student responded that the only time that was interesting in his class was when Steve would talk about his import/export business. Steve had discussed the numbers and how he had made money. All of the students agreed that was cool.

Steve went on to explain, "I didn't know it at the time, but this instant, borne out of desperation, was pointing me toward my real vocation—teaching entrepreneurship to low-income youths." To Steve that means teaching the fundamental concept of "buy low/sell high." When Steve mentioned this, I remembered that as a new father, when I was holding my little girls as newborns, I told them, "buy low, sell high," and I would add, "and keep the difference."

Shortly after that enlightening dinner, Steve began teaching a special class called "How to Start, Finance, and Manage the Small Business—A Guide for the Urban Entrepreneur." Needless to say, this class became very popular. In Fort Apache of the South Bronx, 100 percent of Steve's students started small businesses and reported back to him, saying there were positive changes in their lives as a result of taking his class. Steve even found that this class had a major impact on lowering absenteeism, dropout rates, teen pregnancy, drug use, drug dealing, and violent crime among the students who took the class and got involved in entrepreneurial activities. The class was an overwhelming success.

Steve's Nifty Idea

In 1988, after seven years of successful teaching, Steve decided to move on and launch the National Foundation for Teaching Entrepreneurship (NFTE). Steve pronounces the initials "nifty," which is a catchy way to talk about a very serious and outstanding organization.

"NFTE's mission is to teach low-income youths the basics of starting their own business by creating a curriculum, training teachers, and providing graduate services," Steve says.

The mission of the organization is to provide every low-income youth with the knowledge to pursue economic self-sufficiency. To make ends meet, Steve's brother and father contributed $1,000 per month for the first several months while the organization was trying to get off the ground. Steve's brother, a CPA and a financial whiz, later left a higher paying job to come in and help organize the finances. In his typically modest fashion, Steve says his brother is really a co-founder but does not get the deserved credit. It is great to see the family support, but clearly the ideas are Steve's.

Steve believes that low-income youths are actually better suited for entrepreneurship than others from middle class or affluent backgrounds. Steve believes that "street smarts" are translatable into "business smarts." As he described in a speech he gave, "I know a secret that, if fully understood by our government, business, and community leaders, could have enormous positive implications for the future of our society. Simply put, the secret is this: Children born into poverty have special gifts that prepare them for business formation and wealth creation. They are mentally strong, resilient, and full of chutzpah. They are skeptical of the hierarchies and of the status quo. They are long-suffering in the face of adversity. They are comfortable with risk and uncertainty. They know how to deal with stress and conflict."

It is fascinating to hear Steve talk about this subject. He certainly has the experience to know what he's talking about. I have often wondered how many entrepreneurs had wonderful childhoods, got great grades, and got their MBAs at Ivy League schools. My observation, admittedly very unscientific, is that the group would be extremely tiny. Lots of entrepreneurs are dropouts like me. I didn't complete an academic degree until my experience at Vienna's Diplomatic Academy at age 50. Certainly many entrepreneurs, when you scratch below the surface, started with less-than-ideal childhoods. Steve is absolutely committed to the idea that low-income, at-risk youths live in an environment where they can learn the risk-taking skills important to succeeding as an entrepreneur that kids in safer, stable environments never experience.

But, of course, in the depressed areas of the United States or similarly in the former Communist countries, young people are often not taught the actual skills necessary to succeed at business. That's where NFTE comes in. NFTE's mission and success are fabulous, yet the execution is not terribly complex.

NFTE provides basic programs offering entrepreneurship training to low-income youths both in school and in after-school programs. NFTE also has developed state-of-the-art teaching materials that are available for purchase to anyone involved with youth services. They have trained and certified a growing number of teachers. Most recently, a partnership with Microsoft has enabled NFTE to build a powerful online learning center for budding entrepreneurs. All materials and the services benefit low-income, at-risk youths in the United States and abroad.

As of the fall of 2000, NFTE had more than 35,000 graduates. As a comparison, in 1988, the first full year of the program, 200 students graduated. In addition to the students NFTE has served directly, it has trained teachers. Through the end of 2000, it has certified more than 1,500 teachers who work in 42 U.S. states and 12 countries. The operation is growing both directly and through licensing. The management and the approach of going to larger scale are absolutely incredible. Lots of entrepreneurial organizations go though periods where they have good ideas but can't make it to the next level. NFTE is a remarkable organization that has grown to an international scope that will really make a difference.

Part of being a good entrepreneur is knowing when to be a listener. Steve is always careful to listen to his "markets" for feedback. He is sensitive first to the youth he serves, but also to those who donate funds and evaluate his progress. An entrepreneur, whether in the for-profit or not-for-profit world, needs to find experience and ideas from others. A nonprofit needs to develop links to others both as a fund-raising mechanism and for ideas that will enable it to grow.

Steve has assembled an impressive board of directors as well as other related advisory groups that include some of the best business, academic, political, and journalistic minds one can imagine. Everyone from Jack Kemp, the former Secretary of Housing and Urban Development (HUD), Jeff Raikes at Microsoft, Theodore Forstmann at Forstmann Little, John Whitehead, the former chairman of Goldman Sachs, and David M. Dinkins, the former Mayor of New York, has found value in serving NFTE in some capacity. On the academic side, Professor Jeffery Timmons at the Center for Entrepreneur Leadership at Babson College, Dr. James I. Cash at Harvard University's Business School, as well as professors at Stanford and Georgetown universities, and others from equally renowned centers of learning have found in NFTE a program of great importance.

Part of the beauty of many large entrepreneurial organizations is that they are the result of a simple, focused idea. In Steve's case that is part of what has really made NFTE a success. The need to do something to help low-income, at-risk youths was amply evident to Steve as he tried to find a way to engage them in his classroom. The idea of turning their risk-taking behavior and resilience in the face of adversity into success in business made sense to Steve. Providing them with the tools was a narrow, focused response. Everything else in terms of how to get the job done becomes a by-product. I think this is a truly excellent demonstration of what entrepreneurial ideas can become.

Steve and Gorbachev

Steve and I have spent hours talking about entrepreneurs. He has been invaluable in terms of his insights into what motivates entrepreneurs. We both agree that the former Communist Central and Eastern European countries, like the left-out neighborhoods in the United States, can benefit from NFTE and similar ideas, but Steve has a further unique insight into the problems in the former Communist countries.

Shortly after Gorbachev decided to reform the Soviet system into free markets, representatives of Gorbachev contacted Steve. During their first 500 days, the Gorbachev regime wanted to change the attitudes of Russian children.

With the trust of the Gorbachev regime, Steve offered to personally go to the Soviet Union and provide a training session. Children chosen from all over the Soviet Union were flown in to live together and work with Steve.

This was an eye opener for Steve. Even after 150 class hours, these students still understood virtually nothing about entrepreneurship. As Steve says, they couldn't handle the basic retail concepts about businesses that his students normally learn in the first or second class. All they had ever been exposed to were collectives. The whole idea of private ownership and for-profit business was so foreign that the fundamentals—marketing, making a profit, inventory control—just didn't take with these kids. Steve was disappointed and wanted to do more, but the new Russian authorities considered the venture a success and complete.

Things have come a long way since those days. Because of freedom of the press and a greater general exposure to worldwide activities, students today in the former Communist countries do have a greater appreciation of basic business. Still, a lot of mind-set problems linger. Even today in my software company in Budapest, when we first put in a compensation structure for programmers to account for different experience levels and the complexity of work they perform, the programmers objected. They thought everyone should be paid the same. They believed the idea of differentiating pay just because they do more or better work wasn't fair. We're past that now, but it's interesting to see how the Communist mind-set lingers.

What Do the NFTE Students Learn?

As one of NFTE's graduates put it, "My dream is not to die in poverty but to have poverty die in me." NFTE teaches the skills and gives kids the tools to help dreams like this come true. I don't believe it's about teaching people to become entrepreneurs per se. People like the student above have that within them. The question is how to encourage their entrepreneurial interests to flourish and grow. Steve gives them the tools to be entrepreneurial and supplies positive role models that are also an important part of the formula.

NFTE does all of this through five main programs. The first is "exposure sessions," which are taught either through public schools or community-based organizations. The idea here is to raise the awareness of concepts like negotiation, sales, market research, return on investment, business plans, and other fundamentals of private enterprise.

The second program area is BizTech, which is online entrepreneurship. Microsoft has been an involved partner in this program. A variety of 15-, 25-, or 40-hour Internet-based entrepreneurship learning centers have been set up to include quizzes, games, virtual field trips, and many other modern techniques that (I confess) today's generation is far more apt to master than I would be.

The third component of NFTE's education is through the fundamentals program. Its 54 hours of instruction include guest lectures, field trips, and business plan development activities. The objective is teaching the basic skills for starting a business, being part of a community, and succeeding. Students are shown the countless opportunities that exist and examples of people who have made it.

The fourth area of teaching is the core program itself. This is a 108-hour entrepreneurial training program that covers the vast spectrum of skills and knowledge necessary to start and run a small business. Steve Mariotti's three-module curriculum is contained in the 600-page book he wrote titled *How to Start and Operate a Small Business: A Guide for the Young Entrepreneur*. It covers, in addition to the basics of starting up the business, how to understand income statements, return on investments, advertising, cost benefit analysis, and, importantly, business ethics. The class includes visits by guest lecturers and field trips to real businesses, and it is taught by certified entrepreneurship teachers who are all part of NFTE's teacher training program.

The fifth area of activity focuses on providing ongoing support for graduates of the previous four components. NFTE has developed a wide variety of "graduate" services. Even though it is an awesome task, NFTE tries to stay in touch with every graduate.

All of this adds up to a tool kit for aspiring entrepreneurs. It's a terrific combination. You can't teach somebody who has no desire or lacks an innate, risk-taking mind-set to be entrepreneurial. But you can coax a dormant entrepreneur out of hiding by giving him or her the power to succeed. I think this is true in the left-out areas of America as well as in many areas that were formerly Communist.

While NFTE helps some children to become entrepreneurs, I believe that is only one way to judge the program. From what I can see, it helps people become better citizens. Through NFTE's training program, people learn self-respect, respect for the free market system, and something about individual empowerment. Steve is modest and does not over-promise.

"What we're doing is not a cure-all. It's not a Vitamin C, and there still are a lot of things that need to be figured out," he says.

But clearly, NFTE is changing lives. People are becoming better students and employees. In general, NFTE is a positive force in making society a freer, more stable place.

How Has NFTE Grown?

Many entrepreneurial companies founded on good ideas either fail outright or don't make it to the big time. What I'm calling the big time is that extra level of growth that only comes with an intense focus and dedication. Imagine you are seated in a 767 that has just started its engines and is powering itself into the air, charging the massive engine to its utmost. It is that extra dynamic thrust that increases the speed and takes you to 30,000 feet. Many businesses, whether for-profit or non-profit, simply never make it to 30,000 feet.

I believe the reason most don't scale the way they might is simply because the founder can't adapt and is unwilling to give up control. Entrepreneurs usually have limitations, which are the inverse of the traits that gave them their initial success. Often entrepreneurs are control freaks. They do everything themselves and make sure it's done in the way that they perceive as the "right way."

In Steve's case, he did several things that helped him grow at a quick and substantial rate. For Steve and NFTE, an important transition occurred when he brought in a new CEO to take over the tasks at which he wasn't best while he continued with those at which he was best. He brought in Michael Caslin, who has become an integral and terrific partner for him in this venture. Many entrepreneurs never give up CEO positions. Later they find that while their leadership was critical for the organization for many early years, at a certain point they become a liability unless they make a personal transition. Steve Mariotti made a graceful and helpful transition at a critical time.

Steve followed a second strategy that both nonprofit and for-profit companies also can and should follow. Steve surrounded himself with great advisors. He brought in people with recognized names like the Honorable Jack Kemp and David Dinkins, as well as lesser-known but integral members of the business and academic communities. These are people who could help with ideas and advice, people who could help raise money, people who could help raise the awareness of the organization—

all individuals who were important to NFTE's future. In short, Steve has been open to sharing and learning and listening. Listening is a critical skill for entrepreneurs.

Finally, under the direction of NFTE's CEO Michael Caslin, NFTE is making great use of high technology. For example, BizTech, NFTE's Internet learning site, offers an online curriculum. Students anywhere in the world can access information about entrepreneurship 24 hours a day, seven days a week. NFTE is constantly improving its lesson plans and, by utilizing this technology, it makes itself more available to students at all economic levels and to the whole world. Not every entrepreneur can make the changes required to allow an organization to grow. I see a parallel to a parent who is on the one hand close to and very involved in his children's lives and on the other hand knows when to let the children grow up and go off on their own. Many entrepreneurial founders experience some unwillingness to let their "children" grow up without them.

Real People Having Real Success

Every year NFTE celebrates the spirit of entrepreneurism with an awards dinner in New York City. The evening brings together young NFTE graduates who are just embarking on their careers and well-known adults who have already made their mark. NFTE teachers who have made a difference are also honored at the dinner, which is held in one of the city's great hotels.

Steve is accomplishing lots with this simple idea. He is honoring the achievements of the teachers and the young entrepreneurs who have passed through the program. By honoring the adult recipients, who have included notables like William Donaldson (founder of Donaldson, Lufkin, and Jenrette), Diana Ross, and Doris and Jay Christopher (founders of The Pampered Chef), Steve is building a cadre of role models for all future NFTE participants.

The 10 young entrepreneurs who are selected each year represent only a small part of the thousands of kids who have benefited from Steve Mariotti's vision. One of NFTE's graduates is Jimmy Mac, owner of Bulldog Records in New York City. Now in his late 20s, Jimmy started his first business managing sports figures when he was only 15. Today,

Bulldog Records works with companies like Time-Warner and Electra. Jimmy is still involved with NFTE as a volunteer and credits the organization with helping him develop needed business skills.

Another NFTE success story is Maleka Lensy, who is now a college student. While she was still in high school in Washington, D.C., she started a catering company named Classy Productions. Classy Productions worked for clients like her local Chamber of Commerce and the Washington, D.C. Board of Trade. She believes that NFTE is partly responsible for her resilience and helping her through the business plan writing process. Each of these entrepreneurs and many more like them bring to NFTE some special reserve of courage and willingness to take chances that NFTE then helps shape into acceptable forms of entrepreneurial activity. These kids themselves evolve into great role models for their inner-city neighbors. What a formula for engendering success!

Steve also started a program at Riker's Island prison teaching prisoners entrepreneurial skills in the hopes that they might redirect future activities once they are out of prison. While far from a cure-all, early numbers have shown fewer repeat offenses by NFTE graduates from Riker's Island.

Steve knew after a few minutes teaching entrepreneurship to at-risk kids that he had found a winning formula. That conviction also has been validated by other sources, including Harvard's Kennedy School. A recent study by the Kennedy School surveyed all nonprofits across the United States, and NFTE was ranked in the top five for the sustainability and growth formula it had developed.

NFTE teamed up with Brandeis University to evaluate its own programs and confirmed that it had developed a model for teaching entrepreneurship that was worthy of development to greater scale. The Brandeis study, performed when NFTE was five years old, confirmed that entrepreneurship could be taught. NFTE program attendees as a group created more income-producing businesses and became more career-oriented and adept at information technology than comparable peers not exposed to NFTE's programs.

Another exciting result of NFTE's programs is that 70 percent of older NFTE graduates went on to post-secondary education. That's a higher percentage than for all high school graduates in the United States. I'm perhaps most impressed that NFTE's graduates also have a proven record of increased responsible civic behavior. Responsible entrepreneurship can and should be encouraged throughout the world, and, if NFTE's programs do that, then I think they should have a presence in every country around the world.

What Makes Steve Tick?

One day Steve and I were talking about the merits of nonprofit businesses, and he surprised me by saying he would rather be making lots of money.

"I was starting to get really good with my business when I switched careers," he explained. "I think sometimes I should have waited another 10 years so I could help fund this organization myself. Then I wouldn't need to do fund-raisers."

He went on to talk about problems with nonprofits in a more general sense.

"You know I always tell my students that it would be much better if you could work for social change in 'for-profits' because, from an entrepreneurial standpoint, you can share ownership with your employees. One of the best inventions of all time is a stock option. A not-for-profit can't do that. There are also psychological limits on salaries, and I think that is very destructive."

At the same time, Steve believes some organizations are better suited for being nonprofits. NFTE is one of those. In his case, the motivation he has is the same: helping the children that NFTE serves achieve their goals.

As Steve sees NFTE grow and succeed in changing the lives of troubled youths, people in prisons, and students both in the United States and around the world, he feels a real sense of gratification.

"On a daily basis I couldn't have a better life."

Steve went to a college graduation recently of some former NFTE students that he had taught. During a special ceremony, two of them were recognized for extraordinary achievement. In their speeches they brought up NFTE and talked about how they remembered their first business cards, the importance of writing thank-you notes, following up on what stocks are in the paper, how to buy wholesale and sell retail, and on and on. Listening to that, Steve said, gave him one of the best memories he has. He recalled the joy he felt that day and remembers every day by staying in touch with the graduates of the program. For entrepreneur Steve Mariotti, it's all about making a difference in the lives of children.

Things Aren't Always What They Seem

For Frank Volk, Knob on the Lake almost meant personal bankruptcy. For the people living there, it was a deteriorating property. For the lenders and creditors, it was a disaster. From the perspective of most real estate investors, it was a lemon!

For me it was paradise, a great opportunity, the greatest quantum leap in a 24-year-old's career! It was the biggest rush I could imagine. It was challenge, excitement, and opportunity. I felt very lucky and thrilled to get into the eye of the storm where others perceived only disaster. Where angels fear to tread, entrepreneurs often rush in!

For Steve Mariotti, getting mugged was humiliating. It left scars. He was devastated. He questioned values and doubted himself. His life was changed. Most people would have perceived Steve as the least likely person to want to help the kind of youths who mugged him.

Throwing himself from the frying pan into the fire, Steve became a teacher in tough neighborhoods. He decided to face his fears by going right to the source of them. Out of all these adversities blossomed NFTE.

To most people, at-risk, low-income youths represent problems and people to stay away from, people not likely to change for the good. Steve is absolutely right in his unconventional view that these same low-income, at-risk youths represent potential entrepreneurs. They can take their "street smart" skills and use them in a positive way. I believe that people in the formerly Communist countries likewise can turn their toughness in learning to survive the oppressive Communist system into positive, legitimate success in free markets.

Oftentimes things that appear dismal in a certain light, with a creative change in perception, turn out to be very different. I eagerly anticipated the challenges of Knob on the Lake because my perception was different from that of most people. Perhaps my unshackled imagination, hard work, and luck changed the reality. It was similar for Steve and ultimately for the NFTE youths.

Steve overcame personal challenges and developed an innovative program to help youths find legitimate success. Contrary to most people, he sees that adversity can become a powerful energy for entrepreneurial success. Creatively looking beyond the obvious is a beginning. But Steve has shown that by harnessing perceived negatives of low-income, at-risk youths, he can help turn them into powerful forces for good— for themselves and their communities.

Chapter 5

PARADISE IS
SEVEN KINDS OF BREAD –
GERRY HARGITAI

When Gerry Hargitai was 18 years old, he was desperate to leave communist Hungary and see what was out there in the rest of the world. While visiting nearby Yugoslavia, and risking his life in the process, he sped through the heavily guarded border crossing between Yugoslavia and Austria on a small, borrowed motorcycle. Through luck, timing, and who knows what else, the guards did not shoot.

Gerry Hargitai

After reaching freedom, he eventually made his way to Canada and the United States and learned about business. With the fall of Communism throughout Central and Eastern Europe, he made what some might consider an odd choice. He chose to go back to Hungary and start a business there to teach business skills to the Hungarian people.

After a misstep with his first idea, he founded California Fitness, a multilevel marketing company selling vitamins and nutritional supplements. Financial problems almost shut him down several times. Also, the Hungarian drug companies, owned by former Communist bosses, did everything they could to drive him out of business. Day by day, he managed to stay in business and now the company is thriving with well more than 160,000 independent distributors in more than 30 countries.

── ✦ ──

Escaping Communism

An endless drizzle of rain slicked the road as 18-year-old Gerry Hargitai approached the Yugoslavian-Austrian border. His cold hands gripped the handlebars of the 125cc East German motorcycle he'd borrowed from a cousin, and he shivered. He wondered if the Yugoslavian border guard would take aim with his machine gun. A stream of deadly bullets would have ended the dream that he had nurtured over the months he had planned his flight from Communist Hungary.

Gerry's desperate escape from Hungary was more than 20 years ago, but his voice still trembles with emotion as he recounts his experience.

"I couldn't turn back. I was too scared, and, if they saw me, a young guy with Hungarian plates, I would have been in great trouble. My passport didn't allow me to travel so far into the Austrian border area, so, when I finally got there, I knew that I had to try. If I didn't, I would go to jail. My only choice was to keep going."

Gerry remembers how his body tensed and sweat mixed with rain as he focused on maneuvering the little motorcycle past the guards and through the slightly open barrier. He had only the clothes he was wearing, a false passport, and the equivalent of about $100 in deutsche marks in his pocket. As he approached the first border gate on his borrowed motorcycle, he saw guards talking with the driver of a car they had stopped. Farther on, he glimpsed the second border gate: It was open. Revving the engine, Gerry sent the small bike speeding through the gates that separated Yugoslavia from Austria. He got past the guards by going as fast as the motorcycle could, and by being willing to risk getting shot in the process.

"I was very scared. Scared of the different languages, leaving home, scared of the border guards. I can still feel it today, riding through the gates and wondering if I would get bullets in my back...but the Yugoslavian guard did not shoot."

Gerry left his home and family behind, risking his life to cross that border. When I asked him why he left, I expected that he had great plans for his future, or a philosophical pearl of wisdom to share. But he said, "I heard that in Sweden there were seven different types of bread, and in Hungary there were only two. I wondered, was it chocolate, vanilla? How do they make it? I wanted to see it. I had no plans for the future in terms of jobs."

He wanted to know what other kinds of bread there were in the world! This was the amazing motivator for an 18-year-old. When Gerry and I discussed it, we both laughed. It was hardly what I thought would motivate someone to risk his life, but, in a way, it's exactly what freedom is all about. Being able to freely explore the world, including finding out about little things like different kinds of bread, should not be restricted.

In addition to learning about the world's breads, Gerry had other plans.

"I thought I was going to become a world champion in motorcross racing! I knew that I would never have enough money to buy a Western motorcycle. Ever since I was a child I wanted one. I thought that if I go to the West, I would be able to buy a motorcycle and become the world champion."

Gerry had no intention of ever returning to Hungary, telling only his mother of his plan to escape to Austria via Yugoslavia. She had been a saleswoman and Gerry's role model for his own youthful entrepreneurial activities.

"One of the things that helped me leave," Gerry remembers, "was that my mother's two brothers and a sister had left Hungary in 1956 and emigrated to Canada. So at least my mother knew that the stories we heard about America were not true—about there being no medical coverage and people having no jobs. That is what the propaganda was telling us."

Gerry's uncles and aunt had emigrated during the Hungarian rebellion against Communism. Soon after, the Soviet army effectively closed Hungary's borders. One of Gerry's uncles, John Czinege, now a successful Canadian businessman, was only 16 years old when he left Hungary. While Gerry had only heard about him from his mother, who spoke proudly of her brother, this unknown uncle was an important role model to him. He had been a freedom fighter during the 1956 revolution, responsible for dropping Molotov cocktails into the Soviet tanks from a city bridge. When it was clear that the Soviets could not be overthrown and would retaliate against the rebels, Gerry's young uncle joined thousands of others who escaped before the Iron Curtain firmly closed. A little more than 20 years later, Gerry followed.

The Reluctant Storyteller

When I first met Gerry Hargitai, I liked him instantly. He is a quiet, soft-spoken, straight-talking man. He is hard working and should be an inspiration to any young Hungarian entrepreneur. We are separated by age, upbringing, and nationality. But we share a feeling of mutual understanding and common ground. We are both entrepreneurs, but, more importantly, we share a belief in the ideals of responsible entrepreneurism, though Gerry had never thought of it with that terminology. He innately believed you could be an entrepreneur doing well for yourself while doing good for others. Meeting Gerry and hearing his remarkable story also confirmed my belief that there is what I call a "hidden entrepreneur" in many people—people like Gerry—regardless of where they are born. Despite the suppressive history, there are many entrepreneurs-in-waiting throughout Central and Eastern Europe. Some are in full bloom; others are dormant and untapped. Some people become entrepreneurs in spite of difficult environments. But we will never know how many additional productive entrepreneurs there could be if the environment were more encouraging.

Gerry is a hard-driving entrepreneur who, like any of us, takes pride in his accomplishments. Yet he is very reluctant to talk about his success. Like most successful entrepreneurs in former Communist countries, he keeps a low profile. It took some coaxing for him to share his story for this book. When he finally agreed, he said, "Craig, I'll do it for you. This is an important story for people in this part of the world. I want them to know, if they follow their dreams they can succeed like I did."

Gerry hopes that by learning about him, Westerners will understand the struggles to make legitimate businesses work in these countries. More importantly, he wants to inspire other Central and Eastern Europeans to follow their entrepreneurial aspirations. Many successful, responsible entrepreneurs he knows do their best to camouflage their success. They fear both organized crime and the resentment of masses of people who are still struggling to find their place in the new and frightening world that replaced Communism.

It has been enlightening for me to meet people like Gerry. He helped me understand that years of Communism created a society in which a few powerful bureaucrats lived a pampered, isolated existence, surrounded by luxury items, but with food unavailable to the ordinary citizen. Immediately following the fall of the Communist governments, corrupt politicians and even organized criminals moved into the void, creating lives of incredible richness for themselves at the expense of working people. It's no wonder that ordinary people, even in Hungary, which has done far better at transitioning than most other former Communist countries, can't imagine a life of wealth without assuming that it was created through unethical use of power or criminal activity. Sadly, there are not enough well-known, truly positive role models like Gerry. Yet, with people like Gerry who are willing to come forward, perhaps we will see some real, positive role models for future entrepreneurs, one entrepreneur at a time.

Yugoslavia Was "Economically Successful" Communism

Gerry grew up in Hungary, a Soviet satellite country with a state-controlled economy. Many consumer products we take for granted, they simply did not have. One of six children, Gerry enjoyed bananas as a treat only when an uncle came to visit from neighboring Yugoslavia, a country that in those days he describes as being far more modern than his homeland. Christmas brought relatives from Yugoslavia bearing gifts of chocolate and oranges. These luxuries were totally unavailable in Hungary. Looking at Yugoslavia today, it is hard for me to see that other Communist countries once regarded it as so much more advanced. Yet in Gerry's Hungarian youth, Yugoslavia was the rich neighbor. What we in the West might regard as small differences, such as the availability of fresh fruit or chocolate, meant the world to those across the borders in the Communist-ruled 1970s.

Gerry lived near what was then the Yugoslav border. He was fortunate to obtain a travel permit allowing him to cross into Yugoslavia. This meant that he could make a little extra money by being entrepreneurial, even before he had ever heard the word entrepreneur.

"I used to go to Yugoslavia 20 years ago to buy jeans and other easily transportable consumer products," Gerry remembers. "I bought jeans and Persil, a laundry detergent. I'd bring them back to Hungary and sell them."

Gerry's early entrepreneurial ventures were a natural response to his desire to make some extra money. I identified with these efforts, which were similar to my childhood Greenrivers stand and numerous other ventures. The difference between Gerry's story and mine is that in America, entrepreneurial creativity is not only legal but also encouraged. People want to support the enterprising young American child with a lemonade stand. Gerry, on the other hand, had to be a part of the underground economy that was not government approved but developed nonetheless as a way to trade scarce goods.

Not Quite There—The Life of a Refugee

After his escape in 1978, Gerry first lived in a refugee camp in the countryside outside of Vienna. He was processed and then given "official refugee status," which enabled him to leave the camp and look for work. Gerry has told me many times that life in the refugee camp was frightening and dangerous. He remembers that he didn't want to stay in the camp.

"It wasn't a stable situation. That year, there was a really big riot and a number of people died fighting in the camp. There were Molotov cocktails thrown. If people didn't like you, they would pick you up and throw you out the window." One of Gerry's roommates was killed when struck by a broken bottle in a fight in their room. Gerry decided he had to get out of the refugee camp.

Around parts of Vienna, there are small family-owned vineyards and wineries that have been passed down through the generations. They survive only through the labor of all family members, and the few non-family members willing to work for the low wages these small wine farms can pay. Eugene Kelemer owned one of these farms and offered Gerry his first opportunity. Gerry was happy to get a job on the farm. He left the refugee camp as quickly as possible, moving to Vienna and sharing an apartment with friends. Mr. Kelemer not only gave Gerry a job, but he treated him as an equal, not as a refugee. In fact, to this day, Gerry and Eugene Kelemer, who lives in Vienna, remain good friends.

When he called his mother to tell her about the job, she was sure her young son was lying about his salary. She also could not understand why people would be as nice as Gerry described. He told her that he earned 15,000 shillings in about five weeks. She did not believe him. This was 20 times the average monthly wage in Hungary.

Once he was able to converse in German, Gerry quickly found an even better job. He became an assembly line worker at a Grundig television manufacturing plant, a job he held until he left Austria. His position was so financially lucrative he did not even bother to try to convince his mother about his new salary, though whenever possible he would have those he knew who were going to Hungary smuggle some money back to his family. Over time, he even saved enough money to buy his cousin a new and better motorcycle than the one he had "borrowed" to make his escape.

Gerry's official refugee status enabled him to travel freely in Austria and other Western European countries. This was an experience he was never allowed in Hungary. During his first August at Grundig, he learned that European workers were entitled to a paid holiday. Every August they actually got one month of paid vacation time. Gerry went to Italy.

"It was like nothing I had ever experienced before," he says. "They gave you a month's wages and sent you off on a holiday. So I went to Venice to see the ocean for the first time, and that was an experience. We slept in the car because we didn't have enough money to rent a hotel room. Nevertheless, it was a great time."

As Gerry spent more time in Austria, he began to long for even greater freedom. The Austrian system was too regimented and familiar, not the place he wanted to settle. Always mindful of the uncle he had never met, Gerry decided to emigrate to Canada. He went to live with his uncle in British Columbia in a small fishing village, 100 miles from the Alaskan border. With family help, Gerry adjusted to Canada well. As a political refugee with family sponsors, he applied for citizenship and quickly and proudly became a Canadian citizen.

Welcome to North America, Land of Opportunity

Gerry worked at a variety of jobs in Canada. At the same time, he listened to every motivational tape he could find. He also worked hard at perfecting his English and decided to move to the United States. He had always heard that that was where the action was. He was getting himself ready for a bigger future.

A Canadian passport meant free access to the United States. And, with his Canadian passport, he went back to Hungary in 1984 to visit his family. By the mid-1980s, life in Hungary was getting a bit freer. It was great to visit, but he was happy to leave Hungary again. A few years later, when it was clear that the political situation had improved, Gerry began thinking about business opportunities for Hungary. By then, Gerry was living in Los Angeles. He had become deeply immersed in sports fitness and training. He became a sales representative for a health product from his sports club, and he watched with great interest as the political situation changed in Eastern Europe. Day after day in 1988 and 1989, Gerry and a friend, a fellow Hungarian refugee, brainstormed at a beachside table in Los Angeles to create a business they could one day take to Budapest.

Thinking about what those changes would mean for him and his country of birth, he had an inspiration: There were no coin laundries in Hungary. He also realized that there was no one in Hungary selling health products like those he represented in Southern California. After a decade away, he wanted to return to Hungary and pursue his entrepreneurial ideas. He also felt passionately that he could help others to improve their lives without having to leave their homes behind as he did.

Returning Home

Gerry and his Hungarian friend, George Szabo, drew up a business plan to build American-style launderettes and put them in large apartment buildings in Budapest. He shared his business plan with an acquaintance, John Ritch, who was the senior staff member for the Democrats on the Senate Foreign Relations Committee and a successful real estate entrepreneur in Washington, D.C. John was intrigued by the idea and financed the venture to get the laundry business started. They were sure the business would be a hit.

Gerry returned to Budapest in May 1991, installed coin-operated washers and dryers in apartment buildings in Budapest, and waited for business to boom. To his chagrin, he found that most Hungarians wouldn't pay to use the modern laundry machines. They preferred their old machines and the traditional hand-washing methods.

As is often the case in entrepreneurial activities, things did not go as planned. For Gerry, as the laundry business was failing, a sideline activity caught fire. Gerry had begun a business on the side selling vitamins and fitness products. He had brought 96 bottles of vitamins with him from California and went door to door to gyms in Budapest to sell them. At that time, vitamins were virtually nonexistent in Hungary. Gerry's efforts were met with overwhelming response. Within six months, he had more than 100 customers. The fact that his vitamins were American made them a great hit.

Despite lots of effort, the laundromat business simply didn't work. Gerry came to realize that getting people to change from using simple, nonautomatic washing machines to his new ones would be a long-term process. His coin laundry business was doomed. With entrepreneurial resilience, he decided to focus on his growing health products business. Gerry started a vitamin sales multilevel marketing club and hired an assistant. He began to think big.

California Fitness Begins

Gerry's business plan was simple. He would import name brand vitamins from the United States, mark them up, and sell them through a network of friends, who would receive commissions. Based on recruiting additional friends to join the sales network, they would receive a higher level of commissions. The business grows through an ever-larger network of friends and family. The multilevel strategy was perfect for the widely connected, family-oriented society in Hungary. But, unfortunately, Gerry's Hungarian partner unexpectedly died soon after the company's formation. His partner was in the process of raising a $35,000 loan for the business. With his death, the loan efforts fell apart. Gerry had lost a business partner and needed funding.

Without the loan, the business Gerry had named California Fitness did not have the cash flow to purchase needed inventory. Even worse, sales were booming! Gerry sent urgent telegrams to John Ritch pleading for cash to purchase the vitamins for his growing network. He was actually worried that his customers would beat him up if he didn't deliver soon. Now he needed not the $35,000 his partner was to invest, but, instead, $300,000 to buy inventory and fill the orders he had in hand. Fortunately, as Gerry says today, "just in the nick of time" John Ritch came through and loaned Gerry $300,000.

Gerry wanted both to sell vitamins and to help family, friends, and others in the region who "didn't know what it was like to be entrepreneurial, have their own business, or pursue a dream." He was trying to create a business and help as many people as he could along the way. It became clear, very quickly, that a multilevel marketing concept with good products, like health supplements and vitamins from the United States, and a system that encouraged individual involvement, would work well in the former Communist countries. It was a perfect tool to help people learn about individual rewards for productive efforts. Gerry would encourage participants to become their own boss with a very small investment. In the process, they would learn the benefits of free markets.

"In addition to the very low start-up costs, typically $10, people had a chance to learn entrepreneurship from their sponsor [the person who brought them to the network] and company-run training seminars," Gerry explains. "It's practically for free, which is important to people with no capital to invest. More importantly, as naive as it may sound, California Fitness was started based on family values. The first members were my mother and brothers, relatives and friends. Now we all get ahead by helping each other to succeed. One of our mottoes is: You cannot be successful until you make others successful."

Gerry's vision is reflected by successful multilevel companies in the United States like Mary Kay, Avon, Amway, and more recently, Excel Communications.

"When my mom asked me how to go out and sell the products, I told her go see the people you love and tell them what you feel about using our products. She went to her friends, got eight people involved, who in turn got more people involved. She ended up with 4,000 members. That is really how the first people approached our business and how it has spread to the other countries," Gerry said. "I'd like to tell you we are such smart people or have some special way or knowledge, but the truth is, most of our members care more about helping people than about the business itself. Of course, it does not hurt if they make good money by helping other people, across borders and cultures, to live a healthier, more balanced life. My experience is that people like to help others. We've created the right environment, and most of our people are living the responsible entrepreneur's life."

California Fitness officially started business in 1991, but the network with members started February 1993. On its first day, it acquired 10 new members. On the second day, it added another 60. By the end of the first month of operation, the California Fitness network had 3,000 members. Membership tripled by the end of the second month, and, one year later, California Fitness claimed more than 100,000 members—approximately 1 percent of Hungary's total population! Clearly, there were a lot of people ready to buy into the entrepreneurial life Gerry espoused.

"I noticed that people wanted to belong to something, something that gives them the sense of a club with other types of people who think like they think," Gerry says. "They want to belong to something that is worthwhile, and, of course, the need for money is a big reason to join California Fitness. People were coming because they wanted to live a happy lifestyle, have the promise of a better life, and a better financial future."

The Establishment versus the Entrepreneur

It wasn't long before California Fitness network's success was all too apparent to the large formerly state-owned Hungarian drug companies. It prompted a vigorous response by some of them, who felt the best way to compete with Gerry was to put him out of business any way necessary. Controlled by former Communist bosses, the drug companies engaged in derogatory attacks, maligning California Fitness network products in television, radio, and print advertising. They said that the American vitamins were injurious to consumers and would cause birth defects in children. Gerry's company was slandered by one dirty trick after another. With truth on his side, he hung in and fought each incident of lies with factual counterstatements.

Gerry's troubles continued when suspect "consumer protection" inspectors attempted to seize and shutdown the 35 California Fitness warehouses over a period of a few days.

Gerry knew that once the warehouses were sealed, it would take him months of court action before they were operative again. His brother, on the advice of one of the company lawyers, recruited 20 rather large new employees and they physically resisted the inspectors by linking arms and barricading the doors to the largest warehouse. Finally the inspectors left, vowing they would be back in force in the morning. That night, Gerry's staff removed $1 million worth of vitamin inventory by ferrying it away in car trunks. For many months afterward, the vitamins were actually sold from car trunks. From then on, for a number of months, all new inventory coming into the country was hidden. The warehouse was a series of cars. Entrepreneurs always find creative solutions to what seems impossible, even under the pervasive bureaucratic corruption in Hungary in the early 1990s.

Over a two-year period, California Fitness and its wide network of members gained public acceptance and respectability. Finally, as the business and political environment improved in Hungary, the Hungarian government left them alone, and the business became visible and mainstream again. The company expanded throughout Central and Eastern Europe, and then into the European Union. Gerry's charismatic leadership and faith in individual entrepreneurship has inspired literally tens of thousands of Eastern Europeans to join his company. It is the number one multilevel marketing company in most of the countries in which it operates, with both a direct sales force and a growing number of retail stores.

Serbian People Are Entrepreneurial!

One of California Fitness network's most successful countries prior to the Kosovo NATO bombings was the Federal Republic of Yugoslavia, which is made up of Serbia and Montenegro. To my surprise, Gerry explained that the Serbians were extremely entrepreneurial people and were an important part of California Fitness. I was amazed when he showed me a videotape of a Yugoslavian California Fitness network meeting held in Belgrade in the fall of 1997. The 3,500-seat convention center was almost full. People cheered boisterously as various sales representatives were honored for their performance. To me, it was like watching a revival meeting, yet Gerry himself is soft-spoken and modest, unlike the stereotypical revival minister.

Gerry gave a 45-minute impromptu speech, striding back and forth across the stage, and then down into the audience. I asked him later how he prepared for his speeches.

"I know where I want to start and where I want to finish," he said, "and then I just say what I really believe."

Speaking from his heart that day, Gerry focused on the idea of "The Dream," emphasizing again and again, "All the things I have achieved started with only a dream." He continued in softly accented English, "Take my advice. Select your dream today, now, set your goals. Do something for them, and you will achieve them." As he walked through the crowd, Gerry made clear, "There is no difference between you and me." Men and women, dressed in business suits and sweat suits alike rose to clasp Gerry's hand. He told them about his escape from Hungary, describing his fear as he crossed the Yugoslavian border on that little motorcycle. Then he added emphatically, "You can make it from nothing."

Gerry is living proof that there have been tremendous successes in Central and Eastern Europe, even during the difficult first 10 years of transition from Communism. I was amazed watching the video at how captivated the Serbian people were with Gerry's message. He wove an international theme of success and hope that transcended the political quarrels going on outside the Belgrade auditorium into a belief system for the participants.

It is ironic that less than two years after such an exciting high point in Belgrade, Gerry's Serbian network faced virtual ruin as a result of the NATO bombings related to the war in Kosovo. Serbia had been one of California Fitness network's biggest markets. It will take years to recover. Yet the Serbians have remained among California Fitness' most loyal members, selling vitamins while a war raged in their country. Serbian California Fitness members were more interested in their growing business than in fighting against their neighbors.

The Kosovo War Hits California Fitness

Gerry struggled with enormous problems that the war in Kosovo created for his company: the slowdown in the economy and subsequent reduction in disposable income, the fear of his 40,000 members to leave their homes to sell the product, and the impossibility of importing the vitamins they needed to fill orders. A major dilemma was the loss of all corporate accounts based on the dinar, the Yugoslavian currency, as well as the freezing of all hard currency accounts. When the banks were closed during the NATO bombing, California Fitness kept operating, but only at a large loss for every day of business. California Fitness bought bicycles for its employees so they could travel to work. It took the "California Fitness" signs off its retail stores, fearing reprisals similar to the vandalizing of the McDonald's in Belgrade. McDonald's and possibly other "American" companies were a symbol of America and thus were in danger because Milosevic and his followers were preaching hatred and violent reprisals for NATO action.

In Yugoslavia, dinars could be exchanged for hard currency only by companies that had export sales from Yugoslavia. In his case, Gerry set up a separate business selling Yugoslavian products like raspberries, paintbrushes, and logs to gain access to hard currency exchange. While an unexpected diversification from the vitamin and health product business, this was a creative way to keep California Fitness alive. American entrepreneurs generally do not experience such extensive barriers to operating a business. Untraditional competition, currency crises, unethical and anti-private sector governments, and organized crime can make for a treacherous and unpredictable playing field. These kinds of problems certainly limit the numbers and success of entrepreneurs, but Gerry and many others I have met simply greeted each obstacle with a new solution and kept on going.

Stronger, Larger, "Fitter": California Fitness Network Expands

In only eight years, California Fitness network has grown from a dream to a multimillion-dollar, multinational company. Gerry Hargitai's dreams are very big though, and he plans not only to expand the membership base worldwide but also to develop a broad health product line to complement the vitamins. The company has products tailored to individual blood types. Through research and development, it is always looking for improved health supplements. California Fitness is at the forefront of health improvement efforts in Central and Eastern Europe.

Gerry takes the "responsible" part of entrepreneurship seriously and has created company programs that support the community. He has developed a corporate blood donor program, and he provides free company products to nonprofit organizations serving people in need. California Fitness network members receive free medical consultations, the company sponsors the Hungarian Fitness Federation and other national fitness federations in the region, and manages Fit Kid, a fitness program for schoolchildren. He has also created the International Fitness Federation in 47 countries, which fosters programs like Fit Kid, and others aimed at helping improve fitness.

The company-sponsored fitness program for children is part of Gerry's dream of offering hope to young people. He envisions the program teaching them about physical education and good nutrition, but also instilling in the children the idea that, if they work hard, they can be winners. The last part sounds very much like the American Dream, doesn't it?

If Gerry has any regrets, it is the schizophrenia that overlays responsible entrepreneurial life in the Central and Eastern Europe region (CEE). He told me that, unlike the United States, which has active groups such as the Young Presidents Organization for successful entrepreneurs, the CEE provides no such support system. In fact, he doesn't socialize with other entrepreneurs, preferring like most of them to keep a low profile. Despite his concerns for his personal safety and his occasional wistful desire to move to the United States, he continues to travel extensively, selling the California Fitness network. His business has taken him to the Czech Republic, Poland, Yugoslavia, and many other countries. In each, he tells his story, encouraging others to find and reach for their dreams.

Today, California Fitness has approximately 160,000 independent distributors, or members, operating in 32 different countries. The company provides a commission check every month to thousands of people in Central and Eastern Europe alone, with some checks being more than $25,000.

John Ritch, who made Gerry the original loan for California Fitness, went on later to become Ambassador to the United Nations in Vienna. After John retired as an Ambassador in early 2001, Gerry asked John to become Chairman of the Board of California Fitness, and John accepted. To Gerry's credit, he finds highly qualified people like John who believe in him and in turn makes sure he never lets them down.

Entrepreneurship Triumphs Over Ethnic Prejudice

Much has been made of the ancient ethnic animosity that seems to exist in many parts of Central and Eastern Europe. An argument also could be made that similar, though not as historic, rivalries exist in the United States as well: African Americans versus Hispanic Americans; Chinese American entrepreneurs threatening Korean American grocers; middle-class Caucasian Americans feeling rising pressure from many different minority groups. All of these conflicts have received their share of the media limelight. My own experience has been that when people are working together to create an enterprise, they put aside their differences and work as partners for a common good: an improved economic future. I was pleased to hear Gerry echo some of these same ideas recently. As I see it, his business is the epitome of inclusion.

"In my experience with the California Fitness network, the ethnic divisions are gone when people have an economic future," Gerry says. "They no longer hate each other. As an example, each year we take the best managers on a week-long trip to a nice place. Last year it was the Canary Islands. Eight nations were represented there. We organized many sports events, and, of course, immediately teams wanted to be formed according to nationality. I said we have to do mixed ones. Most of the players could not talk to each other due to language differences, but during the games they really came to understand and like each other. Those people who played on the same teams have stayed friends."

Like Gerry, I believe that people are more tolerant when they are not struggling for economic survival. Responsible entrepreneurism is one important way that the West can encourage the people of Central and Eastern Europe to work together to create a viable future for their region. Any regional recovery plan should include a specific goal of creating multinational working teams, which will enable people of different ethnic backgrounds to reach the understanding that California Fitness network members have: By working together they can reach their common, shared goal of economic success. This same concept also applies to neighborhoods in the United States that have been left out of the American Dream.

"Our network is very multinational, and we have done many international seminars. How is it that in our company the Romanians no longer hate the Hungarians, and they invite each other into their homes to stay? Why is it that the Czech people in the California Fitness network do not dislike the Slovaks? Why is it that the Serbs, Hungarians, and other nationals work so well together and help each other in this company? How do you create the feeling of being on the same team? By having them involved in the game of entrepreneurship," Gerry said.

Looking Forward

Gerry is an example of the type of entrepreneur the world needs. He makes a positive difference. He leads, sets a positive example, creates jobs, and shows that responsible entrepreneurism works.

Gerry and I have become good friends and frequently exchange ideas. As an investor in his ventures, I have found him to honor every commitment. I hope to make additional financial investments with Gerry and to be a partner of his forever. He is a man of true integrity who has been good for Hungary and this troubled region of the world.

Chapter 6

THE TRAIN OF HOPE –
DORAJA EBERLE

Doraja Eberle grew up in a very stable and wealthy Austrian family. She was rebellious as a child and her parents pressed her to receive training as a social worker. She rather quickly learned that she enjoyed this type of work and found pleasure in helping others.

During the Bosnian War in 1992, Doraja watched nightly the horror of the human suffering and felt an overwhelming need to go there to find a way to help. Over time, her desire to help kept creating innovative solutions to problems. Her organization, Farmers Helping Farmers, provides food and supplies, but most importantly, builds homes for people displaced by war or disaster. As of June, 2001, they had built 400 homes and brought 1000 trucks of supplies to Bosnia.

Doraja Eberle (right) talking with a volunteer.

In 1998, Doraja Eberle did the near impossible. She moved 900 tons of desperately needed food from Germany to Bosnia. All of the large international aid organizations had turned down the food because they could not move it. Ms. Eberle said she would take the food without an immediate plan to get it done. She eventually brought the "Train of Hope," as her train was dubbed, into Sarajevo against enormous odds.

— ✦ —

Entrepreneurs Don't Always Seek Personal Financial Gain

One attribute that ties all entrepreneurs together is hope. Whether operating in the for-profit world or the nonprofit world, entrepreneurs must often be optimistic to a fault in order to succeed. Occasionally this point of view creates a hero, as in the case of the inspiring Doraja Eberle. The public is often unaware of the entrepreneurial characteristics of those in the nonprofit world. Still, many of the challenges in former Communist countries are the same for nonprofit and for-profit entrepreneurs: tricky management issues, bureaucracy, corruption, and raising money.

Entrepreneurs—whether nonprofit or for-profit—need to take risks, lead people, inspire action with vision, and just plain follow up to make things happen. Creative, nonprofit risk takers like Doraja and others I have met in Central and Eastern Europe are turning the world upside down with their actions and making it better for those in need.

Of the hundreds of not-for-profit organizations in Central and Eastern Europe today, some are effective; many are bureaucratic and wasteful. Some are entrepreneurial; most are not. Professional managers run many nonprofits, and, while they can be very good organizers, they may lack the vision, passion, and risk-taking nature of entrepreneurial leaders. One woman's compassion and unwitting entrepreneurial skill have really made such a difference. Doraja Eberle and her husband Alexander run a remarkable organization, and the effect they have on people has been remarkable.

A Family in a 1200-Year-Old Castle with No Heat

When Kathy and I traveled to various parts of Austria to pay calls on government officials, the embassy personnel set up meetings with different groups and prominent citizens in each area. In Salzburg, we made a call on the Baron and Baroness Mayr-Melnhof. The Baron and Baroness own vast tracts of land and castles throughout Austria. Their primary home is a lovely, 1200-year-old castle outside of Salzburg. The ancient structure has no modern source of heat or air conditioning. During Austria's lengthy winter, their heat is provided by immense, tiled wood-burning stoves, as it has been for generations.

Titles were officially forbidden in Austria in 1918 after Austria and Germany lost World War I. But to this day, despite the law, titles are still used. Baron and Baroness Mayr-Melnhof are in their 70s. They are very elegant, kind, and interesting people. The Baron has held a number of senior government positions. Today, he continues to operate his family's extensive land holdings. He and his wife have 10 children. At our first meeting, sitting in one of the castle's drawing rooms, we met a couple of the children and their spouses. This included their daughter Doraja Eberle and her husband Alexander.

We had heard about Doraja, but nothing anyone had said really prepared us for meeting her in person. Doraja is one of the kindest, most impressive, and passionate people I have ever met. She is also an extraordinary entrepreneur. She reminds me of another very great and selfless woman: Mother Teresa. Doraja, like Mother Teresa, has dedicated her life to helping others and is impatient with inactivity, only wanting to spend her time and effort doing things that truly help others.

Although we only spent a short time with Doraja the first time we met her, our conversation was comfortable and very open. I knew that our paths would cross again. It was evident in her passionate description of the work she does that, despite her humility, she has been influential in many people's lives. Doraja has a key entrepreneurial trait: She is a charismatic leader and a visionary.

Early Background

Both Doraja and Alexander were born into wealthy Austrian families. Doraja describes herself as having been a very difficult child and teenager. Her parents, with gentle but firm pressure, encouraged her to attend Salzburg's Social Academy, where she would be trained as a social worker. She quickly realized that it was the right profession for her, but said, "The years of study were very, very hard. My first years in the profession were unforgettable because I noticed how different I was from the others. For 20 years of my life, I thought that everybody lived the way I did. After a few years working with lost children, prostitutes, and drug addicts, I realized how thankful I was to have grown up in a loving family."

Doraja and Alexander were married in 1980. "He is always around me," Doraja says. "I'm always the one who talks; he is always quiet. But he's the important one on our team."

In my experience of knowing them as a couple, they indeed are a great team. Doraja and Alexander could have chosen to lead lives that were full and comfortable. Instead, Doraja became a social worker and Alexander a CPA. Their passion is reserved for their two children and Farmers Helping Farmers, the humanitarian aid group they founded to assist those in need in the war-devastated areas of Bosnia and Kosovo.

Mother Teresa Enters Doraja's World

Doraja's similarities to Mother Teresa are not accidental. She says a meeting with the legendary woman changed her life.

"It was in the autumn of 1988, and someone had asked for my help with the Family Congress in Vienna," Doraja remembers. "It was a very impressive conference, and one influential speaker was Mother Teresa. On the last day of the conference, someone came to me and said, 'Mother Teresa would like to speak with you.' I said this could only be a mistake because I didn't know her. I mean, I knew who she was, but she didn't know us. This person insisted and said, 'She wants to see you tomorrow morning.' When I got home, I found a little cross and a letter expressing thanks for my many efforts in this congress."

Doraja explained to me that at the time she had received the letter and cross, she assumed a similar thank you was sent to everyone who had helped on the conference. Doraja reread the personal, handwritten note, which said, "Never forget, with God everything is possible."

"The next morning, Alexander and I met Mother Teresa," Doraja says. "During those five minutes, she made the impossible possible. Mother Teresa told us that within four months we would receive a special child from her hands. It is impossible to describe what happened to me in the following weeks, but I will never forget the motherliness I felt at that very moment, without having my child in my arms."

During their first eight years of marriage Doraja had had 12 miscarriages. After a special treatment in a London clinic, instead of getting a baby, she got a dangerous case of Hepatitis B and had to stay in the hospital for many weeks.

"Alexander and I had decided not to see any doctors after that, but to put our lives in the hands of God," Doraja says.

After her meeting with Mother Teresa, Doraja felt her prayers were being answered. Doraja and her mother flew to Delhi where Mother Teresa handed her a beautiful six-month-old girl. The adopted daughter was a dream come true, but there were problems.

"She was very ill," Doraja says. "When I said to Mother Teresa that I was afraid she was going to die, she turned around and said, 'Listen, God has chosen you to be the mother of this child, so it is now up to you if she stays alive or not.'"

One year later, the family of three was joined by a second addition— a son.

"Antonious was also six months old. He was very healthy and strong, and we brought him home in June 1989. Now more than 10 years have passed, but not a single day has gone by that we do not remember the wonderful gifts we receive through our children."

Doraja truly approaches every day of life as a gift and looks for the positive in every action.

"I have to go there."

The former Yugoslavia was a peaceful and prosperous neighbor to Austria. Under Tito's Communist leadership, Austria's relationship with its neighbor was far better than with Soviet-controlled Hungary or Czechoslovakia. Yet, post-Cold War, post-Berlin Wall, post-Tito, for complex and ill-understood reasons, the former Yugoslavia has now been divided into six little countries of more or less distinct ethnic groups that seem to have nothing more pressing to do than attempt to annihilate each other. In the process, the possibilities of a broader conflict and potential World War III loom.

But without even such an expansive view of the risks of these conflicts, the horror of their barbaric ways is reminiscent of the Holocaust. The distances between Austria and these countries are small, like traveling from New York to Washington, D.C. But the real distance, measured not in miles but in the quality of people's lives, is a massive chasm.

The Bosnian War in 1992 was on the Austrian television every night. Doraja knew she had to work to stop the human suffering. Watching news programs at home, she was horrified by photographs of weeping refugee children. She felt an overwhelming urge to go there, even though she wasn't sure where "there" was.

"I was watching the television. My babies were one and two," Doraja remembers. "I saw the sad pictures of the innocent children in Bosnia, and I said to my husband, all of a sudden, 'I have to go down there. Please let me go there.' I didn't know where 'there' was, but still, he said 'yes,'" she laughs. "We still talk about that 'yes.'"

A Young Soldier Who Changed Doraja's Life

Doraja's work all started with a trip to Zagreb in 1992.

"The war had just begun," she says. "I'd never been to Zagreb before, so I asked someone where there would be a place to sleep. They said there was a convent where I could go. I went to the convent, and that night the priest said he had to go to the hospital because a young man, a soldier, called and asked if he could come. So I asked, 'May I come with you?'"

"What I saw there was a young soldier, probably 25 years old, with no arms and no legs. At his side were his beautiful young wife and a little child. While he spoke to the priest, I had a thousand thoughts. He can never hug his wife again, he can never earn money for his family, and he cannot even commit suicide if he wants to. When we left the hospital, I asked the priest, 'What did this young man want? What did he say?' The priest told me the soldier wanted him to come and pray with him, and thank God that he was alive."

Doraja gave me a minute to think, and then continued, "So that was the key for me. That soldier made my life better because of what he said. Now I will give all my life for other people to make their lives better. That was the day that I started to be there for others. I never met him again, and I don't know what happened to him, but every day he is there in my mind. And that was the beginning. The beginning of something that we couldn't imagine."

At the dawn of the 21st century, it is hard to imagine such an epiphany, but this surely was one for Doraja. I have often thought of this discussion with Doraja and wonder how few people ever have an experience that moves them in the way Doraja described. There is no doubt in my mind that Doraja is a very spiritual person who is open to experiences that will enrich her soul and empower her. Her meeting with the young soldier did exactly that.

Developing a Vision

The next day the priest escorted Doraja to an area south of Zagreb where hundreds of farmhouses had been destroyed. Doraja didn't know what she could do to help, so, through an interpreter, she asked. The people were living in cellars with candles for light and no running water. They had refused to leave their homes. They told Doraja that she was the first person who had asked what they wanted and who didn't bring them things they didn't need. What they did want was to stay in their homes. Doraja looked around and saw only hovels.

"I had never built a house before," Doraja says. "So I came home, and my husband and I remembered a television show about betting on crazy ideas. There was a bet that said, 'Do you think that 100 men can build 100 wooden houses in 100 hours?' We remembered that and called the show's producers to ask where we can find the people who built the wooden houses. We saw one of the houses the next week and asked them to build one for us in our garden so that we could learn how to build them. Then we wrote 100 letters to 100 friends. I think in the next week we got the money for the first house. One house cost $5,000. That is how it all started."

Today, through an assembly-line approach and with careful engineering, each house costs only $3,500. This includes appliances, a full bathroom, and a sleeping loft for an 800-square-foot house. Doraja's leadership and inspiration has encouraged her Farmers Helping Farmers team to keep innovating, whether it's to build these houses or to deliver care packages or food for an asylum for the mentally ill. Doraja's voice is always filled with the simple, profound conviction that what she is doing is right and good. I've seen many people moved to tears as a result of simply listening to her tell her story. Whether building homes or providing food and tools for farming, she is always bringing hope to the "poorest of the poor," the silent, desperate victims of war. Although she does not consider herself an entrepreneur, to me she is the essence of one. She has a vision, grasps its core, convinces others to participate, and follows through.

It's important to note that Doraja's organization doesn't give people things they don't need or support them in a way that makes them dependent. Instead, she listens to her market, finds out what the people need, and empowers them with tools, animals, seeds, and so forth to live independently so that they can rebuild their own lives. Far too often, I have seen people and programs in impoverished neighborhoods in the United States fail to understand this critical point. Instead of teaching people to fish, they keep people dependent by giving them a small amount of free fish. Just prior to going to Vienna, I was spending much of my time working on programs for inner-city neighborhoods. I had the opportunity to meet with former President Bill Clinton on these matters and exchange a number of letters exploring ideas. He was troubled about the plight of people in America's inner cities. Toward the end of his administration, President Clinton still was putting a major press on exploring solutions to decade-old problems. While progress is being made with programs such as Welfare to Work, there is much more to do.

Building an Organization on Principles

In the more than eight years since her first trip to Zagreb, Doraja's Farmers Helping Farmers, using only volunteers, has built more than 382 houses for the elderly, the handicapped, and the destitute throughout Bosnia, Croatia, and Kosovo. The organization also runs a "godparents" program. Through this program, six times a year, 780 families in Austria, Germany, and Italy make care packages for families in the war zones. Doraja is adamant that the personal nature of the packages is essential to their mission.

"It makes all the difference that we are like postmen," she says. "Their names are on the packages and that makes it easy for us to give and easy for them to accept. It wasn't from me; it was from a 'godparent.' People are ashamed to be dependent on humanitarian aid. I've watched mass distribution, and it doesn't work. It reduces people to act like animals."

Thinking out-of-the-box enabled Doraja to come up with the godparents program, addressing both the needs for direct assistance and the problems of mass distribution. Farmers Helping Farmers establishes a long-lasting relationship in the tiny villages it assists. Creative ways of looking at problems has enabled this organization to make a real difference.

"Alexander and I go in first," Doraja explains. "We decide if our team of 40 people can help. We prefer little villages because we want to help everybody there. We prefer areas where Muslims, Serbs, and Croats live together, because we want to make a point when we build our houses, side by side, that they won't be separated again. We stay for up to a year and a half. They get a house, seeds, tools, and animals. We take care of a school and pay the salary for a doctor and a nurse. We cry when we leave because we know them very well. But when we have to go, we say there are others now poorer than you. And they understand."

For Doraja, keeping things simple and being true to her mission of personal support, implied in the name Farmers Helping Farmers, means no fancy office or overhead of any kind. The office to this day is Doraja's kitchen table and the organization is 100 percent volunteer. Doraja and Alexander, who both work more than full-time at this, receive no compensation. They utilize three trucks, which were gifts, old but thanks to volunteer repair work, still working. There are another 10 to 20 volunteers with trucks to add to the monthly caravans bringing supplies and food to those in need.

Failures Are Necessary for Success

So often, I have found that the best entrepreneurial successes come when we don't know enough about something to realize an idea "won't work." A positive attitude and a refusal to hear why something can't be done are often how what seems impossible becomes reality. Such is the case with Doraja.

Doraja is a real entrepreneur in the best sense of the word. Her explanation of the success of Farmers Helping Farmers reveals how entrepreneurs take risks and learn from experiences. For example, the godparents program is an incredibly successful part of her aid program, but it came about because of analyzing failures. Like many good entrepreneurial ideas, it was born out of necessity when an earlier version failed.

"We have learned from our mistakes within the past few years," Doraja says. "One mistake was mass distribution. It should be avoided. It is so much against human dignity that at the end of the 20th century people still have to fight for a pair of shoes or a piece of bread. We have found 780 godparents. These families regularly pack food parcels for their special families. We learned to put people's names on the packages. When they see that it is especially for them, often they cry. And the godparents also feel a special attachment. They pack the boxes with loving care."

Suspicion born of Communism still hangs over these people. Communism made entire populations dependent on the state. Now, though Communism is banished, many people find it hard to believe that people like Doraja and her team want to help them and expect nothing in return. Doraja recognized that simple aid is not enough. It must be given in a way that rebuilds self-worth in people who have been dehumanized by the machines and soldiers of war. The promises she makes are not empty.

"The good thing about our houses is that when we started our program, we promised a house and we fulfilled the promise in four days," Doraja says. "A house is so much more than a roof and four walls. Nobody believed us. I've seen what other organizations' promises mean. The people get the fence, the brick, and the wood thrown in front of their land. That is their house. Things get stolen; the wood gets wet, so there's no house. So, I said, we can do it another way. We promise a house on Sunday night, and by Friday we move them in. They are the handicapped, the elderly, the desperate, and we give them a house to live in. That gives them hope."

A New Challenge—Kosovo

Doraja had a well-tuned apparatus for dealing with the war-stricken areas in Bosnia and Croatia. She and Alexander knew how to juggle the needs of their two young children and the many volunteers who are the backbone of Farmers Helping Farmers. From her kitchen table command center and the garage depot provided by her father, she successfully managed the growing humanitarian organization. Then came another phone call from the newest hot spot in the former Yugoslavia.

"In Kosovo, when the war started, at the worst time, a friend asked if we were going to help. I said no because Kosovo is so far. I couldn't go there. I still had little children. If I could go there, I could go to Rwanda too," Doraja remembers.

Having decided that Farmers Helping Farmers could not go to Kosovo, Doraja was amazed when an outpouring of packages and donations earmarked for Kosovo began arriving unannounced at her home.

"People just seemed to think we would be helping," she said. "They brought things, and we had to rent a tent, and the tent became bigger and bigger. By the end it was 28 meters long, and people came with trucks until we were paralyzed. So we said, 'Okay, what can we do?' And everybody brought money— you just don't know. Very often we ask why people trust us. Why do they put $1,000 or even $10,000, just like that on the table? When we asked people they say it is because we go there personally."

Inundated by contributions, Doraja realized that she had to respond and set about figuring out how. Large, established aid organizations told her they didn't need the donations she was ready to give them. She turned instead to a private citizen, a woman who had been working in Albania for seven years named Mariana Graf. Mariana said she would help Doraja, and, within a month, Farmers Helping Farmers became one of the first aid organizations into Kosovo after the NATO bombing stopped. In a matter of weeks, they had rebuilt the roofs on 77 homes destroyed during the war. Farmers Helping Farmers is an incredible, efficient entrepreneurial organization. Its volunteers are fluid, respond to challenge with a real "we can do it" attitude, and do not flinch from taking a risk. They have a truly entrepreneurial attitude: The worst they can do is not to try.

Raising Money—A Critical Need for Every Enterprise

The Young Presidents' Organization (YPO) is a selective worldwide network of chief executive officers of companies. I was a member for about 25 years until I turned 50, the mandatory retirement age. YPO holds educational meetings all over the world, including three or four annual "universities," which are weeklong seminars held in different cities throughout the world. Often, the seminar subjects are specific to the location of the meeting, but at the same time, there are a wide variety of speakers.

In 1998, YPO held its annual Family University in Salzburg, Austria. Ironically, this was the meeting where I became reacquainted with Steve Mariotti and learned more about Doraja. Even though Salzburg is a few hours away by car, we hosted a number of events at the Ambassador's Residence in Vienna to help make the university more interesting. Most of the YPO University took place in and around Salzburg, where very little happens that doesn't include Doraja's parents, the Baron and Baroness. They were in the small group of honorary chairpersons, brought in as part of the advisory council for the university.

A number of pre-planning meetings were held. Kathy and I attended one of them in Salzburg, and there again were Doraja, Alexander, and one of Doraja's sisters, who was actively involved, as well as other friends and family. Early on, Peter Whitehead, who chaired the Salzburg University, and Jon Fischer, who heads up YPO Education, made a decision to have Doraja take a major role in this university. Peter had grown up in Salzburg and knew and respected Doraja and all of her achievements.

She agreed to lead an "academy," which is a side trip for a smaller group prior to the actual seminar. She took 40 YPOers, including families with children, to show them what Croatia was like and how the Bosnian War had affected the people. Those participants experienced the trip of a lifetime, and Doraja and her husband developed lifelong friends among the group.

At the Salzburg University, Doraja gave one of the few keynote speeches. She spoke from her heart, and, knowing Doraja, I knew she had no written speech. She was simply going to tell her audience of several hundred who she was, what she did, and why. Literally, by mid-speech, she had the audience in tears. Doraja spoke in an honest manner that few of us share with others, much less hear from anyone.

One of her stories from that speech sticks in my mind.

"In September 1997, we started a new project in Bosnia in a little enclave between Croatia and the Republic Srbska. You can only reach this area by ferryboat," Doraja began. "30,000 people live there, and everybody had to leave in the war. Now, the first 18,000 refugees had returned, and we were with them and brought them whatever we could. This area has been completely destroyed. There are no schools and no factories. A Catholic priest asked me if I wasn't scared because there is a psychiatric clinic with 400 patients there, and for more than one year no one had taken care of them. An hour later, I was there. We found 400 patients eating grass with water that had been flavored with salt. The 100 people who help them had not been paid for a year. They had no medicine. They had nothing," Doraja recalled.

"Very often the problems are not about money," she said. "When we arrived 400 people had no spoons, no plates. And this is five hours from Salzburg. So Alexander went shopping, and for $100 he bought 3,000 plastic plates and spoons. We gave them back their human dignity for $100. You can do so much for very little money."

I am not sure that Doraja knew that Mother Teresa had been a keynote speaker for more than one past YPO University. Like Mother Teresa, Doraja really doesn't have much time or interest in giving speeches, but she knows when to make exceptions. I am glad that she did for the YPO meeting, as it created a massive amount of interest in her project and encouraged fund-raising that continues to this day. It also helped some people with workaholic personalities and little knowledge of or interest in regions with human suffering to develop a new sense of perspective.

At the end of her speech, I stood just outside the ornate ballroom where Doraja spoke and was amazed to see so many in the audience deeply touched. Doraja had made a connection with virtually everyone. There were a few lighter moments when people laughed and other moments when they cried. Throughout her speech Doraja held people of all ages spellbound.

In the question-and-answer session, the members asked how they could help. The answers actually came from other audience members. Doraja is not one to make a typical pitch for donations. People just want to give after knowing the good being done. Some money was raised immediately. But later, Pat Beach, a member from Ann Arbor, Michigan, took it upon himself to set up an American foundation, Friends of Farmers Helping Farmers U.S.A. c/o his company Captac Financial Group, Inc. which provides tax-deductible status for U.S. donors and passes all monies on to Doraja's organization. Another member, Michael

Neundorfer, from Cleveland, arranged for Doraja and Alexander to come to the United States, visit various YPO chapters, and introduce them to Farmers Helping Farmers. In the process, the organization raised even more money. In the first year following the YPO speech, more than $1.5 million was contributed.

Doraja's accounting system is quite simple. The money that is raised is spent on good work as quickly as possible. If she raises more money, she builds more houses and feeds more people. Because there are no administrative costs, 100 percent of the money that comes in goes out to meet the needs of the poorest of the poor.

Moving 900 Tons of Food

In the spring of 1998, Doraja took an urgent phone call from U.S. Army Colonel Levens at the U.S. Defense Logistics Agency in Garmish, Germany. He was frantic. He had 900 tons of surplus foods that had to be removed from his warehouse immediately. His generous offer had originally been accepted by a large nonprofit organization. Doraja was interested, but her group was considered too small. Then the group that had said yes found out it simply could not move that much food. Already turned down by a big nonprofit, Colonel Levens heard one after another of the large, humanitarian organizations operating in the region also say no. They all declined because they couldn't tackle what they saw as a huge problem: how to move that much food so quickly from Germany to Bosnia.

Colonel Levens needed the food containers, which filled the immense Army warehouse, removed within 48 hours or he would have to destroy the perishables and ship other foodstuffs back to the United States. Somewhere along the humanitarian workers' phone chain, he was given the phone number for Farmers Helping Farmers, which had not earlier been considered a serious prospect. When Doraja heard the Colonel's offer, she didn't need the 24 hours he gave her to think about it. She just said, "We'll take it." She didn't need to consult anyone. There was no board of directors. No forms to fill out. It was simple. Like a true entrepreneur, she didn't give a moment's thought to how the logistics would be managed, she simply took the risk. She leapt at the chance to obtain all that precious food for needy people and knew she'd figure out the rest later.

Her first idea was to recruit trucks and run them day and night. After Colonel Levens explained that the quantity of food he had to give away wouldn't fit in even the 36 trucks that Doraja had planned to use, she went back to the drawing board. Disappointed, her close associates thought there was no way to move the food in time. Then Doraja thought about a train.

Doraja wanted to move all the food, including tons of valuable coffee, from Garmish, Germany, to Sarajevo. She had never rented a train before; in fact, she didn't know if a private person could rent a train. She also did not know that sections of the tracks were destroyed in the war and that trains simply were not making the trip to Sarajevo since the war. In short, she did not know this was impossible! The 48-hour deadline gave her little time, so she simply kept moving forward, refusing to accept the negative.

She found out that she could rent a train. She did so. Soon, she had it on a siding by the warehouse. Doraja, Alexander, and her best friends Landolf Revertera and Klaus Gollhofer—with handcarts and their own backs—filled 37 boxcars with the surplus food. They inventoried each boxcar and printed numbers on the sides before the train set out for Sarajevo. Doraja soon discovered that trains had not been going regularly to Sarajevo in nine years and that areas of the tracks even needed repair. But she kept working and hoped for another miracle.

The Farmers Helping Farmers train traveled from Germany, through the lush green vineyards and countryside of Austria, through tiny Slovenia. It rumbled its way through the devastated villages of Croatia and in several places was delayed because tracks needed fixing. But mile by mile it moved forward toward Bosnia.

Somewhere along the way, the local Mafia got word of the train and its valuable cargo and hijacked it. When Doraja heard of this, it took several calls to locate the Mafia operation holding the train. They were offering its release for a ransom. Then, her amazing secretary, who pretended to be a Serb, reached for the telephone and made a most impressive call. Impersonating the secretary to a famous Mafia boss that she knew of, she yelled at the Mafia operatives and ordered the release and return of the train and its contents. To everyone's shock, the trick worked. The train was again back on the track and moving in the right direction. When the train finally reached the area of Sarajevo, Doraja could see that the train cars were no longer in the same numerical order they had been when they left Germany. But there were still a total of 37 boxcars, and the contents were mostly intact. Still this was not the last problem.

As the engineer slowed the lengthy train in preparation to pull into the station, the stationmaster slapped his hat on his head and hurried down the tracks. He forced the train to halt well before reaching the station and ordered that the engine be uncoupled from its precious cargo. He then demanded payment of 3,000 deutsche marks—about $1,500 U.S.—before he would allow the train to continue into the station.

As the hundreds of eager refugees and peacekeepers watched, Doraja coolly analyzed the situation. She knew that the obviously nervous stationmaster was hoping to benefit personally, which is rather typical for border crossings in all parts in the region. And yet, she didn't want to set a precedent of Farmers Helping Farmers paying bribes. Looking him squarely in the eyes, she requested an immediate meeting with both him and Sarajevo's mayor. A few minutes later, in the mayor's office, accompanied by Alexander, Landolf, and Colonel Levens, Doraja calmly turned out her pockets and said, "I have no money. I can get money from the bank, but it will require a letter from both of you requesting the payment and explaining what it is for."

Sheepishly, after hasty consultation, the stationmaster agreed that no payment was necessary. The orders were given, the engine was recoupled, and the train inched its way to the platform. The United Nations Peacekeepers and Colonel Levens, who had been waiting for four tense days for its arrival, greeted it. The train was late, but it had made it. Eager hands reached out to help unload the cargo. A cheering crowd of hundreds, including Serbs, Muslims, and Bosnians, peered down the tracks, alerted to the train's arrival by its piercing, triumphant whistle. The "Train of Hope," as the press dubbed it, had finally arrived in grateful Sarajevo, thanks to the unfailing optimism of Doraja Eberle.

Responsible Entrepreneurism by Example

Knowing Doraja has helped me clarify the essence of what responsible entrepreneurism really means, whether you're out to make a profit or engineer a better world. First, entrepreneurs are all about missions and passions. An essential part of any successful venture, whether for profit or not, is having a clear vision of where the organization is going. Doraja is a visionary leader. Her passion and her absolute commitment spill over to everyone else on the team who labor for Farmers Helping Farmers wholeheartedly and without compensation. Second, Doraja's perseverance and single-minded "can-do" attitude are examples of what entrepreneurs do best. She didn't think, "Here are all the reasons why taking 900 tons of food to Sarajevo is a dumb idea." She thought, "I'll take it. Somehow I'll figure out how to get it done." That's what entrepreneurial risk taking is all about. Finally, Doraja's sense of ethics, leading her to refuse to pay bribes and figure out ways to outfox both the local Mafia and government officials, illustrates the best of responsible entrepreneurism.

Perseverance, creativity, and having a mission and a vision for the future are a large part of what being an entrepreneur is all about. Raising needed money, taking risks on ideas, failing sometimes, and starting again: These are all entrepreneurial traits. Doraja is all these things and more.

When it comes to the "responsible" part, I think of ethics, which of course is a relative and debatable concept. Being responsible is giving back in some way to one's community. Doraja is the essence of this. Teaching entrepreneurship in Central and Eastern Europe doesn't have to and shouldn't be just about creating profitable enterprises. People like Doraja give back to the community in so many ways. Profit is far from her goal, but a sense of entrepreneurial spirit is key to her success. What is exciting is that the entrepreneurial spirit can be focused on such disparate goals: from building better bricks to building homes for refugees. Entrepreneurs can be the engines for a train of hope that can produce more responsible entrepreneurs and make the world a better place.

People Just
Want Him to Succeed —
Albert C. Black, Jr.

Albert C. Black, Jr. lives his professional and personal life by the philosophy he advocates: an absolute commitment to his faith, to his family, to his friends, and to the free-enterprise system. His career as an entrepreneur has never distracted him from his civic obligation to the communities where he works and lives.

Albert C. Black, Jr.

Mr. Black was born in 1959, the youngest of seven children, and raised in the Frazier Courts housing projects in South Dallas. He graduated from the University of Texas at Dallas with concentrations in business and political science and received his M.B.A. from the Cox School of Business at Southern Methodist University (S.M.U.) in Dallas.

Following college Mr. Black became an entrepreneur—one with an agenda to create a successful business in the inner city community where he grew up. He founded the firm that is now known as On-Target Supplies & Logistics in 1982 and served as President while performing most of the operating duties in the early years.

Since 1982, On-Target has grown into a diverse and profitable corporation, distributing office supplies, as well as administering the logistics of warehousing and delivery services for companies throughout Texas, Oklahoma, Louisiana, Arkansas, and Missouri.

While his commitment to his community is the driving force of Mr. Black's professional life, his priorities are his faith and his family. Mr. Black works and resides in Dallas, Texas. His wife Gwyneith Navon Black, a lifelong partner in business, as well as family, serves On-Target as Vice President of Business Relationships and is a key architect in helping Mr. Black achieve his dreams.

— ✦ —

Albert Senior Saw a Better Future for his Son

Albert Black loves symbolism. He even loves the responsibility of being a symbol himself. On the desk of his office at On-Target Supplies & Logistics in Dallas is a doorknob from Dallas' old Baker Hotel. Albert's father was once the doorman for the legendary hotel, which was a meeting place for what Albert calls "the highwaymen" of Dallas: the city leaders of the 1950s and 1960s whose names eventually were assigned to Dallas' major freeways. But today, Albert is the one who's opening doors, as the president and CEO of the company he built, as the first African-American member of the Young President's Organization in Dallas, and as the first African-American chairman of the Greater Dallas Chamber of Commerce.

One of Albert's biggest disappointments is that his father, Albert C. Black, Sr., who died in 1987, didn't live long enough to see this major political and social shift in Dallas.

"I do regret that he wasn't there in that room of 1,200 people when the gavel was passed to me and to hear the sound of that glass shattering when I became the first African-American chairman of the Dallas Chamber in its 91-year history," Albert says.

The old Baker Hotel where Albert Senior was doorman had been the meeting place for the Dallas Chamber. And Albert Junior knows his father would have taken pleasure in seeing him lead the organization.

But Albert's father was there to see him defy the odds. Born in 1959, the youngest of Albert C. Black, Sr. and Gladys Black's seven children, Albert grew up in the Frazier Courts public housing project in South Dallas, an area plagued by high crime and unemployment that for decades has been left out of progress. Albert vividly remembers the days when he was on the receiving end of President Lyndon B. Johnson's landmark social services programs.

"I grew up in a time that was very interesting in this country. I wasn't conscious of it then, but in hindsight, I see some of the things that triggered my desire to be an entrepreneur," Albert recalls. "Back in 1965 and 1966, President Johnson was waging his 'War on Poverty,' commonly referred to as 'free-lunch' programs. I remember sitting on the porch and seeing these big trucks roll through the neighborhood. During the summer, little children would be riding with their fathers on these trucks handing out the food. I used to feel so embarrassed that these white men with these white children in these white trucks would be driving through a black community passing out free lunches. Somehow I resented it even at that early age. The children's group I was a part of was learning to get something for free. But the children in those trucks with their dads were learning free enterprise. Their dads were getting paid on a government contract."

Albert learned another key lesson counting his father's tip money from the Baker Hotel. While he conquered simple math, his father talked about his customers, Dallas' business power elite.

"He let me know from early on that I could be one of those people," Albert says. "He told me that I could be every bit as big as they were if I got a good education."

And now he is. Albert made it. He is all his father dreamed of and probably far more. I have often wondered why some people can overcome difficult circumstances, like growing up in a public housing development, while others become part of the negative statistics that stereotype those largely inner-city neighborhoods. Albert was lucky to have a close family with parents who saw hope and opportunity for their children. The American Dream is available for some in low-income areas, but it is clearly not as accessible as it is to those of us who grew up in the white middle-class America of the 1950s and '60s. Certainly strong values and constant encouragement from his father made a big difference for Albert.

"I was fortunate enough to have a father who taught me a lot of things, including how to look someone in the eye when I was shaking his hand and the value of a good education," Albert says. "A lot of kids don't have that today."

Young Entrepreneurship

The company Albert started in 1982 as a young college graduate with his wife, Gwyneith, has grown from $10,000 to more than $40 million in sales and from two employees to 150 as of the writing of this book. It is still growing and represents incredible success by any measure. But Albert's entrepreneurial leanings began, like my own, at a young age.

Despite our growing up thousands of miles apart and coming from different ethnic and socioeconomic backgrounds, as entrepreneurs, our stories have many similarities. I started out selling Greenrivers drinks, my own unique version of the proverbial lemonade stand, at age 10. I was 12 when I started to build a lawn-mowing business. Albert also began his foray into free enterprise mowing lawns at the age of 10.

"At the risk of sounding extraordinarily corny," Albert says, "I fell in love with the free enterprise system at a young age. The idea of exchanging goods and services for a predetermined price was so exciting to me. I learned early on that as long as I could maintain my health, I would never be unemployed. And I learned this growing up in a community that had very high unemployment. Free enterprise is something that ought to be, and can be, blind to our backgrounds."

When Albert was 10, he borrowed a push mower from the public housing project's maintenance department and began cutting his neighbors' small yards for 75 cents to a dollar a piece. Albert eventually saved enough money to buy a power mower and cornered the market at Frazier Courts. He grew his venture into Best Friends Lawn Service, a business that eventually helped fuel the origins of On-Target.

My own lawn-mowing venture was also a source of education, and I owe a lot of lessons to my father. He gave me my first contract: $6 to cut the family lawn. He also taught me the difference between gross and net by charging me $1 for each rental of his lawn mower. As the business grew, I decided renting the equipment was a bad deal. I approached my dad for a loan to buy a riding mower. He loaned me $450 for the equipment but charged me the highest bank interest rate plus 2 percent because he said I was a poor credit risk. This incensed my grandmother—his own mother—and she wouldn't speak to him for months.

My lawn-mowing business grew and even now, almost 40 years later, I remember how excited I was to get a house with two acres as a new customer. I felt like life could never get better. To this day I remember thinking, "Wow! $25 every time I cut and edge this huge lawn. What a deal!" This is also when I became a manager. My first employee was my brother Scott, followed by other kids from school. I soon learned that management was a lot harder than just doing the work myself. Making sure people showed up and worked was a whole new area of business skills to learn.

As I look back, though, I probably had a lot easier time than Albert did. My neighborhood had more customers with bigger lawns, a better ability to pay, and desire to have someone else do the work. Albeit expensive, I still had a loan from my father. For Albert it was a slower, more difficult process of growth. Eventually, I lost interest in cutting lawns and my business slowly disappeared. Albert actually built up a large enough business to sell. I admire his approach all the more because he faced many more obstacles.

Living on Adrenaline

After graduating from W. W. Samuel High School in Dallas, Albert attended Eastern New Mexico University on a football scholarship. He finished his undergraduate education at the University of Texas at Dallas (UTD) while keeping up with the clients of Best Friends Lawn Service. There at UTD, he fell in love with Gwyneith. He had known her all of his life, because they both grew up in Frazier Courts and she was the sister of one of his best friends. But as students, they learned they had even more in common, including the desire to start a life together.

After college, Albert took a job as a doorman working the nightshift at Texas Utilities Company. It was the only time in his life he has ever worked for someone else as an employee. With his days free, he and his new bride, Gwyneith, started On-Target. Albert says he was so focused and passionate that he can't remember ever feeling depressed or discouraged.

"Those were the days of four-hour rest," Albert says. "I worked at night to earn an income so that I could build my company during the day."

Here Albert and I share another similar experience as young entrepreneurs. The first several years after I started Hall Financial as an 18-year-old, the company existed on such a shoestring budget that I worked 40-hour-a-week outside jobs to help make ends meet and pay the losses my business was incurring. As Albert and I and many other entrepreneurs can attest, many sacrifices and hard work go into making it. It may seem success just comes to some people, but most entrepreneurs in the early years are just surviving, moving toward success in very small increments.

Albert originally founded On-Target Industrial Maintenance and Supply Company, Inc. as a custodial service and supply firm. In the early days, Albert and Gwyneith performed most of the operating duties. As a young landlord of a college rooming house, I did the same, not only going to school, but working as a janitor for extra money. Albert and I both had a burning desire to succeed and little could get in our way. Certainly neither lack of sleep nor having to do the dirty work ever stopped us.

But Albert's drive didn't make him one-dimensional. Even though the success of On-Target was his primary passion, Albert stayed involved in other activities that nurtured his beliefs and value system. For example, he has always been involved in politics. He and I first met when my wife Kathy was running for mayor of Dallas. Albert was a big supporter of Kathy. He used to drive her around South Dallas and introduce her before the many speeches she gave to the African-American community there. Kathy was outspent five to one and lost the race to a former Republican Congressman. But even when the campaign got tough, Albert was always there as a loyal, steadfast friend. In the next election, she and Albert worked on a campaign for another friend, Ron Kirk, who became the first African-American mayor of Dallas.

Quantum Leaps and Big Decisions

On-Target's first big shift came four years into its existence when Albert and Gwyneith decided to phase out janitorial services and refine their focus on supplying products. It may not have seemed so important then, but refocusing the business turned out to be a great move. Two years later, in 1989, On-Target signed a five-year, $3.75 million agreement with Texas Instruments to supply computer and copier paper. Today, On-Target serves a five-state area and 14 of the top 100 Texas companies from four locations: two in Dallas, one in Houston, and another in San Antonio. And On-Target does far more than just supply computer and copier paper. The company now provides a wide variety of supply and logistics functions. On-Target has developed a series of supply chain management capabilities that provide its clients with a broad range of integrated products and logistical services. In the fall of 1999, On-Target signed a multimillion-dollar contract with communications giant Alcatel to source, procure, warehouse, assemble, and distribute installation kits for switching devices.

The company's primary goal was again changing, becoming more logistics and less supply oriented. In time, this change also would prove to be key. On-Target's goal was to provide seamless management of supply and distribution requirements. While the company still supplied copier and computer paper, computer products, and custodial supplies, it now provided venture management, logistical services, desktop distribution, material handling and dock management, centralized receiving, local area distribution, and mail room operations. Again, Albert was redefining his business to stay up to date with his customers' needs.

"The hardest time came after we figured out we were really onto something, when we had to shift out of the start-up mode into a mode of growth," Albert says. "At that point it became very difficult because of the realization that the opportunities were not endless. I had to build a management team when I was used to doing things myself."

For the first time, Albert had to hire managers who were not members of his family. He had to find a way to build loyalty, something he had never had to worry about before because of the innate trust and loyalty he had come to know from working with loved ones.

"Here the entrepreneur had to get political as the one who decides who gets what, when, where, why, and how. The great compromise begins," Albert recalled.

Over time, the company has grown and changed. At the same time, Albert and Gwyneith have changed. Today, Albert takes special pride in the fact that he sits on the Advisory Board of Texas Utilities and counts the company, where his father once served as doorman, among his largest customers.

"I love the symmetry of that," he says.

He also loves the "pure poetry" of the fact that his wife, Gwyneith, has gone from being a resident of a Dallas public housing project for her entire childhood to serving as a director of the Dallas Housing Authority board. Gwyneith's partnership has been essential to the growth of On-Target. As the company's vice president of business relationships, she has targeted the top 100 corporations throughout Texas as an effective approach to building market share and growth in profitability. She has also been a part of reinventing On-Target's business strategy to meet the demands of an ever-changing marketplace.

After former President Bill Clinton mentioned Albert as one of six influential business leaders in his 1998 State of the Union address, Gwyneith had the opportunity to meet the President. From Frazier Courts to The White House, Gwyneith has been a constant force at Albert's side, a reminder of his past, present, and future.

It's my experience that a few key decisions cause big jumps in a business's growth. I like to call them quantum leaps. For Albert and Gwyneith, focusing on supplies and getting out of the janitorial service was a quantum leap. But another big key was realizing they were not only in the supply business per se. In other words, they were in the business of having the right supply need of a customer met at the needed time, down to supplying the right desk in the right place at the right time. Too often, I have seen businesses fail or be lackluster by not being focused and defining exactly what the business is all about. Thoughtful decisions helped On-Target grow and succeed, just as they have made many other businesses take off and reach the stratosphere.

Albert's Secret Weapon

The real growth of On-Target began with the Texas Instruments contract. But just how did a little company like On-Target get a five-year, $3.75 million agreement with Texas Instruments? Was it price? A new technology? A better mousetrap of any kind? The answer is simple, yet most people would probably miss it. On-Target's secret weapon was that people want to help Albert succeed. The late Jerry Junkins, Texas Instruments' chairman and CEO at the time of that contract, wanted Albert to make it in business. Why? Albert is incredibly personable. He is charismatic, charming, and, frankly, downright loveable. He is fun, clever, quick, and sincere. He's no phony, but he's also not what people expect.

In addition to awarding On-Target a key contract, Junkins wanted to help Albert dream big. To expand his horizons, he asked Albert to come along with some other high-level businessmen on an international trade mission to Japan. Albert, of course, accepted. This is but one of many examples of the personal relationships that Albert has been able to cultivate to help On-Target grow.

Albert is astute. In the early days of building his business, affirmative action was on the way out. At the same time, big corporations like Texas Instruments and other On-Target customers were still concerned about being politically correct. The use of African-American minority suppliers has been and remains of real interest for some concerned executives. Albert plays those cards in the right way without overplaying them. He has a special knack for befriending anyone, including chairmen and presidents of big companies. He lets them know that it is important to help him because helping him is a way of helping others who have been left out of the American Dream. Moreover, they can count on him to deliver. He also appeals to the hearts of successful executives who want to take him under their wing as a son of their own.

While Albert is an African-American entrepreneur from humble beginnings, he knows how to relate to the white corporate establishment. They believe in him because he does not let them down. They also believe in him because he is aggressive and confident in an understated way. And he's always interested in learning something new.

Albert used to say to me, "Teach me about real estate," so Kathy and I invited him to become a partner with us on a project in Texas. A redevelopment of a historic property, it was fraught with complicated financing and construction issues. Albert became a co-general partner and put an equal amount of money in on a pro-rata basis. He also worked at helping on various issues with the city. I got him involved because he could help, but also because I want to see him succeed in real estate like he has in other areas. If he wants to and I can help, I'll always be there for him. I'm not alone in this feeling.

Young President's Organization and the Greater Dallas Chamber of Commerce

The Young President's Organization (YPO) membership is by invitation only. The Dallas chapter historically has been made up of successful white, mostly male members. To the credit of the Dallas chapter, Albert became the first African-American member.

When Albert wanted to join YPO, I was excited and supportive. Once in YPO, there are subgroups of members called Forums. I was in a Forum group with Albert. Forums are supposed to meet once a month and discuss personal and business matters with the condition that all conversations are confidential. I was always impressed by Albert's courage to talk about a lot of things that were uncomfortable for others to hear. His goal was to say what he believed even if it was not popular with the group.

Albert makes waves in a way that demands respect. He does not forget who he is or where he's from, but you know he is bound for higher opportunities. As if joining YPO wasn't enough, Albert also worked his way up the ladder in the Greater Dallas Chamber of Commerce. To get on the board of directors in the Dallas Chamber, you used to have to be a true good ol' boy. It usually meant being a banker or big corporate executive, certainly not an African-American entrepreneur from the projects. Again, as in so many other things, Albert was the exception.

After years of paying his dues, in 2000, as the Dallas Chamber's first African-American president, Albert used the bully pulpit to talk about how the mainstream white community in Dallas could and should help the areas of Dallas' southern sector that have been left out of economic progress. He talked about how Dallas could be a greater city if the business community pulled together and embraced diversity. Albert spoke out, but more importantly he set a new course and agenda that turned a stagnant organization into a place where people are finally thinking about new ideas and getting things done.

"I like to shake things up," Albert has said time and again.

And with his work on the Dallas Chamber, he has certainly done just that. He spoke out early about the need to bring technology and telecommunications companies to southern Dallas and then was instrumental in bringing Southwestern Bell to the area. He was also a key part of the push to locate and later expand a campus of the University of North Texas in southern Dallas. Albert also jumped full force into the Dallas public schools controversy. Dallas public schools had long been plagued by in-fighting and a revolving door of ineffective leadership. Albert said it was time for the Dallas Chamber to get involved in the search for a superintendent and encourage the board of trustees to stop bickering and start working for a common goal: a better public school system for Dallas.

Together with chamber leadership, Albert presented six points to make Dallas public schools better, then told the school board, "We're going to be in your face until the Board gets it done."

As the Dallas Chamber had never taken an active role in school politics, Albert was met with significant opposition. Many of the chamber members were from other areas of the Metroplex or sent their children to private schools. But Albert kept pushing, insisting that the Dallas Chamber, in looking out for the greater good of the business community, had an obligation and a responsibility to make the public school system that serves the majority of residents a positive mark instead of a negative mark against the city.

Getting Ahead Means Education, Education, Education

Albert puts great stock in new ides. To build his company and the loyalty of its employees, he says he began to mechanize the fundamental principles of the organization. Among the greatest of those is education. On-Target requires every employee to pursue continuing education and training. Albert believes in this so strongly that he funds this education. He also embraced the idea himself.

By 1995, he says, running a $5 million business had become second nature to him. The only problem was that On-Target was no longer a $5 million organization.

"The company had outgrown me, and I was coming up short in finding out how to direct and inspire the talented people On-Target needed to continue to grow," Albert says. This is a tough admonition for a guy who unabashedly describes himself as a "natural charismatic leader."

"I was falling short on another level—competency and expertise—and the organization was being depressed because I was not going to be able to hire more competent people unless I knew how to direct and inspire those people," Albert says. "After all, being president of the company had to mean presiding over the company. I had always been the best person for the job, but what worried me was that I was beginning to think it was better for someone else to be the president of this company. For On-Target to reach its potential, I had to reconfigure and go to that next level as an executive."

So Albert took his own advice and went back to school, getting his MBA at Southern Methodist University while also running On-Target.

"While I was in school, my goal was for On-Target's performance to be better every semester than it had the previous semester, and I reached that goal," Albert says, pulling a chart from his desk to prove it.

Albert keeps the chart handy to inspire other On-Target employees to do what he's done. "When I invite people into my office, I ask them, 'How are you doing?' I listen, and I talk to them about education. I let them know that I took the challenge, too. I'm not asking them to go anywhere that I'm not willing to go," Albert says.

Albert has been criticized by some for requiring continuing education across the board at On-Target, but he responds to critics by saying, "Anyone who can't accept an offer like that is probably someone who's not good for the company."

In addition to formal education, Albert invites speakers to talk about life and business experience during informal luncheons with his employees. Albert invited me to speak one day. I enjoyed my opportunity to do this so much that I keep a picture in my office taken that day with Albert and Gwyneith in front of the headquarters of On-Target. Every company develops its own personality, which in the early days often reflects the founders. In the case of On-Target, I found excitement, a positive spirit, and a hunger to learn and grow. The emphasis on all levels of education is omnipresent.

It's the Mind-Set

In the summer of 1999, Albert and Gwyneith and other senior business executives of Dallas accompanied Mayor Ron Kirk and his wife Mattrice Kirk on a trade mission to Europe. At the end of the trade mission, the Kirks and the Blacks came to visit Kathy and me in Vienna. Albert and Ron are two of the funniest people I know. They had each other going with their comfortable banter, and I think I was laughing most of the time they were in Vienna. Still, we also talked about serious subjects like the problems in Central and Eastern Europe and Kosovo and how the ethnic difficulties were similar to the experiences that African-Americans have had in parts of the United States.

Albert explained how he believes entrepreneurship and creating wealth can make a difference for these suffering regions and people. We have often talked about the impact that mind-set has on success and failure and agree that there is a defeatist mind-set and generational cycle that must and can be broken. It was broken in Albert's case in part by a close family, an optimistic father, hard work, and fortunate circumstances. Albert believes education, access to college, and options to other positive life experiences also help make the difference.

Albert believes that wealth can make the difference as well—not in having it, but in using it to help others gain opportunities and access. He believes, as I do, that wealth can be used for the common good. He feels blessed in his life and intends to continue to dedicate himself and his resources to improving opportunities for others.

Helping Others Reach Their Potential

Albert believes in showing others how to reach their potential. "I like seeing people confident enough to venture out on their own and start their own businesses," he says. "I like to think I'm not creating competition, but, if I do, I like to think it would only make On-Target better."

Though Albert says he thinks entrepreneurship can't be taught, he says he believes it can be learned. That is an important distinction.

"Magic Johnson's jump shot can't be taught. You can't take golf lessons from Tiger Woods and go win the Masters. But if Magic Johnson or Tiger Woods make themselves available to be an influence in your life, you can learn from exposure to greatness," Albert continues. "If successful entrepreneurs share their stories, lessons can be learned. The drive and the vision can't be taught, but the ability to get over barriers, the lessons of success and failure—that can be learned."

Having achieved an impressive level of success, Albert now has the luxury of being able to give his time to help others develop their businesses through his leadership at the Greater Dallas Chamber of Commerce. But he doesn't view his role in business development as that of mentor; instead, he says it's a relationship of mutual learning.

"I don't like mentoring programs where one of the parties is viewed as a subordinate. Instead, I like to think of it as 'success partnerships.' That young entrepreneur just getting started has as much to offer me as I do him or her," Albert says.

"At the chamber, we do an extraordinary amount of business planning for young, gleamy-eyed entrepreneurs, and I find myself coming away from some of those sessions with amazing insights from those who have not yet achieved success. It gives me an opportunity to rekindle my own entrepreneurial spirit," Albert says.

Albert spends a great deal of his time these days giving back to his community, working with programs in Dallas public schools and in private schools in Dallas' southern sector.

That's where, Albert says, "entrepreneurship with a soul" comes in. Albert doesn't "come back" to the old neighborhood to help out the underprivileged because it's still his neighborhood. He never left. He and Gwyneith built a new home just blocks from where they grew up in Frazier Courts. On-Target's corporate headquarters and regional logistics center is located in Dallas' southern sector. And its facilities in Houston and San Antonio also have been deliberately located in the inner city.

"Our goal is to improve the tax base and infrastructure for the inner city, hiring tax users and creating tax producers," Albert says. "We can make a difference in the lives of our neighbors and build a better community through the business and economic development of our inner urban areas."

As the former chairman of a task force that analyzed problems in Dallas' southern sector, I certainly agree with Albert's message of empowerment. The Community Development Assistance Corporation (CDAC), one of the forums in which I participated, focuses on inner-city redevelopment. CDAC pooled resources of the Dallas real estate community to make recommendations to the Dallas City Council on neighborhood revitalization and provided hands-on volunteer and financial assistance. Now renamed The Real Estate Council Foundation, work continues to support grassroots, community-based efforts to foster economic vitality.

While his commitment to his community is the driving force of Albert's professional life, his priorities are his faith and family: his wife, Gwyneith, and their three children, Albert III (Tré), 17; Cora, 9; and Oliver, 24, Albert's son from a teenage relationship who came to live with Albert and Gwyneith at age 10.

"Like most entrepreneurs, I have an insatiable desire to control and direct, and I always have to work for that desire not to spill over into other areas of my life," Albert says. "I don't meet very many entrepreneurs with balance in their lives. I work on that."

Boy do I agree with his observation (see Secret #1 in Chapter 15). But like Albert believes, it does not have to be like this. Entrepreneurs need to work at balance.

One place where Albert finds that balance is in his faith. "No matter what your faith is, we all have exams in the end," he says.

You don't have to be around Albert long to see that he's focused on that final exam. By setting an example, by sharing his story, by improving the inner city—not with free lunches but with free enterprise—he's making money, and he's making a difference.

~ Chapter 8 ~

A Milk Canister
Full of Secrets –
Katharine Wittmann

Katharine Wittmann was born in Slovakia to a family with a rich tradition in the dairy business. Her grandfather founded the business in 1891 and had over time created the most modern and largest dairy operation in the country.

During World War II, the Wittmann family was forced into hiding due to their Jewish heritage. After the war, they briefly regained control of the business only to have it seized by the Communists in 1948. In order to help facilitate escape from the country, the family temporarily split up and took different routes out of the country. Katharine's father left carrying only a milk canister that held prized cheese recipes and the Wittmann family trademarks.

Katharine Wittmann

Eventually, the Wittmann family made their way to Canada. Katharine worked her way through college, earned a nursing degree, married, raised three children, and became a Canadian citizen. However, she never forgot about her family's legacy. In 1990, with the fall of many Communist governments in Central and Eastern Europe, she went back to Slovakia to claim her family dairy. For 10 years, she battled corruption and entrenched attitudes to ultimately succeed in reclaiming the family dairy. A great many wanted her to fail. It was only through her determination and persistence that she succeeded in the end.

Katharine is proud to be able to say that in 2001, the dairy celebrates its 110th anniversary, still in the name of its founders, I. Wittmann and Son.

— ✦ —

Diplomatic dinners are rarely interrupted by telephone calls. When a waiter comes with a call for any party at the dinner table, it's usually very important. I can remember two interesting interruptions. One winter evening after a series of avalanches at Austrian ski resorts, Kathy and I were at a large dinner at the British Embassy. Kathy received a call, left the dinner table, and, after further calls, requested that American Command in Germany send Black Hawk helicopters to help in a rescue effort. On another night, at another diplomatic dinner, this time at our Ambassador's Residence, urgent messages were being delivered to the table first to Hans Winkler, the senior Austrian diplomat at dinner that evening, then to my wife. All of a sudden, the dinner was being broken up with phone calls in musical chairs style. It was a tribute to the diplomatic talents of others at dinner that night that at least a semblance of conversation continued at the table while in the back of our minds we were all wondering about the phone calls. That night in 1997 was the beginning of a long-lasting legal and later diplomatic feud over two paintings, both by Egon Schiele.

Robert Morgenthau, the District Attorney in New York, had ordered the seizure of two Schiele paintings on loan from the Leopold collection in Austria to the Museum of Modern Art (MOMA) in Manhattan. Normally, a museum like MOMA would apply for a waiver of any legal jurisdiction for loaned properties, but for some reason in this case, that had not occurred. Moreover, seizures by the government or by private interests, as later would occur in this complex situation, are extremely rare in the art world. To everyone's shock, an international incident over claims of ownership foreshadowed many other more complex incidents connected to the Holocaust that occurred during Kathy's ambassadorship in Austria.

From the beginning to the end of Kathy's term, one complex, Holocaust-related issue after the other surfaced. To her great credit and that of others in Washington as well as Austria, an issue that could have gotten out of control was handled very well. One Schiele painting ultimately ended up being returned to the museum in Vienna. The other is still, as of this writing, the subject of litigation. The crux of the issue is whether the current owners were the rightful owners or whether their right of legal ownership was forfeited because a prior owner had inappropriately assumed title through Aryanization: renouncement of the right of ownership for Jews.

More than 50 years after the official end of World War II, descendents of owners of these two paintings, both now living in America, had hired lawyers to fight for their ownership. In this case, it was a fight over many concepts: art, money, and family dignity. The concept of restitution and trying to bring closure by either giving property back to rightful owners or paying some form of compensation has been an ongoing and difficult decades-long process. Germany was forced to begin to address Aryanization and other Holocaust-related indignities following its defeat in World War II.

Austria has not completely come to grips with its history. Following World War II, for our own political reasons, the United States and other allies labeled Austria as Hitler's first victim. It was a role that Austria easily accepted. Yet in contrast to the old newsreel footage of the angry French along the Champs Elysees watching as Hitler marched down the boulevard, the masses in Austria cheered in support of Hitler's regime. Of course not all Austrians supported the Anschluss, but the numbers of supporters were clearly very high.

This dichotomy made matters complex after the war. Austrians accepted and embraced the Western wartime propaganda that they were Hitler's first victims. And who would expect them to do otherwise? Who would want to claim responsibility for mankind's most frightening display of inhumanity? Clearing the murky history and dealing with restitution have come slowly to Austria. This delay, however, has several ironies, one of which is that Simon Wiesenthal based his Nazi-hunting operations in Vienna after the war because, as he told me, "There were more Nazis in Austria per capita by far than in Germany." It wasn't long after my first meeting with Wiesenthal, who still lives in Vienna, that I was introduced to another victim of World War II.

A Restitution Story

I met Katharine Wittmann, a naturalized Canadian of Slovakian background, just as she was entering the final stages of a long fight with the Slovakian government to regain control of her family's dairy business in Zvolen, Slovakia. In Slovakia and other former Communist countries, property and business restitution is a major issue in the transformation back to free markets. Property restoration is a piece of the complex privatization puzzle that developed in former Communist countries. As Katharine's story shows, it's not an easy puzzle to put together.

While the governments are trying to get out of owning businesses that should be in private hands, abusing the process has proved a great temptation to those in a position to benefit personally. In many cases, it is too great a temptation, as rightful owners are deprived of their former properties, and other commercial assets are sold at bargain prices to insiders. Slovakia is a case in point.

The Escape

I believe the entrepreneurial spirit is a natural phenomenon, and Katharine Wittmann is a classic example. Ignac Wittmann, Katharine's grandfather, established a dairy product business in 1891 in Zvolen, 200 kilometers northeast of Bratislava, then part of the Austro-Hungarian empire. By the end of World War I, the business had grown from a peddler's efforts to become the largest dairy operation in Czechoslovakia. Ignac's son and Katharine's father, Vojtech Wittmann, was a pioneer in the modernization of the Czechoslovakian dairy industry, introducing pasteurization and mechanized equipment from Switzerland for processing cheese. As a very young girl, Katharine was fascinated by the family dairy and cheese business.

The family remained in Czechoslovakia during World War II, though they were forced into hiding because of their Jewish heritage. Katharine, along with her mother and brother, hid in the mountains while her father remained in Zvolen, hidden in the same town where the German Gestapo had taken over the Wittmann home. While in hiding, Vojtech Wittmann designed a new dairy, anticipating the increased demand for milk after the war's end. The new dairy was under construction by the winter of 1947, but it was clear that the Communists were not going to relinquish control of the country and that they, too, would seize assets just as the Germans did. With a handful of suitcases, the Wittmanns fled. Vojtech Wittmann was 50 years old, and Katharine was 10, when the family abandoned its dairy business, land, and home to escape the Communists.

Looking back, Katharine said, "The world as we knew it abruptly came to an end." The family split up in order to escape. In November of 1948, Katharine, her mother, and her brother gained permission to go to Casablanca where her maternal grandfather had fled before the war. Three months later, Vojtech Wittmann also took flight. Carrying a brief-case and a metal milk canister, Katharine's father peddled a bicycle through Bratislava to Austria, and then made his way to Casablanca. The milk canister held prized cheese recipes and Wittmann family trade-marks, which the family zealously guarded for years. Today, Katharine is revamping the same trademarks for marketing, and continues to guard the cheese recipes.

Katharine's New Life

The family moved from chaotic Casablanca to Ontario, Canada. The transition was traumatic, especially for Katharine's father, who was forced to abandon the business he had spent his life nurturing. For more than half a century, the Wittmann family lived a completely different and more difficult life. Katharine eventually worked her way through college, earned a nursing degree, married, and raised three children.

During all of this time, the family business heritage was dormant, not dead. When I spoke with Katharine, a tall, elegant, and composed 60-year-old woman, I asked what motivated her to leave behind her adopted home and her family to return to the land of her birth. She said she had been trying to find the answer to that question for 10 years, ever since she set foot back in Zvolen, Slovakia, in 1990.

"I think we all get involved in something because we desire a certain effect. It's been 100 years, two generations. I can't explain it any other way, but it was destiny and luck that the fall of Communism happened at an age when I can afford to do this. Not financially, but principally," Katharine said. "If my children had been younger, I would have been torn between duty to my children and duty to the past. Now I am at a stage where I can deal with it."

Throughout her life in Canada, Katharine had nurtured the memories of her childhood in a well-respected cheese-making family in Czechoslovakia. She also managed to keep her eye on what was happening in her old homeland. Her latent entrepreneurial spirit took wing when Communist governments throughout Central and Eastern Europe began to fall. She glimpsed an opportunity to regain the Wittmann properties that had been nationalized when she was a child.

Returning Home

The new governments in this troubled region have not made it easy for refugees to return and obtain restitution. In fact, when I asked Katharine if she had received a letter or some notice about the privatization process in Slovakia, she asked if I was kidding. In 1990, she returned to Slovakia with her family to show them where she had lived as a child. During that trip some "old-timers" told her about the restitution of private property. The lingering memory of her father's and grandfather's entrepreneurial efforts prodded this mother and nurse to forge her way through the morass of the Slovakian courts and win back her family heritage. Even though she was only 10 when she left Zvolen, she spoke with tremendous pride of the Wittmann and Son dairy business and said that she was "born with a cheese spoon in my mouth." She was born, as well, with the strong desire to follow in her paternal footsteps, leaving her husband in Canada for months at a time so she could remain in Slovakia, persistently dogging the authorities who had control of her dairy's future.

I can hardly imagine the fortitude and patience she and others like her must maintain in the face of monumental governmental interference and manipulation of the privatization process.

"We have to right the wrongs; restitution is now embedded in the constitution," Katharine said.

It is that glimmer of fairness and making things right again that has sustained her during the past 10 years. The long period of time since the family's departure from Slovakia entitled her to claim only the tangible property, land, and buildings that existed before 1952. The state refused her claim to the entire property including the dairy company, offering instead 10 percent of the company's value, paid in a mix of shares in other similarly privatized companies. She kept fighting, not ac-cepting the first plan as fair or just. Between 1991 and 1995, the Wittmann restitution case was passed between the Slovakian Regional and Dis-trict courts, in Katharine's words, "like a hot potato." In December 1995, after proving her citizenship, residency, identity, and inheritance— and the courts having exhausted all other avenues—it was determined that Katharine was the rightful owner of the land and buildings, but she was not entitled to any of the improvements that had been made in the 40 years since the dairy's nationalization. This meant all machinery currently in the dairy! Katharine was also installed as chairman of the board of the dairy with a mandate to manage the company. She immediately began to modernize and restructure the company, increasing total sales from 5.5 million Slovakian Crowns in 1995 to 9.4 million Slovakian Crowns in 1998— from about $1.4 million to $2.4 million. The privatization process lasted another five years until March 2000. Throughout that period, her good management only increased the attractiveness of the company to outsiders.

Politics and Corruption

In order to run the machinery necessary to operate the dairy, Katharine had to create a new firm called "I. Wittmann and Son," which owned the land and buildings. Katharine ran I. Wittmann and Son, renting the milk processing and packaging equipment and the right to the 240 employees, whom she paid, from the National Property Fund. During these complex and wearying negotiations, Katharine's dairy didn't close for a single hour.

When Katharine took over the Wittmann Dairy in 1996, some of the people who were on her board of governors and in key management posi-tions were the very ones who had fought against her restitution claim. Most of those people later were no longer with the company. Katharine still becomes outraged as she explains why her restitution was so complicated.

"The Agricultural Minister listens to the big farmers and milk pro-ducers," she said, explaining that she firmly believed that there was corruption in the process because the decision-makers wanted to ac-quire the business for themselves or their friends. Two of the major milk producers used heavy-handed tactics to try to force the Wittmann Dairy out of business. Early in the process one of the two antagonistic milk producers informed her that he was raising the price of the milk for the Wittmann Dairy by 10 percent and threatened to cut off the milk supply if she didn't pay. The second milk producer also manufactured milk bags used by the Wittmann Dairy. When Katharine informed him that she was going to switch to milk cartons instead, he threatened that he would cut off his milk supply to her if she didn't continue to purchase his milk bags. She called his bluff, switched to the more modern containers, and continued to receive bulk milk from the producer. But the threats continued. The milk producers who were among her biggest suppliers formed a strong and vocal lobby, and they wanted to take over the profitable and growing Wittmann Dairy.

This type of pervasive corruption jeopardized the privatization process across Central and Eastern Europe. In addition to her producers' blackmail, Katharine faced a network of former Communist cronies in ministerial positions, including the agricultural department, who conspired to throw obstacles in her path and force her to go home, enriching themselves through her failure. Their goal, she believed, was to buy her property for a cheap price or sell it to local farmers paying stiff bribes. This sounds improbable, but unfortunately the story is repeated in one form or another throughout the former Communist countries.

Katharine had been very successful at running the dairy up to this point, but wondered whether she made her own task harder by making the dairy more profitable.

"I'm fighting a lot of men, men who look at me and say, 'What is this woman doing in our way? If we get rid of her, we can have access to this great business.' The Minister of Agriculture, who was a farm manager, has all these friends around him who are my suppliers. There was no legal way they could do this, but with bribery…I couldn't compete with that," Katharine said.

She saw the hurdles moving higher as her energy and resources waned. She believed the Minister of Agriculture was under pressure from his friends in the farm industry to complicate the Wittmann restitution and ultimately force her to give up and go back to Canada.

They Can Take Everything But Your Name

Katharine's saga was complicated to the point of farce. One road-block the authorities used was Katharine's name. Her legal name is not Katharine Wittmann because she took her husband's name when they were married in Canada. But Slovakian authorities would not recognize her married name because she had been married in a church, and the Communists didn't acknowledge church weddings. The catch was that she was not allowed to file a restitution claim unless she had Slovakian residency. But she couldn't claim residency without a name, and the government initially wouldn't recognize her name. She knew that proof of residency was automatic with a passport. When she tried to renew her passport based on having never relinquished it or having been deprived of her Slovakian citizenship, she was told that without a name she could not renew the passport. Finally she legally changed her name back to Wittmann, and with that, she had a passport, residency, and the right to reclaim her family property.

"It suddenly hit me, these people took everything away from me except my name," Katharine said. "Communism can take everything away from you except your name, and that is enough to build on."

Doing What's Right While Others Do What's Wrong

Katharine's passion is so focused on her company that she is a lively reminder of how much was lost during the 40 years of the command economy. The local population mistrusted her, suspecting she was going to strip the company of its profits and disappear. There was also resentment that she returned after such a long time and took over a company that in recent memory belonged "to the people." This is despite the fact that she pays her workers the highest salary in the Slovakian food industry.

Katharine's experience with corruption has made her a vocal spokes-man against unethical behavior, including a tremendous theft problem at the cheese factory.

"The employees have access to cheese and dairy products, so they give the products to people they want to influence. For example, if someone is in the hospital, they bring the nurses dairy products just to make things a bit better for their friends or family."

Many people have shrugged off the graft and bribery that is rampant in this region, saying that it compensates those who do not make a living wage. But Katharine's employees receive salaries at the top of the wage scale.

"In the production of cheese, I was told my factory needed 10 liters of milk, the industry norm. But, you really needed 9.75 liters of milk. Nobody knew that. We were always making more cheese because we had those fractions of liters to work with. The cheese above the norm was hidden somewhere and then smuggled out of the company," Katharine said. "That extra fraction you didn't know about, you couldn't even identify. We found out about this on our own, but we had to do a sting operation with the local police. I held my breath because the police are so incompetent, and they had to catch the criminals red-handed. If they are not caught red-handed you cannot prove anything, because the judges and lawyers can be bribed. Anyway, the police caught them, and the crook had the nerve to say, 'I had an offer to buy this cheap, and I was just picking it up.' You catch them red-handed and they still try to weasel their way out."

Taking the Helm

Katharine believed that she was the best person to run the company when it was privatized, but she wasn't sure about the future. She wanted to find others to help bring the dairy into the 21st century. Her late-in-life management training was effective, though. She had a crash course in dairy economics.

"Six months ago, I couldn't tell you what a pound of butter or a quart of milk cost for us to produce," Katharine said. "We knew what the total production cost was, but not how much it cost to make a tin of yogurt. Now we are just beginning to understand."

One of Katharine's recent innovations was to start a company-owned store on Zvolen's main street. A great competitive advantage is that her dairy is located just a few minutes away. The tiny storefront also stocks competing products, a marketing philosophy that is quite unusual for this small town. The store is open from 6 a.m. to 6 p.m. Unfortunately, the interior of the store is so small that there is always a line of people outside waiting to enter. For many, the long line is too reminiscent of the Communist period, so Katharine would like to build a bigger store.

The Battle For I. Wittmann and Son Goes On

Since January 1996, Katharine had been actively managing the dairy, although she really didn't know a thing about the business until she started learning by doing. She proudly announced that her dairy purchased 30 percent more milk in 1999 than it did in 1996 to support its increased production. Even though she was a Canadian citizen, a program sponsored by the U.S. Department of Agriculture, involving volunteer experts in a variety of agricultural areas, enabled Katharine to accelerate her learning process by going to the United States on the Cochran Fellowship Program. She invited two of her important suppliers to attend with her, hoping to gain some favor with them, while enabling them to learn firsthand about modern milking processes. She feels very strongly that Slovakia needs expert help in all areas.

In her early days in charge, Katharine owned the dairy but only rented the equipment. She didn't just want to own four walls and a roof, so she entered discussions with the Slovak American Enterprise Fund (SAEF) to help her fund the purchase of the equipment. It was no paltry sum. The National Property Fund had set a price of $1.6 million. In January 1999, Katharine was given 30 days to raise the money to acquire the remainder of the dairy operation, or it would be put up for sale.

Katharine began to work closely with the SAEF, which had a congressional mandate to invest money in Central and Eastern Europe. SAEF has so far not had a great track record in Slovakia and has lost money on a number of investments. Still, Katharine thought SAEF was the best prospect. She wanted a $1.6 million loan from SAEF, for which it would receive equity in the company. An initial loan package was approved by SAEF, which would have allowed Katharine to take full control of the dairy, although the loan terms were not particularly generous.

To her great surprise, in April of 1999 she read about her loan in the newspaper. SAEF had in fact approved not only her original loan request, but also an additional amount, making her financial assistance package the largest ever in the Slovak food manufacturing industry. The 100 million Slovakian Crown loan (roughly $2.5 million) was contingent on meeting a number of stipulations that were added after the approval of the initial loan of Slovakian Crown 60 million, and would eventually have allowed SAEF to control the company. Katharine was irate.

"The deal they were offering was very one-sided," she said. "They would have ended up with everything and left me with nothing. I said no. It was very difficult. When I came back to Slovakia after Christmas 1999, my back was up against the wall."

Katharine decided to push back and bluff the Slovak government into believing she was about to close down the dairy. She asked the Privatization Board to remove the machinery, which it "owned."

"The local political party knew that if this company went under, they would have to answer for it. They couldn't steal the buildings just to keep the machinery there. Finally, they realized they had to find a win-win situation or they would be held responsible for losing 240 jobs."

Katharine's courageous, gutsy move challenged the local authorities to act on the part of their constituents. The asking price for the machinery was dropped from 60 million Crowns to 10 million Crowns in March 2000. Katharine came up with the money, and, after 10 long years, finally put the I. Wittmann and Son Dairy fully back in family hands. To her great delight, her company now has the attention of international food companies.

To me, Katharine Wittmann is a hero. She has fought for what is right and fair with courage and dignity. No matter what happens from here on, standing up for the truth will be her ultimate victory.

Responsibility to Entrepreneurs and the Free Market

Katharine Wittmann's long quest was finished. She had won. Then, unexpectedly, a major European consumer products company made her an offer for the dairy at a good profit. At first she thought maybe she would sell a portion and hold on to some part. Then she decided she should sell it all and move back to Canada. Her mission was complete.

"I believe I have done the right thing," she told me. "I. Wittmann and Son's trademark and logo will endure. The family company has been regained, saved, resurrected, and put on its feet. Its future in the global community is secure."

Katharine deserves tremendous credit for her perseverance and willingness to fight for what is right. She was buttressed by her enthusiasm for the American system.

"I admire the Americans for their pioneer attitude, for the 'let's go ahead and do it' attitude."

Wherever possible along the way, the United States championed Katharine's cause. The Cochran Fellowship Program helped her in her early days as a dairy entrepreneur, and SAEF attempted to provide her financing for the future. The U.S. Embassy staff also helped. Like Western entrepreneurs all over Central and Eastern Europe, Katharine provides an incredibly important lesson in capitalism for her fellow Slovakians.

"We need to do more than tell them how to do it," Katharine says of her fellow Slovaks, echoing a major theme of this book. "We need to show them how and help them. Create the solution, and then help them implement the solution."

Chapter 9

At 83, He Started a
New Business –
Bernard Rapoport

Bernard Rapoport is consultant to American Income Life Insurance Company, which he founded in 1951 and served as Chief Executive Officer and Chairman of the Board until 1999.

In June of 2000, Mr. Rapoport, at age 83, started over again by deciding to purchase Southwestern Life Insurance Company. Though many his age

were content to be retired, he viewed the sale of his long-time company as an opportunity to begin a new challenge and new chapter of his life. After owning Southwestern Life for less than a year, in early 2001, due to the significant improvement in operations he had already been able to achieve, the company was purchased by Swiss Re at a significant profit to Mr. Rapoport and his shareholders. One must suspect that he is already searching for his next challenge.

Bernard Rapoport is the former Chairman of the Board of Regents for the University of Texas System where he received a Bachelor of Arts degree before he began his business

Bernard Rapoport

career. Mr. Rapoport is frequently tapped for important boards and committees due to his highly tuned business sense and passion for issues of importance. He was appointed by President Clinton as a member of the Advisory Committee for Trade Policy and Negotiations. He is a member of the Library of Congress Trust Fund Board, National Hispanic University Trustee Emeritus, Horatio Alger Association, Economic Policy Institute, and the Joint Center for Political and Economic Studies.

Mr. Rapoport resides in Waco, Texas with his wife. Together they support many charitable causes, particularly literacy programs, through The Bernard and Audre Rapoport Foundation.

— ✦ —

He Makes a Difference

The first time I met Bernie Rapoport, he told me he was in love with my wife. He had entered the room like a thunderbolt, turning all eyes with his booming Texas twang. "Hello, darling," crooned this six-foot, lanky gentleman and then enveloped Kathy in a warm hug. With Bernie, I later learned, you always get a hug.

Although I have now ascended to Bernie's hug status, at that first meeting more than a decade ago, I was still relegated to a quick, strong handshake. What I didn't know at the time is that for several years Bernie had viewed himself as matchmaker for Kathy and had had another good friend, Jim Sale, picked out for her when I came along. Kathy's friendship with Bernie dated back to the early 1980s when she moved to Dallas and got involved in Democratic politics. To many, Bernie is "Mr. Democrat," a supporter that local, regional, and national candidates have come to know and love as someone they can trust. His advice, creative thinking, and financial support have been appreciated for decades by a long list of Democratic candidates from the precinct level to the Oval Office.

At one of many Democratic National Conventions, Jim Sale recalls someone asking him if Bernie was there in the hall that night.

"'Not yet,' I told him," Jim recalls. "'You don't hear the room buzzing, do you?'"

Indeed, Bernie has an incredible energy to him that does stir every room he enters. And if you don't feel the energy, you definitely hear the robust laugh or resounding voice.

Today, Bernie has a warm relationship with both Senator and former President Clinton. I first learned that Bernie was a frequent visitor to the Clinton White House in 1996 when Kathy and I hosted a small dinner party for Hillary Clinton while she was in Dallas campaigning for the re-election of the Clinton-Gore ticket. As I watched and listened to Bernie that evening, I began to better understand his passion for politics. For many, politics is about power and access to power. For Bernie, I can truly say it's about how to improve people's lives. Over the years, I've never heard Bernie advocate changes in policy or laws to benefit his business or personal needs. He is simply a believer that people in power can make a difference, and so Bernie unabashedly shares his opinions on how to create a better America for everyone.

Jim Sale tells a story about going to Washington with Bernie on behalf of the Veterans Land Board to try to protect Texas' right to issue tax-free bonds that in turn helped veterans purchase land and homes.

"Bernie knew every Democratic senator in Washington and even though no other state was lobbying for this law, thanks in large part to Bernie's charm, it was passed, and thousands of Texas vets have benefited. It's a program Texas should really be proud of," Jim says.

Why was Bernie so successful where others had failed? Because his interest, Jim says, was completely unselfish. He was asking for help on behalf of those who needed it.

At 83, one of the nation's wealthiest and most successful men, Bernie has been named by *Fortune* magazine to the list of America's 40 most generous philanthropists. He made the list in 1998, the year he donated $5 million to the Jerusalem Foundation and $15 million to his alma mater, the University of Texas. He was also selected in 1999 to become a member of the Horatio Alger Association of Distinguished Americans, an organization that annually recognizes people who personify success through hard work and courage.

Much like the namesake of that distinguished organization, Bernie made it on his own.

The Fear of Having Nothing

Like many great entrepreneurs, Bernie's motivations to succeed began very early in life. Born in San Antonio on July 17, 1917, one of Bernie's earliest memories is coming home from school to find all of his family's furniture out on the street. It was not uncommon during the Great Depression for evictions to leave families with no roof over their heads. Bernie's family, like so many, lived on the edge of homelessness, and one day found themselves on the street. Though now he knows how precarious his family's finances were, at the time, he says he didn't think of his family as "poor." Yet he says he knows that the fear of having nothing, of being put out on the street, has been a powerful though subtle motivator in his life.

"We always had enough to eat," he remembers.

And he always knew that there were others less fortunate—an important lesson he learned from his father.

Bernie's father, David Rapoport, was a Russian exiled to Siberia for working against the czar. Sentenced to death, he escaped in 1910 by walking 600 miles to Belgium. Relatives helped him emigrate to the United States, where he landed in San Antonio, joined the Socialist Party, and went to work peddling goods from a pushcart on the streets of San Antonio's West Side.

"Workers of the world, unite. You've nothing to lose but your chains," is a phrase Bernie often heard his father say with great conviction. As a boy, it held little meaning for him, but throughout his lifetime, and especially in his insurance business, he would discover the power of the people.

Bernie's mother, Reva Feldman, emigrated to the United States from the Black Sea town of Sevastopol. She moved with her family to Fort Worth and had the opportunity to meet David Rapoport after her father, who was a kosher butcher, traveled to San Antonio. Reva was raised a Hasidic Jew, rigidly observing the teachings of the Jewish faith. Bernie remembers his father going to the synagogue only once—for his bar mitzvah. And so, he says, he learned about God from his mother. From his father, he learned about the power of education.

Bernie and his sister, Idell, were encouraged to question everything. Their father spoke Yiddish, Russian, English, and Spanish, and, because they lived in a Mexican-American neighborhood, the children, too, grew up speaking Spanish. Music was also an elemental part of their life. Bernie played the violin, Idell the piano. Reading was a daily requirement and, Bernie remembers, by the time he was a teenager, he had read Marx, Dostoyevsky, Upton Sinclair, Turgenev, Tolstoy, Pushkin and, for fun, the mysteries of Sherlock Holmes.

For a year and a half of his life, reading was Bernie's only pastime. When he was 13 and rushing home after Yom Kippur services at the synagogue, a car hit him. Without enough money for the best medical care, the accident left one leg permanently an inch and a half shorter than the other. With the help of tutors, Bernie kept up with his schoolwork from bed. And though he's had a limp ever since, it's never stopped him from staying out in front or from even now playing tennis on a daily basis at 6 a.m. when he's at home in Waco.

Growing up in the 1920s, Bernie vividly remembers being called a "Jew boy" as well as witnessing many anti-Semitic and anti-black activities that marked the era. He says his family always sat in the back of the bus to show its support.

"My father called the racists 'ignorant,' which made me work even harder in school not to be," Bernie says.

Bernie's studies—he graduated from San Antonio's Thomas Jefferson High School as a member of the National Honor Society—and the strong influence of his parents helped to shape his own personal value system. Bernie could never tolerate people who dislike others for the color of their skin or their religion, and he could never understand why people who have a lot aren't willing to share it.

Despite missing much high school classroom activity due to the long recovery from the car accident, Bernie earned a scholarship to Drake University. He had to pass on the opportunity though, because additional expenses were too much for his family to handle. The University of Texas (UT), however, was a relative bargain. Bernie attended and graduated in four years for the total cost of $1,440 for tuition, room, board, and expenses. He worked his way through school making $40 a month as a credit manager for Zales.

"I didn't make good grades in college because I didn't have time to study," Bernie remembers. "Getting a degree was all I worried about."

Bernie loved the university and is a proud alumnus. His days as head of the Board of Regents are what many call the UT System's "golden years" of expansion into communities across the state. Bernie was in fact instrumental in bringing the UT System to poorer areas of San Antonio, making a college education geographically accessible to a much larger population of previously disadvantaged students.

"Dreams with deadlines are opportunities realized."

Like many of his peers, Bernie married young. In 1940 at age 22, he was both a newlywed and a new graduate from the University of Texas. During the war years, Bernie stayed home to man the jewelry store because the injuries to his leg landed him 4F and kept him out of the service. In the jewelry business, Bernie got his first taste of being an entrepreneur. He opened his own store in Waco and put on a few auctions on his own. While he was still working in the jewelry business, he began to sell life insurance on the side with his father. He soon found out that he was pretty good at it. In 1950, Bernie, the son of a pushcart salesman, went to work full time selling life insurance for Pioneer American Insurance Company. His primary audience at the time was union members—no easy target in a right-to-work state.

Bernie's life as a salesman and entrepreneur teaches an important lesson: Success for him was anything but overnight. But even when he was struggling, he always had dreams of great success and a plan to get there through hard work.

In 1951, at age 33, Bernie and his wife's uncle, Harold Goodman, decided they could improve on the insurance product Bernie was selling. The pair founded American Income Life Insurance Company with a $25,000 loan on his uncle's credit. In the early days, Bernie says, he worked long hours and lived on as little as possible—a meager $300 a month. The company bordered on insolvency on a day-to-day basis, but Bernie never quit. He had a nugget of an idea and an underserved niche: union members. He tailored his product and his marketing to this unique audience, and he never stopped working the concept. He even insisted that every salesman in the company join a union. It was a great marketing gimmick, but typical of Bernie, it wasn't a façade. He believed in the power of the people and the ability of unions to improve working conditions and treatment of American workers.

In the early days at American Income Life, Bernie started a practice of checking in on every salesman weekly by phone to discuss what had been accomplished the week before and what was going to be accomplished in the week to come. Even today, at age 83, Bernie keeps up the practice. On Saturday mornings, the calls start at 6:45 a.m. and last until around noon.

Bernie's weekly calls helping salesmen to set goals and stick to them are consistent with the philosophy he has always applied to himself.

"Dreams with deadlines are opportunities realized," Bernie says.

This is vintage Bernie Rapoport. Without discipline and a program, dreams are just that. Bernie always made sure his dreams became opportunities by coming up with a plan, making sure it worked, and then getting it done.

The Bernie Rapoport Appreciation Committee

After a decade of working to build American Income Life—in stark contrast to the myth that entrepreneurs get rich quick or the success stories of today's dotcom millionaires—Bernie says his net worth was probably only around $100,000. By 1977, Bernie had built American Income Life from $25,000 borrowed capital to a company with more than $100 million in assets. His company had come through some hard times, but he was seeing the light at the end of the tunnel. That year Jim Sale founded the Bernie Rapoport Appreciation Committee. His tongue-in-cheek pitch was to round up 100 "charter members" to buy 5,000 shares of American Income Life. The brash invitation to invest would never make it by today's regulatory standards, but in 1977 it flew.

These were the days of Texas' "Good Old Boys Network" when business was based more on relationships than asset consideration. Bernie was someone who did everything for everyone. People liked him, and, like so many other successful entrepreneurs, people wanted him to succeed. So they wrote the checks, became investors, and many years later, if they stuck with him, they got rich.

In a letter dated July 28, 1977, Jim wrote, "While building this multi-million-dollar enterprise, Bernie has been a great friend to his business and political associates. He truly encourages, respects, and supports his fellow man. He is a happy warrior."

Jim called the Bernie Rapoport Appreciation Committee "an opportunity to intelligently seek capital gains in one of the fastest-growing companies in the Southwest." And his prediction proved true for all of the takers. Those who invested $25,000 and held out for the long haul eventually had an investment worth half a million dollars, Jim says.

The Making of a Philanthropist

In 1988, Bernie orchestrated a leveraged buyout of the company, retaining 20 percent ownership. With that move, he and many others realized great wealth. That same year, he and his wife of more than 60 years, Audre, established a foundation with $75 million to begin giving back to the community. An empty phrase to some for its overuse, to Bernie "giving back to the community" is a powerful force for change as well as what he calls a "positive form of greed."

Bernie puts it this way: "If you play marbles and win all the marbles, if you don't give some back, you won't have anyone to play with."

Bernie sometimes sends a conflicting message with his words and deeds. He often says he can't stand "do-gooders" and he thinks everyone should be greedy and do what's in their own best interest—like giving back some of the marbles so they can stay in the game. But I believe Bernie truly cares about other people. He makes charitable gifts because they help build a future for people who otherwise would have no future. His philanthropy emphasizes people learning to take care of themselves because he really believes if you have a small group that just takes advantage of other people, eventually you have a diminished economy. Bernie lives by that creed, and I happen to agree with him.

You could say Bernie won all of the marbles in 1994 when he sold American Income Life to Torchmark for $563 million. He was 77 at the time, but Torchmark kept him on as chairman. In September of 1999, at age 82, Torchmark's Board of Directors asked Bernie to take the post of Chairman Emeritus, an honorary position. So, he retired. For two months. Then he decided it was time to start looking to buy a new business.

Starting Over at Age 83

At 83, Bernie, along with a group of partners that included another Texas insurance legend, John Sharp, bought Southwestern Life Insurance Company out of bankruptcy. Bernie is back at it again. And so is Jim Sale. He's resurrected the old Bernie Rapoport Appreciation Committee and made John Sharp an honorary member.

"No one has ever lost money investing with Bernie Rapoport," Jim says. "He knows his business."

Bernie owned 20 percent of the company, but he is certainly not just an investor. He is actively involved in the remaking of the company and scoffs at the idea of retirement.

"I'll have plenty of time to do nothing when I'm dead," Bernie says. "After all, living is the thing you do now or never."

Encouraging Others to Take a Chance

When Kathy and I began to consider the possibility of seeking an ambassadorship, Bernie is one of many friends we consulted. As you might imagine, his attitude was, "Go for it." During this period of exploration, we visited another friend from Democratic politics, Robert Krueger in Burundi. Bob was sent to Burundi after an unsuccessful race for a Senate seat. He had been appointed to a U.S. Senate seat from Texas to fulfill the term of Senator John Tower after Senator Tower was killed in a plane crash. During his bid for a full term in the Senate, Bob came across as too intellectual and not connected to the people. After he lost, found a new challenge in one of the toughest spots in the world—Burundi—as its U.S. Ambassador. While Kathy and I were traveling in Africa, we took a side trip to see Bob. While we were there, we traveled to a displaced person camp by United Nations helicopter to see just some of the challenges of the area.

The United Nations helicopter landed on the western boundary of the displaced person camp in Burundi, and we were immediately surrounded by soldiers bearing machine guns. In disbelief, we saw behind them a seemingly endless number of African children running toward us. From the air, we had seen the camp with its makeshift housing and open ditches for a sewage system.

We had flown over four different villages, ghost towns with war-ravaged remnants of homes partially standing, before landing here. Bob led the tour along with local government and U.N. officials. As we walked up a gentle slope, I looked back into a sea of faces, well more than 10,000 people, most under the age of 12, each trying to follow our every move. At that point, with the most people possible within earshot, Bob gave a short speech using a translator to relay his words to the crowd. Enthusiastic and hopeful, the crowd cheered this interest in their plight.

Burundi is just one place in the world where the United States, often through its ambassadors, makes positive changes. Seeing this firsthand deeply affected both Kathy and me. After our experience there, we decided to seriously consider seeking an ambassador position for Kathy. We also learned that U.S. dollars can have a huge impact in these hot spots. We were happy to give money to local missionaries Bob knew and respected. To our delight, we found out Jim Sale had also sent money. In Burundi, we saw another of Bernie Rapoport's sayings in action.

"Money is a means, not an end."

Bernie is a perfect example of the fallacy of the myth that entrepreneurs are only in it for the money. While it's true that Bernie is competitive and fought hard for the best price for his company, I've often heard him say, "Money is a means, not an end."

More and more these days, Bernie spends his time working to help others. Though he says he can't stand "do-gooders," Bernie, Audre, and the Rapoport Foundation do a lot of good. The foundation has a focused interest on programs that aim to strengthen young people, especially through education.

It's not surprising that the foundation's Web site, www.rapoportfdn.org, is chock-full of quotes from Bernie's lifetime of reading. Bernie keeps a collection of quotes, constantly updating and sharing it with friends. One of his favorites graces the home page of the foundation's Web site:

> "I believe in the perfectibility of man, because this is the only working hypothesis for any decent and responsible person."
>
> —Dennis Gabor in *"Declaration"*

Though Bernie and Audre certainly have the means to live a grand life, they still reside in Waco in a modest home. The only large room in the house is the library, which has a section reserved for the Russian authors Bernie read as a child and still loves. You'll rarely see Bernie in anything but a plain blue or white shirt, and you'll never see him in a $750 suit. In Dallas for business or pleasure, you'll find him at one restaurant: The Palm. No fancy fusion cuisine for him. A steak will do, thank you.

"I never wanted anything in my life but a red scooter," Bernie remembers. And for a kid whose father never made more than $4,000 in a year, wanting that scooter was like wanting the moon. So when he and Audre spend an afternoon every week tutoring children in a Waco inner-city elementary school, he understands the desires and the hurdles these young kids face.

Bernie and Audre are part of a widespread literacy effort in Waco called the Waco 1,000. Supported by the Rapoport Foundation, this effort organized 1,000 people in the community to spend an hour a week teaching kids to read in elementary schools.

"America doesn't care about people enough," Bernie says. "Twenty percent of our population lives in poverty. It's a disgrace."

This strong pronouncement is typical of Bernie, a man who puts his money and his time behind his opinions. That's why his foundation puts its resources into people, because Bernie believes education is the key to breaking the cycle of poverty. That's why, he believes, the GI Bill is the greatest piece of legislation ever passed.

"My pop used to think that everyone who had money was crooked and did illegal things," Bernie says. "I told him I was going to go out and make a lot of money, and I asked him what he thought about that. He said he wouldn't be sure about me!"

Bernie reminisces like this about his father in the familiar way that comes from growing up in a close-knit family. He knows firsthand that in addition to learning from books, kids need to learn from their parents.

Bernie often tells a story about one of the students he was reading with at a Waco elementary school. The nine-year-old, Rena, was having a hard time, and, when she finished reading, Bernie gave her a hug and told her he loved her.

"She looked at me and said, 'Don't give me that crap; nobody loves me.' I was stunned, and for a minute I didn't say anything. Finally, I asked her why on Earth she would say something like that," Bernie says.

He later found that the girl was being raised by her aunt because her father and mother were out of the picture.

"I know it's better than being in a home or something, but that's not the way kids should live," Bernie says. "Kids should be with their parents. We need to work harder to make that happen."

Not surprisingly, Bernie's foundation is working towards that goal with very young children and a program called Parents as Teachers that involves parents in the Pre-K programs at elementary schools in Waco.

Bernie as philosopher, intellectual, and entrepreneur has a lot to share. And with an unparalleled amount of energy and discipline, he shares his wisdom every day.

Though Bernie spends a lot of time thinking, at 83, he doesn't spend much of his time pondering his own mortality. He does, predictably, have a quote to share on the subject:

> "Faith in immortality was born of the greed of unsatisfied people who make unwise use of the time that nature has allotted us. But the wise man finds his life span sufficient to complete the full circle of attainable pleasures, and when the time of death comes, he will leave the table, satisfied, freeing a place for other guests. For the wise man, one human life is sufficient, and a stupid man will not know what to do with eternity."
>
> —Epicurus, Ancient Philosopher

Throughout his remarkable life, Bernie has inspired people, including me. In his own company, he has nurtured many entrepreneurs, helping them to realize the potential of an innate spirit that he insists can't be taught. Bernie inspires others, in part by being a bigger-than-life character, but also by being willing to take time to encourage other people. He takes great joy in seeing other people do well.

In contrast to some professional corporate managers, most entrepreneurs I know are not threatened by the success of other people. That's why they frequently build organizations in which people can be entrepreneurial.

Bernie truly enjoys inspiring others to think and to learn. Some people send out fruitcakes at Christmas. Bernie has his own book club with an ever-growing mailing list. Each year he picks a book that he finds interesting, provocative, or educational to send to everyone on the list. It's an appropriate gesture for a man who appreciates literacy and holds a thoughtful concern for the written word. It's indicative of a man who wants to inspire others to think and to achieve their potential.

More than anything else, perhaps, Bernie Rapoport is an original. Yet he has much in common with many of the entrepreneurs in this book. He's persistent, passionate, creative, and hard working. He gives back to the community. He's a relationship builder, a people person. He's the American Dream realized.

Don't Be Afraid to Take a Profit

As I was finalizing this book, Bernie received a very profitable offer for Southwestern Life from Swiss Re, the largest life and health reinsurer in North America. The offer was an excellent deal for his shareholders, and as such, he decided to sell the company. However, as he enters his 84th year, I know he will be looking for an opportunity to start over once again. I, for one, would enjoy being Bernie's partner in any new venture. He is forever a young entrepreneur in spirit.

Chapter 10

Struggle and Hope in the Land of "Spaga" – Kenny Blatt

Mr. Blatt has spent the past 10 years developing businesses in Central and Eastern Europe and as an angel investor in technology-driven companies in the United States and Europe. His European activities have focused in the media and communications sectors. Prior to Mr. Blatt's entrepreneurial activities in Europe, he practiced law in the real estate department of Sills Cummis and also worked with Coopers & Lybrand in New York. An Atlantic City native, Mr. Blatt has had significant experience in the hotel and casino industries.

Mr. Blatt was instrumental in creating the service industries in Romania and Bulgaria. He founded and developed advertising companies that

Kenny Blatt (right)

have gone on to become partners with J. Walter Thompson, McCann Erickson, and Lintas Lowe GGK; developed and exited publishing companies in Romania which titles included *PC World* and *ELLE*; and created Romania's largest outdoor media company, which has partnered with Advent International, a leading private equity group. As a consultant, he has been active in all aspects of marketing and communications in Europe.

He is a Board Director of the Romanian Foreign Investor's Council, Euromedia S.A., member of the New York New Media Angel's Society and active in numerous political and charitable organizations in the New York/New Jersey area. Mr. Blatt graduated from Cornell University School of Hotel Administration, received his JD degree from Emory University, and completed the INSEAD Owner's Director Program. He splits his time between New York City and Bucharest, Romania.

— ✦ —

A Place on the Fringe of Europe

The ride from Bucharest airport, traveling over pothole-saturated roads and through grimy, industrialized areas that shouted "Communism!" to me, caused mixed emotions. This was especially true as we made the turn onto Unirii Boulevard, which used to signal the entrance to the enclave of senior Communist officials. I wondered what Bucharest, Romania, must have been like in years past. Even though it is rough around the edges and suffers from extensive deferred maintenance, there is a captivating beauty to the city that has been called "Little Paris."

Normally my trips to Romania were quick ones, filled with back-to-back meetings for my consulting roles with the U.S. State Department and the Southeast European Cooperative Initiative (SECI). There were winter meetings in government buildings that lacked proper heat. There were sweltering summer meetings in conference rooms with no air conditioning. But I enjoyed the work regardless of the conditions.

My social time in Bucharest was limited, but I was surprised when I first encountered prices taped in the menus because they changed so often. Inflation rates of more than 50 percent meant prices sometimes rose once or twice a day. I quickly learned not to exchange more dollars than I thought I would spend in a couple of hours.

Romania is a complex country. The people are difficult to get to know, but over the course of my visits, I came to really like the Romanians.

Romania shares borders with Ukraine, Hungary, Bulgaria, Moldova, and Serbia. It also shares the predominant Eastern Orthodox religion with each, with the exception of Hungary. To many Americans, Romania's most well-known export has been its gymnastics teams, which for many years have been among the best in the world. Russia casts an ever-present shadow over the country. Romanians want good relations with Russia, but clearly are trying to turn to the West. This is a critical time for Romania with much at risk.

My Home Away from Home—The Romanian U.S. Ambassador's Residence

Modern Romania really took shape under the harsh hand of Nicolae Ceausescu in the 1960s. A vast program of industrialization transformed the agrarian country into an urbanized, heavily industry-based society, and created a Communist elite with lives of extravagant indulgence.

Communism was truly the time of the "haves" (a very small percentage of the people) and the "have-nots" (everyone else). In 1947, Mrs. Ana Pauker was one of the leading members of the first Communist Party in Romania. Her position allowed her to choose a large house in Kieseleff Soseaua, a fashionable district in Bucharest. The house is still owned by Romania, but is now rented by the U.S. government for the Ambassador's Residence. Former U.S. Ambassador to Romania, Jim Rosapepe, and his wife Sheilah were kind enough to have me as their guest when I was working in Bucharest.

The history of the house reveals a glimpse of the Communist times there. When Mrs. Pauker first moved in, she decided she wanted larger grounds and more gardens. To accomplish this, she simply ordered the demolition of a nearby house and restaurant, with no compensation for the occupants. The former Pauker residence not only has a grand staircase and numerous sitting rooms, but it also houses an indoor swimming pool surfaced with thousands of tiny, handmade tiles. Staying in the former Communist mansion went a long way to shattering my naïve thought that Communism was a system geared toward equality.

The End of Communism in Romania Was Televised

Between SECI meetings, personal travel, and meetings with local and international entrepreneurs, I've gotten some idea of the challenges entrepreneurs face and why it is taking so long for Romania to become a free market economy. I can only try to imagine what living under the rule of Nicolae Ceausescu, Romania's despotic dictator, must have been like. Romanians of a certain age shudder when they recall him. Dictator during the Communist regime, ruler of Romania from 1967 until 1989, Ceausescu was a violent, authoritarian, crazy man. He ruled out of fear, creating a personality cult to rival Stalin's.

Adrian Draghici worked for a government exporting company, and his office overlooked the square where he watched Ceausescu's last speech. In late 1989, the revolution against Communism was sweeping across Central Europe. Ceausescu and his wife, Elena, were trying desperately to retain their hold on the country. Adrian told me about what he saw on a particularly historic day, December 22, 1989.

"It was a confusing time, almost like a dream," Adrian said. "There was a demonstration in the square, and we didn't know what to do, we really didn't know. Ceausescu and his wife, for the first and only time, were openly booed by the restless mass of people in the public square. They were compelled to flee. I saw the helicopter leaving, and I imagined he was leaving the country. We would go home, and somebody would come and take leadership, organize elections, and that's it. It didn't come true like that.

"When his helicopter was forced to land just outside Bucharest, Ceausescu and his wife were captured. Some people held them for three days. Then on Christmas Day, they were both shot as videotape recorded the events to prove to Romanians and the world that they were gone. Otherwise the people would not have believed it."

The People's Palace

In Bucharest, I was amazed by the huge, ostentatious public buildings constructed during Communist rule. Ceausescu was obviously a frustrated real estate developer. Romania's unique Communist legacies are these immense, mostly vacant, and architecturally monstrous creations prompted by Ceausescu's need for self-aggrandizement. Foremost among them is the building known as Ceausescu's Palace or the People's Palace.

In the early 1970s, a few years after he became President of the Romanian State Council, Ceausescu made a trip to North Korea to visit the Communist regime on which he closely modeled his own. Admiring the enormous government buildings constructed under the command of Kim il Sung, he determined to build his own masterpieces in Romania, only larger. Ceausescu detested foreign debt and was fiscally very tight, so, to pay for these monuments, he starved the private economy. The Minister of Health explained to the people that they should live on a very limited amount of food. While people were starving, Ceausescu ordered the construction of a vast, castle-like monument, rivaling the buildings he had seen in Korea. The House of the Republic, as Ceausescu's People's Palace is officially known, may well be the biggest building in the world and has never been fully occupied. It sits at the end of a street that was once devoid of traffic, but is now a patchwork quilt of taxis and private cars.

Ceausescu's megalomania required more than just one monument. He had a vast neighborhood of 18th- and 19th-century homes destroyed to make room for his vision of a haven for the Communist Party elite. He didn't care who was dislocated as a result. A story that a number of people told me was that residents of Bucharest would leave home in the morning and return at the end of the day to find that their home or apartment building had been bulldozed, often with all their belongings inside. Today the streets of Bucharest echo with Ceausescu's all-too-visible ghosts: the looming shadows of buildings no one is quite sure what to do with. Ironically, a portion of the large 10th floor of the People's Palace has now become the SECI-inspired anti-crime center for the region. Slowly but surely, the palace is finally being put to some practical use, though it remains mostly vacant. Now, more than a decade later, construction cranes still wait in areas where construction stopped at Ceausescu's death.

Enter the Western Entrepreneurs—"How Do I Get to Bucharest from Kuala Lumpur?"

During Ceausescu's reign, Romanians experienced a low quality of life. But at least it was predictable. Entrepreneurship was not allowed.

Since the end of Communism, life in Romania has continued to be difficult for many. Democracy is taking hold, and people are enjoying access to information and freedom to travel. But hyperinflation, a lack of experience with freedom, and the leftover mind-set of Communist oppression are making transitioning to free markets slow and difficult. For entrepreneurs, the needs are great, but so are the challenges.

Hope and change began with the first wave of young Western entrepreneurs who arrived in the wake of Ceausescu's death. When Kenny Blatt came to Romania, he had no idea he would turn into a marketing, media, and advertising mogul, nor that he would mentor Romanians such as Adrian Draghici. But over time, that is just what happened.

A restless and well-mannered 40-year-old New Jersey native, Kenny Blatt wanted to be an entrepreneur. Kenny had lived a predictable life back in New York as a lawyer. But when his father unexpectedly died, Kenny knew he had to make a difference—if not to prove something to himself then for his father's good memory. So in 1990, Kenny left the United States determined to make more of his life and see the world. His first international venture took him to Kuala Lumpur, where he joined a group developing a feature film.

"It sounded like fun," Kenny said. "I'd never been to the Far East, and I was ready for a change. Besides, I learned the hard way that life was indeed short and the world was big. Change is one of the strongest catalysts that unleashes entrepreneurial instincts."

Six months later, as he realized that the project was going nowhere, an old business partner of his father's contacted Kenny in Malaysia. He told Kenny that he saw an opportunity for casinos in Romania and he needed a lawyer to negotiate a contract. "Come to Romania," said his father's old partner.

Kenny, a lawyer by trade and an Atlantic City native, decided to go. "Besides, isn't Romania near KL?" Kenny negotiated a memorandum of understanding for the exclusive right to develop 10 gambling parlors on the Romanian coast.

"I said wow, casinos, 23 million people, and six months from now I'll have $100,000,000...this is it!" Kenny remembered.

Confident that this was the business deal that would make his fortune, Kenny returned to the United States. He bought 200 used slot machines that were loaded into a container and soon on their way to Romania. His initial feeling that things were going well changed in short order.

"A month or so into the process, I got a phone call from friends who had heard I was doing business in Romania. They said they had an opportunity in casino gambling. I asked them where and they said Romania. One thing led to another and I ended up with a copy of their memorandum of understanding. It was the identical document I had drafted!" Kenny said.

Rules for the Road

Kenny told me he developed a personal set of rules for doing business in Romania. Rule Number One was that a memorandum of understanding for exclusivity was irrelevant. It was a document that meant something to a Western businessman but very little to the new Eastern European businessman. It could be copied, names changed, stamped with an official-looking but irrelevant mark, and someone, somewhere, would believe that an understanding existed.

"We no longer had exclusivity, and the whole thing was somewhat of a sham," Kenny said. "The person we dealt with gave the document to about 10 parties, each of them taking the prerequisite 'presents,' whether it was consultancy fees, office equipment, or cars. These guys were leading the good life in the early times."

What I really wanted to know was what happened to those 200 slot machines slowly making their way to Romania. Rule Number Two: When the Romanians say, "Send something over, we want to see samples," those samples are not going to be around for very long. Kenny's slot machines were stolen, and two weeks later the container they had arrived in was missing, too. As the markets developed, Kenny was pleased that some laws acted as a deterrent to something like this happening again, but he told me that to the Romanian government officials, this was something they felt they were entitled to after years of suffering. Where Kenny viewed the act as outright theft, his Romanian counterparts had no remorse.

Kenny's story is similar to that of many young Western entrepreneurs getting their start in business in Central and Eastern Europe. All are marked by a series of fits and starts, some of which end up in disaster. The rare one over time resulted in real business opportunities. Kenny is mildly embarrassed by some of his early exploits in Bucharest. Like many others, he was engaged in numerous small trading projects, making $5,000 to $10,000 per trade. Kenny met his business partner, Adrian Draghici, this way. He worked on a commission, selling the products that Kenny imported. Without Kenny, Adrian may never have become an entrepreneur. Kenny provided the spark that set Adrian's below-the-surface entrepreneurial potential into action.

Kenny stumbled onto Rule Number Three working on yet another deal. A delegation from the Ministry of Transport claimed to have $10 million at its disposal to purchase a fleet of public transportation buses. Kenny organized the trip and escorted them to New York and New Jersey, with the promise of a 1- to 2-percent commission. Kenny paid for the entire trip, introduced the delegation to the right people, and then discovered his third rule: When someone claimed to have an amount of money, what they meant was that someday they might have it, and, in the meantime, they really wanted someone else to pay for a trip to the United States for them. In Kenny's case, bureaucrats wanting to see America had taken advantage of him. But Kenny, like a good entrepreneur, did not give up. He tried to figure out a solution to the latest mess.

"My father owned a huge billboard on the Atlantic City boardwalk," Kenny said. "He collected a check from the advertisers 12 times a year, paid the landlord once, and made $250,000 a year. That's good business." Learning from his father, Kenny suggested to his freeloading Romanian travel friends an idea for putting advertising billboards on the old buses they already owned. Adrian became Kenny's partner and helped Kenny formulate the best approach to the bus authority. The Bucharest bus authority agreed to provide advertising space and Kenny and Adrian's empire was born. By 1992 Kenny and Adrian had expanded from billboards on buses to a full-fledged outdoor advertising company. Today they own a successful nationwide billboard operation in Romania.

Kenny is very reflective on those early days. "The main problem at first was that we tried to impose our ways of doing business in a market that had no laws or rules that could be enforced. To be successful, one must not only be patient but also recognize that the playing field you are on is completely different than what you are used to. Don't superimpose your field onto theirs. Understand the differences and adjust your practices accordingly." Kenny went on to tell me that what may be black to us is white to them and on their playing field, white is white.

"If you need to act in a way that offends your morals or ethics, then decide not to play but do not assume that yours is the only way." Kenny's favorite way of illustrating this point is when he shows me two marks, say A and B, and asks me the straightest distance between these points. While we know the obvious answer, the straightest distance in an emerging market may be a jagged line and in that market, that is the correct answer.

The business climate has changed tremendously since those early days. Kenny Blatt and Adrian Draghici have become key figures in the transformation of the playing field in Bucharest. They later added Petra Groiss, an Austrian entrepreneur, as a partner.

A Lucky Lawsuit—The Story of a Romanian Entrepreneur

Adrian Draghici has a calm personality that complements Kenny's intensity and constant motion. He is conservative and handsome with a Latin air about him. He looks the role of a wealthy business financier. Adrian is very composed and brings the right balance to Kenny's intensity.

Adrian had a relatively privileged childhood, growing up as the son of a senior-level Romanian military officer. When he was a teenager, he passed the difficult exam for admission to the Polytechnic Institute in Bucharest. After graduating with an engineering degree, Adrian went to work for a foreign trade company, which specialized in semiconductors. He soon was given assignments that took him out of the Communist sphere and was one of few Romanians who traveled to the West. The Romanians needed some contact with the outside world, and, because of his father's position, Adrian was unlikely to defect. He held what was rare for Romanians under Communism: a passport for official travel.

In 1983, an American company sued the Romanian government-owned trading company where Adrian worked. The Romanians decided to mount a defense rather than ignore the lawsuit. Because of his knowledge of the transactions and his language skills, Adrian was given the job of handling the company's interests during the trial.

"It was very interesting for me," Adrian said. "I started to like the American mentality, the American way of living, of doing business. I traveled two or three times a year for about three years to be in touch with the lawyers. I'll never forget the chance to appear in a court of law in the United States, to raise my hand and to say, 'Yes, I do.' I will tell the truth and only the truth."

Adrian's job eventually included handling all North American and Australian business, requiring him to perfect his English and learn basic business concepts such as letters of credit, guarantees, and conditions of payment. This was all valuable information for what followed the collapse of the Communist system.

Great Expectations and False Starts

Immediately after Ceausescu's death, Adrian said the free market concept was completely unfamiliar to Romanians.

"The only thing people were dreaming about was freedom to speak, freedom to travel, freedom to do what they wanted," he said.

The first year following the demise of the command economy was filled by a sense of euphoria, a belief that with the end of Communism, life in Romania would quickly resemble that of the fabled West. In this sense, Romania, like the rest of the region, had naïve expectations, which 10 years later gave way to frustration, confusion, and even desperation.

After Communism, Adrian explained, the early politicians brought in huge amounts of consumer goods for people to buy, subsidizing the real costs. This gave the public a temporary surge of positive feelings. But it demolished government reserves and ultimately led to hyperinflation. Adrian is saddened and frustrated by what he sees as missed opportunities for the country to make real progress.

"It is going to take another 15 to 20 years to change the mentality of the people," Adrian says. "There is a mentality that the state is supposed to give to us. We are not supposed to have to work hard, and there is no understanding that you can go into private business."

The Moveable Entrepreneur

Petra Groiss, a tall, graceful, young Austrian woman, describes herself as being a "people person." Her self-made entrepreneurial career in marketing and advertising has led her from the country of her birth to London, Budapest, and Bucharest, in search of the challenge of surrounding herself with people with whom she could share her love of the business. By 1995, and after building and selling her own advertising/communications firm in Budapest, Hungary, Petra started looking for other regional opportunities. She found one in Bucharest when she met Kenny Blatt and Adrian Draghici.

The time between Petra's first post-university job and owning and running three concurrent companies in Romania was remarkably brief. Despite the challenges of entrenched attitudes and bureaucracy, the 1990s has been a period of great opportunity in most of Central and Eastern Europe, simply because so much was needed in so many fields. As a junior account executive on the Chrysler-Jeep account in Vienna in 1992, Petra was assigned the task of developing the advertising campaign in Eastern Europe: the least desirable of locations when compared to London or Paris.

"I went to Prague, Warsaw, Budapest…not really knowing what I was doing," Petra said. "It was great fun. It was a huge market, and I was always very open-minded. It was great for me; I was traveling around, meeting new people, and seeing new places."

By age 24, Petra had been hired away from her first agency to be a Senior Account Executive with Saatchi and Saatchi in the Budapest office.

"I wasn't worried about my age," she said. "If you were a foreigner, you were shown a lot of respect. I met a lot of other young people who were put in very responsible positions. Suddenly you are handling a large client just because you are a foreigner, not because you have great experience."

Leaving Saatchi and Saatchi, she started her own company in Budapest. Then she moved from Hungary to Romania in search of even greater "undeveloped" areas of opportunity. Meeting Kenny Blatt facilitated the creation of a new advertising company with Kenny and Adrian as her partners. Petra has made a tangible difference to the many Romanians who work for her company.

"The Romanian people have a history of depending on strong leadership," she said. "They have greater confidence in their ability to accomplish something if the leadership is there. I'm like the mother in the company. I bring the people close to me, teach them values and how to do business, and then gently push them away."

Petra, like Kenny and other Western entrepreneurs who find themselves becoming mentors, draw people in, help them learn what they need to thrive, and then give them the wings to achieve on their own. Petra is also an example of the huge opportunities available to young people with ideas and initiative in the formerly Communist countries of Central and Eastern Europe. In New York advertising circles, competition is cutthroat. By comparison, the opportunities open to young Petra Groiss have been broader and farther reaching.

They Needed Everything!

Rom-KU, the company Kenny and Adrian set up to manage the bus authority business, handled its first successful ad campaign for RJR Reynolds.

"I found a contact with RJR in Geneva," Kenny remembered. "I flew in and met with them, and the rest is history. These people were responsible for the advertising in the region, and I convinced them to advertise on these new yellow buses. They put their Camel brand on the buses, and that was how it started."

Kenny and Adrian went on to become RJR's Romanian advertising agency, partnering with the first international advertising agencies to come to Romania. Their business burgeoned with the needs of the multinationals, a phenomenon similar to the free market life cycle in other former Communist countries.

"The minute the Wall comes down, who are the first two groups of companies to come in? First you have the cigarette companies looking to establish themselves, including RJR Reynolds, Philip Morris, BAT (British American Tobacco), and so on," Kenny said. "Then the second area is beverages: Coke and Pepsi and so on. So, the first industry in the Central and Eastern European countries to develop is the service sector, because that is what the multinationals need."

With this strategic mind-set, Kenny and Adrian developed one service area after another, helping the international consumer products industry find its way in the totally new and undeveloped Romanian market. In addition to the advertising businesses, Kenny and Adrian created magazine companies, personnel agencies, and telecommunications companies.

Teaching What You Know

Kenny uses his American entrepreneurial instincts and role models in everything he does in Romania. He is quick to say that he was lucky to grow up in America. Information about other successful entrepreneurs has helped him develop his drive and entrepreneurial attitude. His view, which echoes Adrian's, is that a real understanding and appreciation for the free market model and mind-set is still missing from Romania. Entrepreneurs can be key in changing things.

In developing his companies, Kenny relied on American ideas. He drew on strategies and programs that he had seen succeed in the past.

"I don't like to reinvent the wheel. I have no ego, so I might as well copy, or partner with someone who already knows how to do it," Kenny said. "For each of my businesses, I have said, 'Great, let's find some young Romanians, train them in the American formula, and go with it.' I know America, but now I'm in Romania, and I want local partners. At the same time, I want international partners who can help with the training. So, for instance, in the personnel area, when I was back in America on a trip, I looked in the yellow pages and found Snelling & Snelling, America's number one personnel agency. I ended up choosing Snelling as our personnel company partner and found some great young Romanians to run it. In each new business, I just tried to intelligently say to myself, 'Who are the biggest and the best in the world? Who would be potential clients for me? How can we train the Romanian employees to be the best?'"

Kenny's formula of working with young people has paid off. Never having been given a chance before, they work their heart out for a decent salary, and, most importantly, for exposure to outside training and a chance to participate down the line in profit sharing or partial ownership of a business. Kenny has sometimes found it hard to retain young employees because as they gained valuable experience working for him, they grew more appealing to other international companies. That's all right with him. To Kenny, helping young people recognize and understand the power of hard work and entrepreneurial risk taking is a reward in and of itself.

Spaga

Western entrepreneurs in Romania face some unique cultural challenges. What we in the West call corruption is a way of life in Romania. Corruption takes many forms. There is a type of corruption I call "structural," that enables life to go on normally for most people. It is related to the entitlement mind-set that developed during the Communist era, and hearkens back even further to the system of serfdom that existed well into the 19th century.

In Romania, one often hears the word *spaga*. Spaga is a "consultancy fee," a "present," or "favor," but in harsher terms, it is a bribe. A typical day doesn't go by without several spaga offerings. From flowers, to a bottle of whiskey, to perfume, pens, and even cash, spaga is employed in one way or another as part of everyday life.

The early multinationals had to learn how to deal with the concept of spaga. Now multinational business managers know that it is a part of successfully doing business in Romania. An executive for an international company with business in Romania told me at a dinner that the key is for the spaga to be in the proper range. It is, according to that executive, "just a cost of doing business." Bribes grease palms in virtually all parts of the distribution system in order to get products into the country and sold, or to get things done better or faster.

But there are other views.

"I personally do not give bribes nor do we take bribes," Petra Groiss said. "But this is my personal way of dealing, because I am a great believer that if you do it once, you will do it a second time, and it will become a habit. I'm responsible for educating people. If I don't conduct business a certain way, I can't expect them to follow. I want to set a moral code. Corruption can have a snowball effect, and it will become a disaster."

"Spaga is a very normal thing. I have to tell you, you get very tempted," she said. "If a policeman stops you, you know all he wants is $1, and he'll get off your back. Or you will waste 30 minutes with official forms and pay a fine anyway. He probably earns $50 a month and needs the money to feed his family. It's tempting. You have to make judgment calls. Not everything is black and white. I do think that things will get better as the standard of living rises. For many people, bribery, giving and taking, is a matter of survival."

As Kenny joked in discussing the uneven playing field in Bucharest, the two jobs he would like to have in a different life would be a border guard or a "consultant" in Romania. The border guards are notorious for accepting bribes: cash, whiskey, cigarettes, or other small consumables. It's one of the key issues that SECI is tackling.

The "consultant" that Kenny referred to usually is someone who speaks impeccable English and offers to help Western businesspeople through city hall or trade bureaus for a few hundred thousand dollars. The consultant tells them the fee is high so he can pay bribes on their behalf. This way the client doesn't knowingly violate American anti-bribery laws. Most of that fee goes into the consultant's pocket. Only $5,000 or $10,000 becomes the spaga at city hall or the trade bureau.

Enter the Age of the Consumer

Kenny and Adrian, doing business in Romania since the early 1990s, smoothed the way for many entrepreneurs to follow. Among those is Fahim Tobur, one of the most contagiously happy, friendly, optimistic, exciting, and outgoing people I have ever met. As a Turkish entrepreneur in Bucharest, he exemplifies the entrepreneurial energy that can move mountains and make the world a better place.

Fahim developed the first new Western-style shopping center in Bucharest, overcoming immense challenges. Even though the government is not helpful or encouraging, the unfilled demand for goods and services is strong and compelling to entrepreneurs with ideas.

A Romanian-Turkish Feast

During a summer trip to Bucharest in 1999, Fahim invited me to a dinner party. Kenny picked me up shortly before dinner, and we drove to a fashionable district in Bucharest. Our destination was an enormous house, owned by our host's company, and used exclusively for entertaining and temporary visitors. It was a magnificent place with attractive grounds. As we entered, we saw guards carrying guns, and I felt like I was attending a party at an ambassadorial residence in any number of countries that I had visited.

The evening began with cocktails for about 25 guests. Most of them were people who knew one another, but there were a few newcomers. The guest list included mostly businesspeople and a few diplomats, which made for a fun and stimulating evening.

It was raining when we arrived, but the weather improved enough for dinner outside on the terrace. It was a great evening. The combination of friendly conversation, extraordinarily delicious Turkish food, and perhaps too much good wine, was great. Fahim was a gracious host. Course after course of fine food arrived. The dinner party went on until the early morning. Fahim sat across from me, and I found him to be a dynamic individual with impeccable English. He is a 60-plus-year-old grandfather with a wonderful wife who seems to thrive on his enjoyment of life.

During the evening I discovered that Fahim was building the first international shopping mall in Romania. What impressed me with Fahim's vision was his desire to take the risk of being the first new mall developer in this region of the world. Why was he doing it? What was it like? I wanted to know more. I mentioned my interest and immediately he offered a tour. Later at 1:30 a.m., despite what had now turned into a fun sing-along, Kenny and I were among the first to depart.

Renovating a Communist Eyesore

The next morning Kenny and I were on the way to Romania's first Western-style mall. On the way there, we saw one enormous, vacant government facility after another. The many construction cranes rusting in place throughout this district of Bucharest were even more shocking.

In a corner of the former government district was an unfinished building. Its ultimate purpose was to have been a Communist Party headquarters. In 1997, the building was privatized through a government auction. The buyer was Fahim's company. Our car pulled up in front of a bustling construction site that was to have been the seat of the Romanian Communist Party.

The sales brochure given to prospective renters proclaimed "Next Station, Bucharest Mall, All Aboard." It described an express train to Romania and symbolized the speed at which Fahim and his associates were developing a consumer complex out of the old unfinished building. As Fahim met us, I was handed a hard hat for the walk through the construction site, which is a typical requirement of any safe construction site around the world. What was unusual about this hard hat was that it already had my name on it.

We began our tour, quickly walking through the 500,000 square feet of construction. The mall includes several cinemas, a bowling alley, food courts, a large hypermarket (a modern supermarket food operation), as well as all the traditional pedestrian areas and numerous retail stores. The center of the mall is a multistory atrium covered by an ornate skylight. Bucharest Mall is as finely done as any Western-style mall I've ever seen. Still, the juxtaposition of completely modern, Western architecture dedicated to consumers, sitting in the middle of Ceausescu's old Romania was fantastic. Are entrepreneurs great or what?

Kenny, Adrian, Petra, and Fahim represent American, Romanian, Austrian, and Turkish backgrounds. Yet in Romania, they all represent the bridge to the future. This is what responsible entrepreneurism is all about. They are doing what they do in spite of rather than because of Romanian encouragement or Western support. Yet, they are making money and, more importantly, making a big difference. A better entrepreneurial environment will encourage more entrepreneurs, maybe even you, and, ultimately, it can build a better free market and democracy for Romania.

Chapter 11

DON'T ACCEPT THE
COMMON WISDOM –
AMBASSADOR RICHARD SCHIFTER

Richard Schifter was born in Austria. When he was 14 years old, Germany annexed Austria and the Nazis took control. As Jews, he and his family were immediately subjected to severe persecution and sought to emigrate to the United States. Under U.S. immigration laws then in effect, only Richard qualified for the immediate issuance of a visa. His parents were placed on a waiting list. They as well as a majority of Richard's extended family died in the Holocaust.

Ambassador Richard Schifter (left) with Lech Walesa while he (Walesa) was still leader of the Solidarity Movement.

He quickly completed high school and obtained an undergraduate degree. He was 19 when he joined the Army, where he served in military intelligence, returning to Germany as a U.S. soldier in 1944.

After the War, he obtained a law degree and entered the private practice of law, specializing in the representation of American Indian Tribes.

He was also active in civic and political affairs in his home state of Maryland, serving for twenty years on the Maryland State Board of Education and becoming its president. He also chaired the Democratic Central Committee of Montgomery County, MD.

More recently, Richard Schifter has served as U.S. Representative on the United Nations Commission of Human Rights, Deputy U.S. Representative in the United Nations Security Council, with the rank of Ambassador, Assistant Secretary of State for Human Rights, Special Assistant to the President and Counselor on the staff of the National Security Council, and Special Adviser to the Secretary of State. In the latter capacity, he organized the Southeast European Cooperative Initiative, which has brought twelve countries of Southeastern Europe together to efforts to find joint solutions to economic, environmental, and social problems that they face.

With the change of Administrations, Richard Schifter left U.S. Government service in 2001 and is once again active in Maryland public affairs.

— ✦ —

Ghosts of the Past

It was a warm, sunny afternoon when my friend Dick Schifter and I left the ornate Chancery building housing the executive offices for the U.S. Embassy in Vienna. We had been in a meeting with various law enforcement agency representatives talking about drug trafficking and other issues affecting Southeastern Europe. Dick had some new ideas to share on how to add real teeth to drug enforcement in the region. From this meeting on drugs to the next on business trade facilitation in Southeastern Europe, Dick led the agenda promoting innovative and creative ideas to address the problems at hand.

Dick is an entrepreneur in government who isn't afraid to take risks. Time and again in his career, Dick took a good idea and did everything it took to make it happen. He has always been a diplomat who isn't afraid to be undiplomatic. In government, good ideas too often give way to excess bureaucracy. Most of the time, this is because individuals care more about covering their backsides than achieving the end goal. That's why it's hard to find a risk taker in government. That's also why we desperately need entrepreneurs in government. We need caring, creative, smart individuals like Dick Schifter, who are willing to do what they believe is right even though there is personal career risk.

On this particular day, I was accompanying Dick, who is formally called Ambassador Richard Schifter, to a wide variety of meetings. As our next meeting was in an adjacent building a block or so away, we walked.

Many Americans think of the embassy buildings as tourist attractions because they aren't only beautiful, but also rich in history. The reality, though, is that they are not generally set up to receive visitors. Much of the business in embassies is either top secret, classified, or otherwise sensitive and, accordingly, the embassies have several layers of security. You can't simply go wandering around without proper authorization.

Naturally, Ambassador Schifter had all the necessary authorizations, and, by the time of this meeting, so did I. Being the spouse of the U.S. Ambassador to Austria got me only so far, but because of my work with Dick, I had applied for and gone through a rigorous process of screening at the State Department that resulted in my top-secret security clearance.

While the weather is not usually Vienna's strongest attraction, this was an unusually pleasant day, warm and sunny, so we kept walking and talking. I knew that Dick was originally from Vienna, but I didn't know the details of his life's journey. As we walked along Boltzmanngasse, Dick began to describe the changes that had occurred in the neighborhood since the time he lived in Vienna.

"Over there, on the ground floor of that apartment house was our synagogue, where I had my bar mitzvah. And a few blocks from here is the house in which I was born," Dick remembered.

He also told me a story related to our embassy building. When he was a child in Vienna, it served as the Consular Academy. By the time Dick was in third grade, he was fascinated by geography and found out that there was a close relationship between diplomatic work and geography. He said that diplomats got their training at the Consular Academy. So, whenever Dick and his parents passed the building that now houses the U.S. Embassy, he would say, "That's where I'm going to go to school." His father finally decided to have a serious talk with him. "We are Jewish," he told him. "Jews don't get jobs as diplomats." Dick was crushed. Fifty years later, when he took his seat for the first time as a diplomat at the United Nations Human Rights Commission, his first thought was that he wished his parents could have witnessed that scene.

One of the things that surprised me early on about Austria was the ever-present relevance of the events of World War II. Throughout the time of Kathy's ambassadorship, issues relating to World War II, restitution, the Holocaust, and anti-Semitism dominated her activities. Dick was enormously helpful to her in an advisory role on many issues of this nature. Working behind the scenes with Dick, the Undersecretary of the Treasury Stu Eisenstadt, and others, Kathy helped resolve many issues related to the Holocaust during her tenure. Throughout her time in Austria, Kathy was an admired representative, spreading the messages of tolerance and diversity she had honed throughout her years in politics. She was extremely successful in helping resolve issues in part, I believe, because she is not Jewish. Often she would find herself in a room between Austrian Catholic officials and Jewish representatives. From her neutral position, she was able to be far more effective.

Toward the end of her service, a right wing party led by Jörg Haider came into power in Austria. Some of Haider's messages were frighteningly neo-Nazi in their tone and content, provoking a strong reaction and sanctions from the European Union. Working together with Dick and then-U.S. Secretary of State Madeleine Albright, Kathy helped implement a more restrained policy on the part of the United States. After the EU sanctions were lifted. Haider again began campaigns with anti-Semitic messages. Kathy stepped up to the plate again, issuing a strong press release and holding a press conference condemning the materials. Others soon followed suit. Kathy was enormously popular with the press and the people of Austria in part because she gave her speeches in German. She was the right person at the right time in the right job.

Before our move to Austria, I never would have believed how front and center these issues would be 55 years after the end of the war. It all became a bit clearer as I listened to Dick explain his old neighborhood to me.

With his eyes tearing up slightly, he described what his life was like growing up in Austria's capital. The Schifter family lived within a few blocks of what is now the U.S. Embassy. In 1938 when he was 15, German troops marched into the country, making it a Nazi state. Dick described how Hitler came to the Heldenplatz, a large square next to the Hofburg Palace downtown, and spoke to a crowd of tens of thousands. He remembers how Austrians cheered as Hitler entered and at every pause in his speech. There was no fighting, no resistance. With the overwhelming acceptance of Hitler in Austria, Dick's life changed literally overnight. His family and all other Jewish families suddenly became outcasts. So did Christians with any Jewish ancestry. Of his more than 20 non-Jewish classmates, only one continued to speak to Dick and other Jewish students. Dick and the other Jewish classmates had to sit on benches in the back of the room, separated by an empty bench from the other students. On streetcars, Jews could no longer take seats. They were allowed only to stand in the space near the conductor.

In December of 1938, Dick finally got a visa to the United States, a difficult process at the time. He qualified because he was born in Austria. His parents, natives of Poland, were placed on the U.S.-quota waiting list, because the United States then controlled immigration through the national-origins quota system. Dick's parents decided not to wait until it was their turn to qualify for a visa. They chose to send Dick to safety. Dick's parents and many other relatives eventually perished in the Holocaust.

Coming to America

What did this 15-year-old Austrian fleeing persecution do in the United States? Dick took advantage of every education opportunity available. He worked hard, quickly finished high school and then, in less than three years, received his undergraduate degree. By the time he finished college, America was also at war, and Dick joined the Army. He served in the Military Intelligence Service and was sent to Europe in 1944. In October of that year, he was attached to the First Infantry Division as the U.S. Army entered Germany and occupied the city of Aachen. His unit was later assigned to other divisions entering large cities such as Cologne, Coblentz, Frankfurt, and Dusseldorf. Dick's fluent German and unquestionable loyalty made his assignment logical.

In early 1946, Dick was discharged but decided to stay in Germany a while longer as an official of the military government. In his spare time, he worked on American programs to rebuild Germany. Long before the Marshall Plan, indeed before the outcome of the war was certain, American officials had been exploring how to help Europe find lasting peace. Rebuilding the economies and helping develop strong democracies even in the enemy nations was the goal to help achieve stability.

Among the many things Dick has taught me are the benefits and responsibilities that come with freedom. He is grateful every day to America for, as he says, "saving my life." In gratitude, he has dedicated himself to helping others in jeopardy, proudly doing so with the strong American values he holds so dear.

"I returned home yesterday," Dick wrote to me recently. "When I presented my passport to the immigration officer, I told him: 'It's 62 years ago to the day when I met my first U.S. immigration officer, when I arrived in this country as a refugee.' The officer to whom I said that then gave me a big smile and said: 'Welcome home.' The fact that the United States let me in to make my home here is why I made it past the age of 21."

It's Not About Collective Guilt

When former President Bill Clinton asked Kathy and me to make a list of countries where she might be interested in serving as ambassador, we put Austria at the top of the list. Still, we had mixed feelings. On one hand Austria was a great central location and close to the new frontier of Central and Eastern Europe, about which we both wanted to learn more. Austria also was a beautiful, cultured country. I had visited there in 1987 and was very impressed. On the other hand was the negative legacy of anti-Semitism. This was a country where relatives on my father's side had been killed during World War II. Despite my mother's German roots, I had been brought up to believe that Germans and Austrians caused these terrible things to happen to Jews.

If anyone in the world has the right to be bitter about the Austrian and German people it's Dick Schifter. And yet, he went on to shock me when he talked about the Germany he lived in as a soldier and military government official after the end of the war. He participated in a program outside his official duties to help Germans embrace democracy. He had a keen interest in helping the German people. I didn't get it; why would he do that?

While it seemed simple to him, it was revolutionary to me. I had heard the words before, but hadn't fully grasped their meaning. Dick explained to me that he doesn't believe in collective guilt. He never held the German people responsible for what happened to his family. Instead, he held the Nazis and the individuals who made decisions and committed the terrible atrocities responsible.

In his early 20s, with the war over, Dick remained in Germany and took every opportunity to help expose young Germans to what democracy was all about. In one youth group meeting, he and a young, attractive German girl translated the American Bill of Rights from English to German. They wanted to read it to the youth group so it could be discussed piece by piece. The young lady who shared Dick's passion to create democracy was not Jewish. As the young woman, Lilo Krueger, and Dick spent more time together, they fell in love. In 1948, they married.

Dick, accompanied by his new wife, moved back to the United States shortly after the wedding. Over the years, they had five children and nine grandchildren. Lilo Schifter is a very accomplished person. At 48, after raising her children, she went to law school and graduated first in her class. She subsequently became a specialist in the field of public utilities law and served for 16 years as a member of the Maryland Public Service Commission. Prior to their 35th wedding anniversary, unbeknownst to Dick, she converted to Judaism. This was all kept as a surprise until the anniversary party, to which many friends, including the rabbi of the synagogue they attended, had been invited. At the party, Lilo announced her conversion and asked Dick whether he now wanted to have a religious wedding. The rabbi, who had performed the conversion, then stepped forward and Lilo and Dick, their children, grandchildren, and friends enjoyed a very special celebration.

Taking Responsibility and Getting Involved

Back from the war with a new, young wife, Dick Schifter didn't waste time. He attended Yale Law School and, upon graduation, set about building a career as a lawyer. He eventually became a partner of Fried, Frank, Harris, Shriver, and Jacobson, a prominent New York and Washington law firm. As a Washington, D.C., lawyer, Dick's activities often involved government and administrative law. Washington lawyers find that it can be extremely lucrative to represent private concerns with government and administrative interests. The pay is good because the stakes are high.

For Dick, money was not the most important measure of success. He became a specialist in a rather non-lucrative area, representing Native American tribes in the United States. He represented Native Americans in numerous matters, collecting lower fees that other lawyers found ridiculous. As an entrepreneurial lawyer, he was not the kind of person who waited for a client to tell him a specific need or function. Dick would initiate ideas to solve problems. Native Americans on reservations lived in squalor. Dick was ashamed to see the incredibly poor housing conditions, so he began to pursue initiatives to help bring about positive change.

Early on, Dick learned that politics are important. He became actively involved in the Democratic Party at the grassroots level as a precinct chairman. Working through political channels, Dick executed strategies to help Native Americans get better housing. He had first planned to write an amendment to legislation or a whole new law and pursue support in Congress. At the same time, he studied and restudied the 1937 Housing Act. He finally decided the 1937 Housing Act provided broad enough authorization to build public housing on Indian reservations. Previously, no one had ever successfully used the act for this purpose.

Dick went to the acting head of the Bureau of Indian Affairs, the senior position in government created to protect the interests of American Indians. This individual, a Native American himself, laughed at Dick's idea, saying, "Sure, can you get a house for me? I need a house, too." He said the administration would never appropriate money to build housing for Indians. But "never" is a word that doesn't exist in Dick Schifter's vocabulary.

It wasn't easy. There were many hurdles. But Dick created support within the presidential administration and the Public Housing Administration (this was before the creation of the Department of Housing and Urban Development) for the need and legal grounds to build public housing on reservations. He then took the leap—an entrepreneurial risk—and made a specific application. On behalf of the Oglala Sioux Tribe, he requested 50 homes to be built on the Pine Ridge Reservation in South Dakota. The request was approved. From there Dick made applications for other tribes and won approval for one after another. Finally, housing standards were brought to more reasonable conditions, and today, thanks in large part to Dick, the United States has a vast program of public housing on Indian reservations.

Becoming a Reagan Democrat

In 1955, Dick and Lilo and their children moved to Montgomery County, Maryland. Within weeks he became active in the Democratic Party. In 1966, he led a citizens' movement that unseated the established county party organization, which had been in control for more than 40 years. For the next four years, he headed the County Democratic Central Committee. The Clean Government standards established as a result of this committee's effort have lasted to this day.

In 1981, Ronald Reagan reached out to the well-respected academic Jeane Kirkpatrick to become the U.S. Ambassador to the United Nations. She was a woman of undisputed credentials. She was also a Democrat from Montgomery County and a friend of Dick Schifter's. Early on in her Ambassadorship, she needed to recommend a new alternate delegate for the United Nations Human Rights Commission. She picked Dick Schifter. He later became the U.S. Representative to the United Nations Human Rights Commission and then served as the Deputy United States Representative in the United Nations Security Council, with the rank of Ambassador.

Then one day a call came from Secretary of State George Shultz. Shultz wanted to recommend to President Reagan that he appoint Dick Schifter to become Assistant Secretary for Human Rights and Humanitarian Affairs. Dick agreed to serve in that position.

Through seven years—the balance of the Reagan administration and into the Bush years—Dick Schifter was the active Assistant Secretary for Human Rights. This was a time when the world was changing fast. Negotiations over human rights issues with the Soviet Union were at a critical stage. As Assistant Secretary, Dick used his position to work for positive change and to make things happen.

Entrepreneurs and Bureaucracies

Dick Schifter knew that he was not creating basic policy. He was influencing it and sketching out the details in his area of responsibility. His ideas, together with those of many others, would influence the Secretary of State, who, in turn, would work with the National Security Council and the President to make those basic policy decisions.

There was one event that was particularly noteworthy. In November 1987, Dick accompanied the Deputy Secretary of State, John Whitehead, to a meeting with the then-Soviet Foreign Minister, Eduard Shevardnadze. After the usual exchange of pleasantries, Whitehead got down to business. He pointed out that there was deep concern in the United States about the scores of persons imprisoned in the Soviet Union for "anti-Soviet agitation and propaganda," or holding meetings of a religious nature without proper authorization. Shevardnadze responded that he understood the point, but then asked what he could be expected to do.

"These are people convicted under the laws of the Soviet Union by courts of the Soviet Union," he told Dick. "I am the Foreign Minister. This is out of my hands."

It was at this point that Dick got into the discussion.

"Mr. Minister," he said, "the laws under which these people were convicted are in conflict with the International Covenant on Civil and Political Rights, which guarantee freedom of expression and freedom of religion. The Covenant, as an international treaty, is the responsibility of the Foreign Ministry. It was negotiated by the Foreign Ministry, and the Foreign Ministry should see to it that it is adhered to."

Dick then cited four articles in the Soviet Criminal Code that he said were in conflict with the Covenant.

"These articles should be repealed and anyone convicted under them should be released," he said.

As his remarks were interpreted to Shevardnadze, Dick thought that he saw a sign of recognition in Shevardnadze's eyes. A few weeks later, one of the Soviet Deputy Foreign Ministers remarked casually to Dick, "We have decided to bring ourselves into full compliance with our international agreements." By the end of 1988, all persons on the U.S. list of those imprisoned for political or religious activity had been freed, and the Soviet Union had begun the process of repealing the laws that forced their imprisonment.

Not everyone had noticed the basic political changes that had taken place in the Soviet Union. By the end of Reagan's second term, some of the people associated with the incoming Bush Administration thought that, influenced by Shultz, Reagan had finally gone soft on Communism. Important negotiations in late 1988 were being hindered from within the State Department on the assumption that this is what the new bosses would want. Dick became aware of instructions that had been cabled to our Embassy in Moscow that would cause the Soviet authorities to believe that the United States was not interested in reaching an agreement in the ongoing negotiations in the Conference for Security and Co-operation in Europe. When Dick saw the instructions, he felt a sense of disbelief that George Shultz, a man whom he knew well, would have approved the cable that went out with his signature. Though Dick was told Shultz had approved it, he couldn't believe it.

Dick, who had been raised by his parents to be an anti-Communist, had himself been a hard-liner on matters involving Soviet policy. But he believed that massive changes had taken place under Gorbachev and that Reagan and Shultz had responded wisely to those changes. Having seen the new instructions, he went to Shultz and asked his position on the issues posed at the conference. When Shultz confirmed that his position had not changed, Dick explained the situation. Shultz was upset that the cable had gone out. The question then was how best to handle the situation. Dick told Shultz that he was on his way to a meeting in Moscow the next week and said he could deliver a message to the Foreign Minister in Moscow. This message would counter the message conveyed through the Embassy. Shultz agreed and together they formulated the message that Dick would carry to the Soviet Foreign Minister. As he escorted him to the door, Shultz told Dick, "Tell them I, too, have problems with my bureaucracy."

Dick left George Shultz's office with his mandate and the knowledge that Shultz, as he expected, was consistent in his policy. This was an important issue, and, if this mission were not properly carried out, talks would deteriorate and likely result in failure to reach agreement at the conference.

Entrepreneurs need to know when to take risks and when to innovate. At this point, Dick became convinced that if he didn't take some risks, persons at lower rungs in the bureaucracy would have countermanded his Secretary's, and indeed his President's, positions. Staffers had gotten Shultz's initials on instructions that modified policy that had been years in the making. Dick was concerned that sentiments in Moscow would now freeze on the incorrect assumption that the United States had changed its position. He needed to get a message to Moscow quickly, suggesting that the Soviet authorities await his arrival there with his message from Secretary Shultz. He thought about passing a message to the Soviets through the U.S. Ambassador to Moscow but then was uncertain about which side the ambassador was on. Only later did he learn that the Ambassador, Jack Matlock, was in agreement with the Secretary's position and would have been helpful. Needing someone to slow down a Soviet overreaction, he decided to contact the Soviet Deputy Chief of Mission in Washington. Dick telephoned him and said that he had a personal message from George Shultz concerning the conference, which he would deliver in Moscow the following week, asking the Soviet Deputy to await that message before taking any other steps.

It was fortuitous that Dick took this risk. Later in Moscow, it became clear that when the message contained in the instructions had been delivered, as Dick feared, the Soviets concluded that U.S. policy indeed had changed. Dick's meetings in Moscow helped repair the damage done by the earlier message, and the Soviets made major concessions on the human rights issues that were on the U.S. agenda. After Dick's visit to Moscow, there were some follow-up meetings as well. And on January 19, 1989, the Reagan Administration's last full day in office, the conference was successfully concluded. The result of all of this was very positive, but at the time it was high risk and took creative entrepreneurial thinking.

After the change of administration, Dick was asked by Secretary of State Jim Baker to continue in his role as Assistant Secretary of State for Human Rights. Entrepreneurs need to have backbone and, as the Kenny Rogers song goes, "You gotta know when to hold them, know when to fold them, know when to walk away...." In the Bush Administration, Dick Schifter became concerned about new policy that affected human rights. He disagreed with the administration's effort in 1989 and early 1990 to befriend Saddam Hussein, an effort that came to naught when Kuwait was invaded. After our success in the Gulf War, he was troubled by the U.S.'s failure to help the Shiites in Iraq's south and to do enough to protect the Kurds in the north. In his third year in the Bush administration, Dick had a sharp disagreement with the Middle Eastern Bureau of the State Department over the text of the annual human rights report on Israel. Dick had not been hesitant to criticize Israel, including Defense Minister Rabin, for actions that violated accepted international standards of human rights. But the draft report espoused by the Near Eastern Bureau, he concluded, used terminology that had been adopted by the PLO in its propaganda campaign against Israel. Curfews, for example, were called "collective punishment," a term that had been used to describe Nazi mass killings during World War II. Dick had to know when to be a team player and when to stand up and do the right thing. After Secretary Baker sided with the Near Eastern Bureau, Dick resigned.

Too Old

Having returned to the private sector, Dick was soon back into Democratic politics. He began to help a new young Democratic candidate for president, someone he had known for the preceding four years: Bill Clinton. When the Clinton campaign hit full steam, Dick was actively involved. After Clinton won the election, the incoming National Security Adviser, Tony Lake, and his Deputy, Sandy Berger, recommended Dick for an Under Secretary's position in the State Department. But the final decision of appointment was to be made by the Secretary of State-designate, Warren Christopher. Dick was invited to meet with Christopher. The meeting was pleasant, but before long Christopher finally came right out and told Dick, "The time has come to turn the leadership of the country over to a new generation." It was Christopher's way of telling Dick that he was too old.

Shortly after the inauguration of President Clinton, Tony Lake asked Dick Schifter to come to see him. He told him that the President wanted to appoint him Ambassador to Germany. To Lake's surprise, Dick turned him down. He explained that Lilo had stayed at home for years to raise their five children, had then gone to law school, and now had a career of her own, serving as a member of the Maryland Public Service Commission. He didn't want to ask her to resign, nor did he want them to live on different continents. He said he would prefer to serve on the staff of the National Security Council. Again, time would show this to be one door closing for Dick with a new and better door opening, as Dick was ultimately given the opportunity to serve on the Security Council.

Entrepreneurs come in all ages. At age 68, Dick Schifter was told he was too old. But at age 76, Dick was still as energetic and committed as he was in his youth. Part of his job involved frequent travel to Central and Eastern Europe, with Vienna being one of his usual stops. He often started his day at 6 a.m. to make a breakfast meeting in downtown Vienna. That would be followed by his typical, intense 15-hour day working for the taxpayers. Dick is one of the healthiest, most productive, and energetic workers I've seen at any age.

A number of months after his encounter with Warren Christopher, Dick accompanied the then-U.S. Ambassador to the United Nations, Madeleine Albright, on a visit to Europe. At one point, they attended a luncheon at the Dutch Foreign Ministry. Not realizing that the meal being served had some lobster in it, to which Dick is extremely allergic, he began to feel terrible. But the last thing he wanted to do was get up from the table and leave the meeting early. If word got back to Warren Christopher, he thought, that would be proof to Christopher that he was right, that Dick was too old. Through sheer willpower he hung through the entire dinner. As they left, Madeleine Albright turned to him and asked: "Dick, what was the matter? In the middle of the lunch you turned green." Entrepreneurs can be stubborn and tough.

How Policy Is Made: Forming SECI

Dick Schifter, "too old" for the State Department, moved to the National Security Council. Dick enjoys his ability to be entrepreneurial and provide initiative and ideas in a variety of policy areas. He considers himself more of an inventor in government than anything else. I use the term entrepreneur, he uses the term inventor, but, either way, there's no doubt that he is far from a typical bureaucrat or politician.

"Most people think of an inventor as somebody developing gadgets and material things," Dick said. "What I believe I can do is invent new legal interpretations, new governmental structures, and new arrangements of how people work with each other. In a way that really is what an entrepreneur does: doing something for the first time that has never been done before."

In 1995, the National Security Council was hard at work on what to do about Bosnia. When the war in Bosnia ended, it was quite obvious that at best there was an unsettled peace. The prospect of stabilizing Bosnia looked huge and problematic. Indeed, the whole region looked like a potential powder keg.

Dick Schifter came up with an idea for an organization that he first called the Southeast European Development Cooperative Initiative. His idea was to form a regional organization that would help support countries as they restructured, readying them to join NATO and the EU. What became the Southeast European Cooperative Initiative (SECI) includes a roster of countries many Americans know little about. They include Albania, Bosnia-Herzegovina, Bulgaria, Croatia, Greece, Hungary, Macedonia, Moldova, Romania, Slovenia, and Turkey. This widely disparate group of countries now works through government officials and business people on such important issues as crime, corruption, border crossings, drugs, energy savings, business impediments, and more.

Since the Kosovo war, the attention being paid to this often-neglected part of Europe is a sign of growing interest, but an interest that is still far from approaching the focus on Western Europe after World War II. The Marshall Plan was unique in history. In hindsight, part of its incredible success was due to bringing together countries on a regional basis, including former enemies. At the time, many thought that Germany and France would never work well together, yet time and the Marshall Plan encouraged the creation of a truly regional Western Europe, today taking the form of the European Union. SECI, while far from as well funded or as all encompassing as the Marshall Plan, does focus on regional needs.

For example, high energy consumption is a regional problem. One SECI country, Romania, has more than twice the per capita energy usage of the average Western European country. The United States, through Ambassador Schifter's efforts, was willing to provide technical assistance to help reduce Romania's energy consumption as a pilot regional project. The big question was who would pay for millions of dollars of capital needs to bring Romania's energy infrastructure into the 21st century? I signed on to help find an answer to that question, by agreeing to help structure the necessary financing.

What I've learned watching Dick work is that a combination of the entrepreneurial approach of "never take no for an answer" combined in government circles with "figure out a new way to get the substance of what you want done" is the process that works. Dick always stays on course and keeps driving his focused ideas until people who initially disagree with them have a concept in which they agree and ultimately bend to his will. In forming SECI, after much discussion and bargaining, the Treasury saved face by changing one word in the title of the organization. Finally and ultimately, the President signed off on SECI. Dick Schifter was on his way.

All this meant the United States actively participated in forming a new organization that would try to coordinate plans for improving security and business conditions to ultimately stabilize the region. The initial goal, though not a requirement, was that this would be a joint effort of the European Union and the United States. In any event, the plan always consisted of the idea that the individual countries in Southeastern Europe would voluntarily become members of this organization and, like the Marshall Plan, they would work together on a consensus basis with outside forces supporting them, but not jamming ideas down their throats.

Making a Little Go a Long Way

The green light from the higher-ups in Washington came, as is often the case, with very little money. (Contrary to what I had thought before being on the inside and knowing better, the United States is very tight on its Foreign Service spending. The image of waste or lavish spending is incorrect.) Dick started making his way to individual countries in the European Union to build support. He hoped this support would include funding. The first place he floated the idea was in Bonn, Germany. He went to the Foreign Minister in Germany and found a sense of excitement and support. Since the Germans rebuilt their democracy after World War II, they have been leaders in Europe in supporting responsible ideas to help others and provide a more stable region. Oddly though, Dick was hearing negative feedback through the unofficial grapevine that this was not so much a Washington plan as a Dick Schifter plan. Some bureaucrats in Washington were trying to undercut Dick's efforts to start SECI. From Bonn, he went to London and on to Paris and Brussels and back again. In each case, he received interest, initial support, and then more rumors that this was not something that Washington was wholeheartedly pushing, but had only given quiet approval.

As time and negotiations went on, it became clear that the key to pulling the European Union firmly into the plan and making it a joint plan would be an endorsement by the French. Dick and several American diplomats had what they thought was a great meeting with the French. But after they left Paris, the French rejected the plan. Separately the EU, with a lot of French insistence, put forward a similar plan for SECI that arguably could have been viewed as a competitive plan. When the French bowed out, SECI lost the sponsorship of the EU.

Ironically, as this was happening, one of the Frenchmen who participated in the initial talks with Dick quietly contacted him after the formal rejection and said how impressed he was with the idea. He offered a few thoughts that might help put the joint initiative back together, and suggested off the record that Dick might look into support from the United Nations Economic Commission of Europe out of Geneva.

In every meeting, Dick had always spoken of the effort to have all of this done on a shoestring. There would be no heavy overhead, but instead a tight organization to help these countries help themselves.

As Dick has told me many times, "A lot of good things simply happen by happenstance." My observation is that most entrepreneurs will say that this is true because with persistence you make your own luck. In Dick Schifter's case, he kept talking about the idea with as many people as he could get to listen, diligently trying to start SECI throughout 1996. His constant optimistic vision, and description of the same to everyone who would listen, is the kind of entrepreneurial focus and vision I often have seen turn an abstract idea into reality. Dick's leadership and vision brought followers who wanted to help. Even people who turned him down actually assisted him to open new doors that ultimately helped SECI. The United Nations Economic Commission ultimately supplied personnel to help coordinate SECI activities at no cost other than reimbursement of travel expenses. The commission liked the idea of SECI and how it would contribute to the United Nation's efforts in the same region.

Before long, Dick had recruited a former Austrian Vice Chancellor, Erhard Busek, for the position of Coordinator of SECI, and also talked the Austrians into providing free office space and a headquarters for SECI as well as a cash contribution equal to that of the United States.

My Involvement with SECI

By 1998, Sandy Berger, then National Security Adviser to President Clinton, had suggested that as the operational phase of SECI was moving forward, Dick should move the whole operation over to the State Department. In the spring and summer of 1998, Dick began asking me to become a consultant and special government employee to help SECI in various projects. I agreed to do so at no compensation. Dick has a special way of getting people to volunteer. I saw more than once that tens of thousands, and even hundreds of thousands of dollars, in personnel and other forms of assistance were donated from individuals, governments, and organizations to support SECI, all a result of Dick's persuasive talents. Dick viewed U.S. government money as his own. He was always looking for ways to do more for less.

My efforts in Southeastern Europe were enjoyable and interesting to me. I'm not sure that I made a huge difference, but hopefully a little here, a little there, does lead to positive change. I primarily worked on an energy efficiency program in Constanza, Romania, which was meant to be a pilot program in modernization of infrastructure and financing energy development. Bringing the area up to date in terms of energy efficiency was enormously complicated and involved putting together not only the plans for how energy efficiency could pay back a loan, but also plans for how a city's fiscal responsibility would be properly carried out. Using energy funds to pay back a loan is something very common in the United States and something I had done with many of our commercial buildings over the years. Retrofitting old buildings usually has pretty good pay back.

The other piece of the puzzle I worked on, however, proved particularly difficult: that is, showing a government entity that owns a building utility and hadn't borrowed money in decades (under Communism there was no such thing as municipal debt) how financing can work. With all this in mind, the complications were unbelievable, and it was an incredibly slow process.

I quickly formed the opinion that commercial banks simply were not going to provide a workable financing solution. In Romania in 1998, inflation was at such a high level that the exchange rate would change dramatically and often. Moreover, interest rates were more than 110 percent per year. The only sources for financing that seemed feasible to me were the World Bank or the European Bank for Reconstruction and Development (EBRD). While we narrowed down efforts to EBRD, I found the whole process of dealing with its bureaucracy extraordinarily frustrating. A huge amount of unnecessary waste and bureaucracy seems to have developed in some of these multilateral organizations.

Border Crossing, Business Trip Facilitation, Regional Crime, and More

Ambassador Schifter had organized SECI to be both a government and private-sector group. He made it clear that SECI could not expect large amounts of foreign assistance. It had to be a self-help program, for which the United States would provide a limited amount of technical assistance. The governments of the Southeast European region signed on and became involved. All activities were conducted on a volunteer or consensus basis. In any given project, not every member agreed to be involved. As it turns out, most of the time, virtually all entities ended up participating. What the organization does is provide a format for negotiation of ideas and, ultimately, agreement on various programs. SECI efforts have led to treaties and other agreements that have been supported by presidents and adopted by parliaments.

But the government activities are not the sole work of SECI. It also has a very active and important business advisory group. I've enjoyed attending these meetings all over Southeastern Europe. Here, Dick's "just keep moving toward the goal" philosophy is hard at work. Who would ever have guessed that one of the most successful Greek businessmen, who is interested in taking an active role in being chairman of the business advisory council, would suggest the idea of having a co-chairman from Turkey? The two co-chairmen are incredibly strong, well-respected individuals who have a real interest in helping the business community in the disparate regions of Southeastern Europe. While historically at odds, Turkey and Greece actually have much in common, being far more developed and far more entrepreneurial than their neighbors. They want to see the region stabilized and their investments in neighboring countries succeed, and they are willing to provide time, effort, and energy to make this happen.

In addition to the area of improving energy efficiency, I had a small role in an exciting project during 1999 and 2000. This was a program to improve border crossings to facilitate trade. Virtually all of the SECI countries today have borders where it takes 8 to 10 hours or longer for commercial trucks to cross with goods. It's not so much because the border guards are diligent in their anti-crime efforts to locate contraband, but more because the borders have insufficient physical infrastructures. There aren't enough lanes to allow for inspections; facilities are antiquated and lack computerization; and the guards are slow, corrupt, and not motivated to do a good job. Worst of all, if it rains, most of the borders have no covered areas. Commerce simply comes to a stop.

Six of the countries involved with the initiative put together a $68 million joint World Bank loan request that won approval. A seventh state's involvement will hopefully be forthcoming with approval of another $6 million loan. This would mean $74 million would be allocated to improve the border crossings. Additionally, the United States, Switzerland, Austria, and Italy are going to provide personnel to help retrain customs service officers. The whole idea is to improve trade facilitation and lower corruption at the borders. A memorandum of understanding between customs directors has already been signed by the six countries, which will lead the way to greater cooperation.

Ambassador Schifter's enlightened view of issues like corruption has a key place in reforming the borders to expand trade and growth in the area. In addition to training, ethics, standards, rules, and laws, higher compensation for customs officers and border guards is needed. Some form of bonus based on collection of overall legitimate fees makes sense. Perhaps free housing, uniforms, and other consideration would help compensate for an elimination of bribes. This kind of detailed, progressive thinking is all part of a plan to move, one step at a time, toward a more transparent and less corrupt system. It won't happen overnight, but it won't happen at all without this kind of effort.

Sometimes Things Just Happen

In late 1997, around Christmas, Dick was meeting with the Romanian Ambassador in Washington to discuss a number of SECI initiatives, including anti-crime work. Because of a lack of cross-border cooperation among the law enforcement agencies in the region, there simply was no effective way to combat such things as drug trafficking, trafficking of people, and the pervasiveness of organized crime. Indeed the only remedy at the time was often extradition. I was surprised to learn that police in this region simply never shared information. Moreover, prosecutors never shared information that could help in the prosecution of criminal offenses that involved crossing borders. Yet the irony is that when you have borders that are so close and crime activities that are occurring on a regional basis, fighting them on a local basis gives the bad guys a huge advantage.

At this Christmas meeting, Dick was in one of his many enthusiastic discussions of the numerous programs he was trying to help establish in the region. When he received a call that the President of Romania was so excited about the anti-crime program that he wanted Romania to sponsor the project in Bucharest, Dick was very pleased. Early in 1998, when Dick began setting up the center in Bucharest, he met with resistance from the other countries. Calls from the President of Romania to other presidents and behind-the-scenes help from the United States resulted in nine of the 11 countries joining the initiative. It took a year, but finally there was an agreement to share information on crime. In May of 1999, in Bucharest, nine countries signed a treaty. Later the 10th, Croatia, signed, and the 11th, Slovenia, is expecting to sign soon. By now, the parliaments of nine governments have ratified the agreement—actually a very fast and speedy approval.

The center itself opened on October 2, 1999, on the 10th floor of the huge People's Palace, which was built "on the backs of the people" by Nicolae Ceausescu, the Romanian dictator. Now the former People's Palace has a working anti-crime center where policemen from countries throughout Southeastern Europe share information and work through computer databases to detect cross-border crime. This also has led to another major initiative of Ambassador Schifter's: a crackdown on the trafficking of human beings, primarily women. Again through the Anti-Crime Center and with the United States and other Western countries providing training, this region is beginning to make efforts to prevent these horrible crimes.

An Entrepreneur Doing Big Things Every Day

Dick Schifter's primary motivation—like that of Steve Mariotti or Doraja Eberle—is not personal financial profit. Indeed it's not even glory or making sure that people know how much he has done to help the lives of others. Most of what Dick does by design is behind the scenes and, to him, it's important that the individual countries and people in their governments take credit for the successes. At the same time, being an entrepreneur in government is exciting and rewarding. As Dick tells me, it's the ability to do "big things and good things every day" that keeps him going.

Dick has his detractors, but perhaps that is characteristic of any successful entrepreneur. Getting things done often means making waves. Dick is truly a risk taker and someone with a lot of inventive creativity.

SECI has accomplished a lot in just these few short years. Simply bringing people together in one room from countries with world-renowned rivalries and hatreds between them is a nearly impossible feat. And then to accomplish true cooperation and progress on important issues such as improving energy efficiency and stopping crime is a phenomenal achievement. I've sat with Dick in meetings involving very controversial issues and seen him write out on a pad of paper a paragraph that brings about consensus. Whether it's large groups or small groups, his focused, entrepreneurial "won't take no for an answer" approach works. He is truly a hero who, as an entrepreneur in government, has made a huge difference in Southeastern Europe.

Chapter 12

THE INTERNET MAKES THE WORLD SMALL AND THE OPPORTUNITIES HUGE – TREVOR CORNWELL

Trevor Cornwell founded Skyjet and serves as chief executive officer of the company, with overall responsibility for all key functional areas. He has extensive experience in all aspects of start-ups. He developed the concept for Skyjet after experiencing business jet travel first hand. After looking closely at the business aviation market and evaluating new trends such as fractional ownership, he determined that air charter companies could more efficiently deliver the service companies need.

Skytech Europe Grand Opening in Budapest, Hungary.

His research took him on a series of road trips to small airport locations throughout the Eastern Seaboard to meet in person with air charter operators, solicit their input, and encourage their participation in the new Skyjet service. He secured financing and developed the prototype site, using a Web design company in Budapest, Hungary (Skytech Europe), and housing the Skyjet server at a data center in North Carolina.

Before forming Skyjet, Cornwell served as a consultant to an Internet Service Provider and an e-commerce start-up, shortly after returning from Europe where he started a media company. Called Word Up! Inc., it produced English-language radio programming serving Central and Eastern Europe and held the exclusive contract with Turner Networks International to sell advertising for CNN in Hungary. Word Up! also developed a daily advertiser-supported, Internet news service. In 1995, Cornwell sold the assets of Word Up! and returned to the U.S.

Earlier, Cornwell founded a not-for-profit organization, National Service League, Inc., which brought business and young people together to aid in the transition to a democratic, free-market system in Eastern Europe. Its funding included the Soros Foundation, the Agency for International Development, AT&T, and others. Before that, he worked on several political campaigns. Cornwell is a graduate of Johns Hopkins University in International Studies. A native of Hastings-on-Hudson, NY, he now resides in Washington, DC.

Author's Note: While the previous chapters revolve more specifically around one individual, in this chapter Trevor really started us on a journey that includes a number of other individuals. Trevor whet my appetite and helped educate me in the basics of technology and the Internet. He introduced me to Viktor Lantos and Tamas Perlaki. From there, I added Cheryl Newman to the Skytech equation. That led to long-time Hall team member Don Braun becoming more active in technology areas and, ultimately, our business relationship with young, American entrepreneur Patrick Brandt. You will meet all of these individuals as well as hear Trevor's story in this chapter.

— ✦ —

Trevor Cornwell and "Entrepreneurial Idealism"

When he was 24, American Trevor Cornwell developed a concept he called "Entrepreneurial Idealism."

"The idea was to use the tools, notions, and fundamentals of business and apply them to not-for-profits," Trevor said.

He put his brand of entrepreneurial idealism to work in Central and Eastern Europe in 1990 with the National Service League (NSL).

"At the time, the Berlin Wall was coming down. Like a lot of people, I was drawn to the notion that the world as we knew it was going to change fundamentally, at least in terms of the way we related between nations," Trevor said. "I was very interested in the idea of making sure when this change took place that our country, which sets the tone for so many, did things differently than we had in the recent past. The idea was to set up NSL as an organization that would use business as a lending library and then have the young people carry the books out to the indigenous community. I wanted to use the skills and tools of business to make things work more efficiently."

Trevor was convinced that a vibrant free market, free press, and focus on a healthy environment were the pillars that would link countries together around the world.

"The idea was to bring together young people who might typically go into business, and let them first spend a year of their lives making a difference. In some ways, NSL was very successful," Trevor said. "One group helped develop a revolving loan fund in the inner city in New York, and then went to Hungary to help develop a credit union."

The experiences of working in inner city New York proved strikingly useful to working in Budapest. By 1993, Trevor was living in Budapest and running NSL. Over time, though, he became disillusioned.

"In a lot of ways, being an entrepreneur in a pure non-profit is the toughest thing that you can do," Trevor said. "There is not a capitalistic interest for somebody to stay involved. Sustaining the interest of employees is difficult."

National Service League was active for about six years, having been intended as a vehicle to help transition countries through the difficult first years after Communism. When I asked Trevor about closing it down, he said that the region had changed so much that the marginal benefit that a non-profit could provide was just not cost-efficient.

Some NSL projects did make it. One of them was an English language radio program in Budapest based on the U.S. National Public Radio (NPR) format. The NSL radio project was very successful and became the doorway for Trevor's move into the private sector.

Trevor started an English language radio program in Budapest that was distributed throughout the region. After a year and a half, he sold it to a small investment bank. The last phase of the radio program he worked on involved an Internet distribution system. This led Trevor into a new and exciting world.

Skyjet.com

Trevor's initial Internet experience convinced him that any new business he pursued needed to be Internet-related. Even as he prepared to move back to Washington, D.C., he was still looking for ideas to apply Internet technology. One day during his travels, he read a magazine ad for a company called NetJets, since purchased by Warren Buffett. NetJets and FlexJets are companies that theoretically sell fractional interests in airplanes. In reality, people commit to a large charter company on a complicated time-sharing concept. The idea is that, on reasonably short notice, the "owners" can use the planes for travel. They are charged an initial amount for an ownership interest in a variety of airplanes and then pay an hourly rate for using them.

Trevor decided that time-share ownership wasn't a great economic deal for everyone who might need to rent a private plane. He decided it made more sense to consolidate the hugely inefficient independent charter operators, linking them together in a way that would allow charter customers to enjoy the benefits of fractional ownership without incurring the upfront costs. Trevor realized that what the market needed was a simple, efficient way of getting dependable, safe, fast service at a reasonable price. Skyjet.com was born.

With the essence of the business in his mind, but very little money to get it started, Trevor headed back to Budapest. He knew that there was a real technological cost advantage in Eastern Europe and that there was immediate availability of well-trained engineers. The educational system the Communists had built with a strong emphasis on math and engineering provided a solid foundation for training computer programmers. Trevor knew that he could move quickly and at a fraction of the cost in the United States if he took the software development idea back to Hungary.

A few people who believed in him initially funded Trevor's company. The original investors included Kenny Blatt and Gavin Susman, as well as two other friends of Trevor's I have not met.

Trevor is a great guy who is easy to believe in. He taught me a lot about the Internet. Ultimately, my company became Skyjet.com's largest shareholder.

Even though it serves U.S. airports alone today, Skyjet.com is truly an international company. Headquartered in Washington, D.C., its

Internet server was in North Carolina. The fulfillment phone number and staffing was in Boston. The applications development, programming, and Web site design work were all contracted to a company named Skytech Europe in Budapest. Skyjet.com's multi-locale organization is proof of the Internet's connectivity and represents the future of business.

Skyjet.com has become an on-demand airline. It is an air charter reservation system that currently services more than 5,000 airports within the United States, and, in time, will go international. Skyjet has more than 650 jets available on call, 24 hours a day, 7 days a week, and is expanding the number of planes and service areas every week.

By mid-2000, Skyjet was clearly a company on the move. Trevor and his team had done a great job. The seed investors had a few million dollars invested. I realized that the next growth phase would have to allow Skyjet to dominate its space. That would in turn demand a different level of funding—many millions more. Meanwhile, we had two unsolicited offers of interest to buy the company. We ultimately sold to Bombardier, the maker of Lear Jets and owner of Flexjets, in a win-win deal for all. Bombardier wanted Trevor to stay and run Skyjet full-time, which meant closing up our other mutual projects.

Trevor is very sensitive, intense, and focused. His goals have always been excellence in executing whatever the plan, be it his non-profit or Skyjet. As an entrepreneur, he has provided jobs to many people, and through his risk taking on new ideas has provided innovation in airplane traffic.

He is hard working. I have never met anyone more willing to hop on an airplane and go anywhere just to make sure a meeting goes right. One of our projects that required this level of attention was called Skytech Europe.

The Rebirth of Skytech Europe

At Hall Financial Group, I am blessed to have great entrepreneurial senior managers. Yes, that's right, "entrepreneurial." People can be entrepreneurs within a corporate culture if the culture endorses and reinforces taking risks. I encourage my senior people to run their areas and do so as if they were 100 percent owners.

At Hall, we are lucky to have Don Braun, who has been with the organization for 21 years, as president of the overall company and head of the technology area. Larry Levey, who has been with the organization for 23 years, is head of development, and Mark Depker, a 31-year veteran of Hall Financial Group, is head of the management area. Patricia Meadows, Valerie Reber, Melinda Jayson, and other long-time veterans help round off different areas of our operations, which involve wide-ranging businesses. The high-tech area is fun for us but represents a modest 5 percent allocation our total invested capital.

Don handled all of the work on selling Skyjet. As part of the sale, we ended up with 100 percent of Skytech.

We quickly decided to invest more money and effort in building Skytech. We were excited by the idea that the Hungarians we'd employed had done a fabulous job on very complicated programming for Skyjet. Bombardier was impressed, and why not: The Hungarian's work had been first class and at a fraction of normal cost. Under Harris Turner, a company called RetrieveIt used software also developed by Skytech that we were hearing was cutting edge. We were impressed enough to become a major shareholder in RetrieveIt. RetrieveIt is a client-based search engine that can accumulate and find specific information for people from a number of other Web sites, then summarize it for easy usage. For people like me, the technologically challenged, this is the tool to make the Internet functional.

To build Skytech, we had to look at our senior management. With Trevor gone, we still had our key personnel, Viktor Lantos and Tamas Perlaki. Viktor is an outgoing, friendly, caring individual with maturity beyond his 25 years. He has a big heart and wants to help his fellow Hungarians. In typical Hungarian family style, he still lives at home with his parents, though in his case as Managing Director of Skytech and an owner, his resources would allow him to live on his own. Viktor attended technical school for five years of computer study with a graphics emphasis. After graduating, he went to work for a large ad agency, where he excelled quickly. But after two years, he felt he could do more on his own. He started Next Dimension, a company that we used to do Skyjet's original graphics and Web site work. Fortunately for us, Viktor agreed to merge his company into Skytech.

Where Viktor is outgoing, Tamas is quiet, shy, and harder to get to know. Like Viktor, he went to a computer school for five years but then added studies in biochemistry and anatomy. Despite his reserved presence, he should not be underestimated. Don Braun and Tamas went to the Silicon Valley to visit a company in which we were considering investing. Don was shocked at how Tamas came alive when detailed high-tech areas were discussed.

Tamas and Viktor are a good team, but we wanted to supplement the youth and technical abilities of Viktor and Tamas with an American perspective, because many of our clients were expected to be American-based companies. Moreover, we wanted a skilled, aggressive, entrepreneurial chief executive to run the organization. For many companies this would mean hiring a search firm and looking for the right manager. We don't do this at Hall Financial.

We start out trying to find people we know. I've always believed in giving people a chance to excel when I think they are capable, even though they may not necessarily have the requisite resume or experience for a given position. Taking someone else's so-called trained person is not in my view the best way to go. Often, they are trained in ways that aren't compatible with the existing corporate culture. At Hall Financial, we like people who have a killer instinct and a burning desire to make something happen, even if they have to be more entrepreneurial in learning as they go.

A couple of years before the Skyjet sale, I had hired Cheryl Newman to help with research on this book, as well as other activities in my European operations. Over time I got to know Cheryl, and she got to know the Hall Financial operations. At one point, she took on an assignment of doing the major Web site formation for the Hall Office Park, a four-million-square-foot development in the Dallas area. Our objective is a whole new redefined concept of office space. We don't believe in just renting space but instead providing an entire park-like setting with extensive modern art. We believe the "new office" is about services from fitness and day care to our concierge arranging for home maintenance or any number of other personal services. It's our "HOP to It" program, HOP being the acronym for Hall Office Park.

As Cheryl learned what we were doing in our office park development and translated this to the Hungarian programmers and graphic designers, a great product developed. She drew on her skills from her undergraduate days at Dartmouth followed by Stanford Business School. She also drew on skills gained as a traveling spouse. Her husband had worked in the United States, Tokyo, Paris, and, most recently, Vienna. In each place, Cheryl had spent her time raising their three children while learning Japanese and French, volunteering, and writing a book.

Believing in her ability to learn whatever would be needed to supplement her current skills, we thought Cheryl could run Skytech. Don and I decided to offer her the CEO position. She quickly accepted, and the team of Cheryl, Viktor, and Tamas was off and running.

Skytech is expected to grow in one year by about 200 percent in terms of revenues and personnel. By the end of 2001, we expect to have 100 employees.

Crossing Cultural Barriers

Early on, with the help of some dedicated Hall team members, Cheryl put together an agenda for the Skytech team to visit Hall Financial Group. The week that Viktor and Tamas first visited Dallas, we had a welcome Tex-Mex buffet for them, an associate's birthday celebration (a monthly event complete with cake and ice cream), dinner in one of Dallas' downtown entertainment districts, and an evening at a typical cowboy dance hall. When Cheryl had asked Viktor and Tamas what they most wanted to do in Dallas, one of the first requests was to go to an amusement park and ride the roller coaster! In one short week, the Hall Financial Group managed to make great progress on its real estate Web site, foster international relations between Texans and Hungarians, and lay some more bricks in the foundation of what I hope will be a long-lasting business relationship.

Based on some of the stories Cheryl related about her first trip to Dallas with the Skytech team, it is clear to me that, intentionally or not, she was the catalyst for a deepening trust between the Hungarian Skytech team and its American owners. There were moments when everyone really relaxed and had fun. Mark Hammans, director of technology for Hall, was instrumental in one of the most frequently discussed memories of that trip. After a management dinner at a nice restaurant in Deep Ellum in downtown Dallas, Mark led the group, minus some senior management who had called it a night, on a brief tour of the area. Viktor and Tamas had wanted to see the infamous Texas School Book Depository and the site where President John F. Kennedy was assassinated. Though it was late in the evening, the site was overrun with tourists, as usual. Viktor and Tamas took pictures. Cheryl was impressed by their knowledge of this part of American history. She hadn't begun to learn much about Hungary until moving to Vienna. When she walked around Budapest with people from Skytech, she occasionally commented on the famous places and names she noticed on buildings. The Hungarians were amazed that she knew anything at all about their country, and touched that she did.

After that stop, Mark guided them to "Dick's Last Resort," one of Dallas' renowned watering holes. The place was packed. A band was playing on the miniscule stage, and the Hall group, including a wide-eyed Viktor and Tamas, watched as brides-to-be and others jumped on the stage to dance and sing with the band. Waiters at Dick's are trained in light-hearted verbal abuse of the customers, encouraging the purchase of pitchers of beer and snacks. They also reward unlikely customers with specially made paper hats, shaped like chef toques, with rude comments written on them.

Their waiter had no idea that Tamas, on whose hat was written, "I haven't got a clue what is going on," is a brilliant programmer. Cheryl's and Mark's hats were equally, if not more humiliating, and so the whole group had a great laugh. Irreverence is not a trait that was encouraged by the Communists who ran Hungary when Viktor and Tamas were growing up, but they proved themselves as quick learners during their brief time in Dallas. The stories they took back to the rest of the Skytech staff have become company lore, and are helping nurture a wonderfully international corporate culture, which is exactly what I hoped would happen.

Back to the Mind-Set

Even the younger generation of Hungarians tends to be very conservative and in some respects naïve about fundamental business tactics, despite their involvement in the New Economy. It often takes some familiarity with the West to inspire true entrepreneurial efforts. The antics at Dick's Last Resort are unusual by Hungarian standards, but they are just symptomatic of broader differences in perspective.

Communism left psychological scars on generations. While the effects are less evident among young people, even the 20-somethings that work at Skytech are in need of exposure to Western business practice and theory. At the same time, there is at least one positive legacy: technical education. Central and Eastern Europe, including the Balkans, may be composed of lesser-developed countries in terms of infrastructure, but they should not be confused with Third World countries. As I have stated before, education in mathematics and engineering is at an extraordinarily high level. This provides a unique opportunity for Internet and technology activities.

With the advent of Skytech, the importance of entrepreneurial activities in the region was no longer an abstract idea to Cheryl, as it was while she did research for this book. Instead, it was an everyday reality. How to motivate people who had never absorbed the work ethic of the West became a great challenge. These workers didn't understand the concept of customer service or why providing project status information was important to the client relationship. They didn't understand why and how marketing was important to developing new clients, or why different people are paid different salaries. These were all fundamental issues that the Skytech team needed to make part of the corporate culture.

Cheryl discovered that Skytech was billing all its programmers at the same hourly rate, regardless of their experience levels or background. When she first attempted to change that system, prompted by clients who wanted the option of hiring a team of mixed talent, she provoked consternation and resistance. One of the founders of the company pointed out that all the programmers came from Budapest's finest technological universities, and in his mind provided the same skill level. On the other hand, some had worked for Skytech for a year and others for a matter of weeks. Frankly, some were better than others and were doing more complex work. Only after additional discussions and the input of a potential client was Cheryl able to convince the senior managers to rank the staff along various criteria, including tenure, knowledge of various programming languages, flexibility, creativity, and English proficiency.

Skywire, Hall, Melanie, and Patrick Brandt

After Skyjet and RetrieveIt, Don began exploring other opportunities in the emerging technologies sector, but continuing our maximum allocation of up to 5 percent of our total net worth for technology deals. We made several early stage investments, knowing that some will turn out to be "singles" or even "strike outs." Every investment can't be a home run. In fact, some of these have gone broke, and we have lost our investments. That's the reality in these ventures.

For us, the Internet and emerging technology are all about meeting and working with young entrepreneurs. Part of our goal in the Hall Office Park was to develop a park that in part catered to young entrepreneurs. In our "tech" buildings, we have "incubator space": "free" rental space for entrepreneurs in exchange for equity in their company. We are organizing group meetings for entrepreneurs every month with outside speakers and discussion groups. We also have what we call a "quiet room" for meditation or sleeping for entrepreneurs burning the midnight oil.

For me, entrepreneurship has always been about networking. The Internet and tech revolution just continue to intensify these basics. It's funny how sometimes things work out. Years ago, Melanie Dulock was the heart and soul of the Hall Financial home office as our receptionist and more. She is one of the sweetest, nicest people you could ever meet. She eventually had a baby and retired to be a full-time mom. But she and all of the people at Hall, including me, have stayed close friends. I'm often kidded because I have a picture of Melanie's son on my desk near my own granddaughter. It confuses people, but that's the kind of closeness that Melanie and her husband have with the Hall family. To make a long story short, Melanie's husband and two other partners started an IT consulting business. One thing led to another, and we ended up as partners in a new business venture called Skywire Technology.

Patrick Brandt, who was one of the executives in Melanie's husband's company, now is our partner, and the CEO of Skywire. Skywire, which targets three vertical markets—the healthcare, financial service, and insurance industries—concentrates on two lines of business: fee-for-service consulting and incubation services through its wholly-own subsidiary, Skywire Labs. I like to think of Skywire Technology as high-level architects doing master plans and general design work rather than working drawings. While Skytech does working drawings, Skywire can design some of the most complex grand scheme plans.

Skywire's incubation activities include providing technology services, strategic and management counseling, a full complement of office/ accounting personnel, and other services through Hall Financial personnel in exchange for equity. Patrick, who is in his late 20s, is a young, aggressive, hungry entrepreneur. He's an entrepreneur first and technical "geek" second. Interestingly, Patrick actually started out in business the same way Albert Black and I did: mowing lawns at age 11. That was followed by lots of other odd jobs, some stock investing at a young age, working as a busboy and, in short, doing everything to make and save money at a young age. After being in and out of various universities, he finally graduated from Southern Methodist University (SMU).

At SMU, Patrick developed several very important relationships. Two relationships are noteworthy: first, the one with his girlfriend (now wife), and second, with his first business partner with whom he co-founded Cyberpix. Cyberpix struggled and would have failed without his wife contributing part of her income and Patrick borrowing to the limit on credit cards. Cyberpix was the first company to integrate event photography into an electronic commerce solution by cataloging and distributing a large number of images. Business customers can view images conveniently anywhere and anytime.

After a long period of struggling, eventually Patrick and his partner raised several million dollars and got Cyberpix on solid ground. The company moved to New York. Patrick stayed in Dallas but still maintains a small ownership position. After Cyberpix, Patrick followed through on a promise to his wife to "get a real job." After only a year and a half of working for others, his frustrations made him reconsider his pledge. It was obvious he was meant to be back in the entrepreneurial world. He joined up with Melanie's husband and the other partners at Network Services Now, Inc., in the fall of 1999. That eventually led to the Skywire transaction with us.

There is no doubt that these are exciting times, and revolutionary change is occurring in technology. When the NASDAQ was booming, we saw too many ventures funded in ways that to us made no sense. Since the bursting of the NASDAQ bubble, for many incubating Internet start-up ventures is over. For us, it is a more rational time to invest. I'm the first to admit that I don't understand technical aspects of new technology and am not patient enough to really try. My role is generally to force these high-tech entrepreneurs to "dumb things down." Entrepreneurs must be able to put things in simple terms. While my time is stretched in many directions, I still enjoy the trips to Skytech in Budapest. It's great to see the people and feel the buzz that's going on there. I also have sideline interests that attract me to Budapest.

Antique shopping and pursuing one of my real passions, art collecting, are two indulgences that have added real enjoyment to my life. Supporting the arts is an important way for entrepreneurs to give back to their communities and something I've pursued as a lifelong avocation. Over the time that Kathy and I spent in Vienna, I specialized in collecting artwork from living artists who created their paintings and sculptures during and after the Communist period. My primary teacher and mentor in this work is Lorand Hegyi, an art historian of Hungarian descent, who, for more than a decade, headed the two most prominent art museums in Vienna. He is the world's leading expert on contemporary Central and Eastern European art. We became close friends, and he introduced me to a number of artists, which has enriched the collecting experience immensely. It has been a wonderful experience to get to know the creators of these works and to be able to more fully understand their motivations and their lives.

A number of pieces I collected during this time were part of an exhibit at the Jeu de Paume, Paris's celebrated contemporary art museum. To see the wire sculptures of Karel Malich, a Czech artist, or the fantastic large-scale paintings of 80-year-old Bohemian Zdenek Sykor exhibited makes me proud to know that I am going to be a minor part of helping bring their works greater exposure.

To me, art and business are a great mix. This high-tech world we live in can truly add to our sense of humanity. Through e-mail and the Internet, I have met and collected art with friends from all over the world, from Australia to South Africa and back again. Not only is the world shrinking in terms of its ability to quickly communicate, but also it is being enhanced by the ability to share quality expressions of the human soul around the world in an instant. Art also brings so much to the work environment. I've included major art installments in many of my office buildings. The four-million-square-foot Hall Office Park will soon be home to a $10 million art installation. Many developers would consider that wasteful, but I consider it the essence of differentiating the product from others in the marketplace. If someone points to a piece and says, "What is that?" it has made him think. Whether they like it or not, we have reached them. Adding art to the work environment brings a balance to what can often be a sterile world.

Windows to the World

A key to the success of the Internet lies in its ability to help us all communicate. Whether we are entrepreneurs or artists in Budapest, Delhi, or Dallas, the Internet enables us to act independently and in concert with others around the world. We aren't losing our individuality; we are sharing it. Our culture and personalities can be communicated instantly around the world. The artists whose works I collect and then exhibit in distant locations help us to understand the way the world really is. I truly believe that if a businessperson in Texas can be moved by the work of an artist from Zimbabwe or Prague, then he has established a fragile link to that person and the culture in which he works. I find it a perfect harmony that the artists are using the power of the Internet to introduce their work to potential patrons around the world. They have found a formula using high-tech and high-touch to create windows to communicate with the world.

What Is Different About Entrepreneurs in the "New Economy"?

Maybe for the first time in history, engineers and people with inventions or intellectual ideas are really able in a large way to prosper from the fruits of their labor. Often in business, it's the entrepreneur that seems to get the big rewards, not the engineers or "nerds." In the New Economy, the early big rewards seem to have gone to more of the engineering and/or intellectual folks than ever before. But as the New Economy matures, the future is not going to be "new" versus "old" economy companies but a merging of these concepts and economies. A constant throughout all the dotcom hype has been the need to have entrepreneurs as the engineers of change.

There is no substitution for many of the common entrepreneurial traits described in Chapter 14. To succeed in the Internet world, you have to have Old Economy realism. There are lots of engineering ideas that work and make money, but then knowing how to start the business and ultimately prosper still requires the same old common traits and skills of entrepreneurs that have existed for centuries.

Many entrepreneurs in the high-tech world are fancy translators. They translate between the needs that they perceive and understand in the marketplace and technologies that they think in theory can be put together. They further translate between the technologies they think in theory can be put together and really smart folks that do the actual engineering.

Whether it's Patrick Brandt with Skywire, Trevor Cornwell with Skytech, Harris Turner and his ideas for RetrieveIt, or an undiscovered creative thinker, entrepreneurs are exploding with new ideas. The Internet is unleashing more entrepreneurs and creating more change than anyone possibly could have imagined just a few years ago. True, we've gone through a financial bubble in technology, one that fortunately in our company we anticipated. We actually shorted the NASDAQ 100 during most of 2000 and 2001, profiting more on that than all of our tech investments to date. Our view was and continues to be that even though the financial bubble got way ahead of the revolution, the technological revolution is real, and the entrepreneurial opportunities are staggering. Not since the Industrial Revolution have we seen a time like this for entrepreneurs. But, that does not change the basics I discuss in Chapters 14 and 15.

Over the next few decades, entrepreneurs will become increasingly important to economies. Nimble risk takers who can make fast decisions are rapidly replacing the bureaucratic organizations of the past because of more and better information. Internet business solutions are dramatically improving productivity and encouraging more successful entrepreneurial behavior.

This is a time of great connectivity between geographical areas all around the world, and between different cultures and people. It is a time of great opportunities for efficiencies and productivity to increase, raising with it the standard of living around the globe. The risk is that some people and countries will be left behind. My hope is that we will recognize this danger and use technology and its opportunities to reduce the divide between the "haves" and the "have-nots" of the world. The opportunities are huge. So are our challenges.

– Chapter 13 –

It's All About Freedom –
Rabbi Arthur Schneier

Rabbi Arthur Schneier, senior rabbi at East Park Synagogue, is internationally known for his leadership on behalf of religious freedom, human rights and tolerance throughout the world. He is founder and president of the Appeal of Conscience Foundation, established in 1965, and spiritual leader of the political and religious leaders in Albania, Argentina, Austria, Bulgaria, China, Cuba, Czech Republic, Egypt, England, Germany, Hungary, Indonesia, Ireland, Israel, Morocco, Poland, Romania, Slovak Republic, the

former Soviet Union, Turkey, and the former Yugoslavia.

Several U.S. Presidents have recognized Rabbi Schneier's accomplishments; notably, he was recipient of the Presidential Citizens Medal in 2001. In 1998, President Clinton appointed him as one of the three U.S. religious leaders to meet with

Rabbi Arthur Schneier (center) at the Appeal of Conscience Foundation, March 16–18, 1999, in Vienna, Austria.

President Jiang Zemin and the top leadership of the Chinese Government for the first official dialogue on religious freedom. He was appointed by

President George Bush as Chairman of the U.S. Commission for the Preservation of America's Heritage Abroad and served in that post until 1995. He negotiated and successfully completed bilateral agreements with the Czech and Slovak Republics, Hungary, Romania, Slovenia, and Ukraine. President Reagan appointed him a U.S. Alternate Representative to the 43rd session of the U.N. General Assembly, and he was appointed by President Carter as a member of the U.S. Delegation for the return of the Crown of St. Stephen to Hungary.

Rabbi Schneier is the recipient of the Grand Decoration of Honor in Gold with Star for Service to the Republic of Austria. He is a member of the Council on Foreign Relations.

— ✦ —

Serbian Religious Leaders and Me

Every day we lived in Vienna, we were reminded of the important events that had taken place in our temporary home. In our library was a photograph of President John F. Kennedy and Soviet Premier Nikita Khrushchev walking up the same front steps that I walked every day. I have heard descriptions of how Kennedy and Khrushchev spent time in the same gardens through which Kathy and I often strolled on summer evenings. Imagine the conversations that took place!

The Ambassador's Residence was also home to negotiations between President Jimmy Carter and Soviet Premier Leonid Brezhnev during the SALT II negotiations. Our first summer in Vienna, former President Carter came to town, and we took him out for a private dinner. We also had him autograph a photograph for us of himself and Leonid Brezhnev at the signing ceremony of SALT II. We hung this in the Residence library, near the photograph of Kennedy and Khrushchev. During the Bosnian War, some of the peace negotiations occurred in the Residence. It was impossible to live in this history-filled home without wanting to also make a difference, even if on a much smaller scale.

I hosted a meeting of religious leaders from Serbia and Kosovo around the time of the doomed peace talks in Paris in March 1999. As politicians failed to hammer out a peace agreement, Rabbi Arthur Schneier of New York, president of The Appeal of Conscience Foundation, brought together diverse religious leaders in an effort to find common ground. The religious leaders each held strong, contrasting beliefs. I hosted a dinner that culminated a long day of negotiations and, no doubt, a great many prayers. Key leaders from every religion involved in Serbia and Kosovo were present, including the bishop from the predominant Eastern Orthodox religion, the Catholic bishop, and Islamic leaders.

Our dinner started late, as negotiations had dragged on. Finally, language was approved for a joint statement in support of ceasing the ethnic cleansing and taking a firm stand for longer-lasting peace. Even within days of potential NATO bombing, there was a sense of importance as the religious leaders began laying the groundwork for enduring, comprehensive peace in the region.

I really enjoyed that evening. Initially, I was apprehensive that I would make a mistake and say something that might insult someone's religious beliefs. My own upbringing, reflecting America's diversity and tolerance, was a mixture of Catholic and Jewish traditions. I learned quickly in Austria that European countries are vastly different from the multireligious and multicultural society of the United States, with America's careful distinction between church and state. In Europe, the link between religion and politics is close. Religious leaders have significant importance and influence. That evening at the residence, I was put at ease as I saw each of these important religious leaders interact as individuals and people of good will. Even those who could not speak English or German with me radiated smiles and expressed themselves through gestures that provided a sense of warm communication.

It was fascinating to watch Rabbi Schneier bring the disparate groups together with carefully chosen words. This tall, wiry man has a commanding personality. He wears his spirit on the outside, putting a positive spin on even the most negative circumstances.

"A river of tears will not nourish the seed of change as deeply as one thread of peace," he said. "It is in this spirit that these religious leaders have gathered in Vienna for their historic first meeting. Each is a thread in the fabric of hope. Each is a strand in the cloth of peace that today, together, we begin to weave."

As I thought about Kosovo and saw how Rabbi Schneier had shown that people at war could come together, I wondered what really could bring a lasting peace. Frankly, I also wondered how much difference these religious leaders could make. But even more to the point, I became very curious to know more about just who Rabbi Arthur Schneier really is. I knew from the briefing papers provided by the Embassy that he was the founder of an American nonprofit organization called The Appeal of Conscience Foundation and that he was a rabbi at a large prominent synagogue in New York. He also had a reputation as being held in high esteem by world leaders. In this first evening, I also found him to be an approachable, down-to-earth, engaging individual and successful entrepreneur in his own fashion.

Learning to Survive

I came to know Rabbi Schneier a bit better on some of his other trips to Vienna, as well as at Park East Synagogue in New York where he is a senior rabbi. The more I got to know him, the more I understood that this man is truly an entrepreneur.

Arthur Schneier was born in Vienna in 1930 to Jewish parents, a circumstance that was relatively unimportant at the time. A few years later this would become the dominant event of young Arthur's life. By the time he turned seven, Hitler and the Nazis officially were in power.

"Overnight I became a pariah. Many of my friends who played with me and came to my home were forbidden to do so, simply because I was a Jew," he said. "We had to be one step ahead of the Gestapo."

"I lost my dad when I was six years old. Later, when I discovered that my grandparents were gassed in Austria, I made a pledge: Whatever I do in life, I was going to study full ordination to become a rabbi in my grandfather's memory."

In fact, Rabbi Schneier is the 17th generation of his family to become a rabbi. As he explained, it was "in his genes" to become a rabbi.

Young Arthur Schneier learned how to survive.

"I basically saw man's inhumanity to man. I saw the beast in man and I saw the best in man, and you know then you survived," he said.

He was lucky enough to make it to America, grow up, and study dual disparate professions: biochemistry, with a master's in physiological psychology, as well as studying for the rabbinate. He considered becoming a psychiatrist, but instead ended up a rabbi who uses his psychology background in international affairs. Dedicating his life to helping others was an outgrowth of his wartime experiences.

"When you survive, there is always a certain amount of guilt: Why did I survive rather than others? If I survived, I survived for a purpose. So that's essentially why I became a rabbi and have done what I'm doing," he said.

We talked about the fact that not every survivor has gone on to public service.

"I can understand that some survivors become cynical and distrustful and paranoid," Rabbi Schneier said. "I can also understand why some survivors turn to God. Fortunately, for myself, if anything, my faith in God became stronger as a result of being a survivor. I have also not lost faith in man. And I am not naïve, but I really feel there is a goodness in every human being and it is just a matter of bringing it out."

Rabbi Schneier has turned anger into energy for positive actions just as many entrepreneurs have turned their own personal crises into successful businesses. It's hard to pinpoint what makes some people find the positive while others become bitter and cynical. Nevertheless, for Arthur Schneier, his survival remains, even many decades later, a focal point of drive and motivation. It also continues to provide perspective, compassion, and sensitivity for any part of mankind that suffers.

In Love with America

As a young 32-year-old rabbi, with a masters in psychology, who had survived the Holocaust and then experienced living with Communism all before finally getting to America, Arthur Schneier was interested in "paying back the opportunities that not only I have but all others have." As he has said many times, he was, is, and always will be "in love with America."

In 1962, Rabbi Schneier became the senior rabbi at Park East Synagogue. This was a quantum leap and a great opportunity for a young, enterprising rabbi. Rabbi Schneier had been serving an old age home, but he says he wanted "the youth, the children, and the community" of a larger synagogue.

He began to develop a long-term vision: development of a new school dedicated to young children. This, of course, was a radical change for the congregation. He had to make others see his vision. The feat would require assembling land in an area that was already fully developed and had no land available. It was very hard to acquire such property, but Rabbi Schneier never thought about letting that stop him. It would require raising money, designing a building, and much more. The idea seemed impossible to many. But as an entrepreneurial rabbi with lots of energy and ideas, Rabbi Schneier just pressed forward.

By 1965, much of the needed land for the school had been assembled.

Rabbi Schneier said. "It had taken years of patient negotiations and perseverance to assemble the property. We were indeed fortunate to acquire the property adjacent to our synagogue. We expected the truism of the adage, 'Ein dabar omeid lifnei ratzon: The spirit of man conquers all.'"

By 1966, Rabbi Schneier was celebrating the acquisition of the last important properties needed from nearby Midtown Hospital. He then proceeded with the design of the building and raising the money. By 1969, the demolition of the buildings on the properties acquired near the synagogue began. A cultural center and Park East Day School commenced construction in 1973 and were topped out in 1975. As a religious entrepreneur and "part-time real estate developer," 1977 would bring the realization of the rabbi's dreams.

I recently toured this amazing eight-story facility that today serves 320 young school-aged children. The positive spirit of youth that fills the building is exciting. With enrollment full, the school, almost 25 years after completion, remains an incredible success. But like most entrepreneurs, this was far from Rabbi Schneier's only dream to be realized.

Standing Up to Khrushchev

Rabbi Schneier's experience prior to coming to the United States had long shown him the importance of the entrepreneur's responsibility to the community around him. After he emigrated to the U.S., one of Rabbi Schneier's first battles as a young rabbi was against Khrushchev. In 1965, the Soviet leader was thought by many to be a liberal.

"But few people knew at that time that he was determined to destroy religion, including Russian Orthodox churches. He wanted every church closed by 1980," Rabbi Schneier said.

Having known Eastern Europe and experienced religious oppression, when Rabbi Schneier heard about so-called economic trials being used to close down Jewish synagogues, he was inspired to demonstrate. He still has a framed copy of a newspaper ad from the January 14, 1965 edition of *The New York Times* in his office with the headline: "An Appeal of Conscience." The ad urged the Soviet government to "end all discrimination against its Jewish community" and announced a protest meeting at the synagogue later that month. Rabbi Schneier worked to collect supporters for the ad, which carried the names of many prominent Christian religious leaders and American politicians. This one event pushed Rabbi Schneier into a new direction.

On January 17, 1965, the protest meeting occurred. Because of Rabbi Schneier's leadership, the mayor of New York, Robert Wagner, who was Catholic, as well as both of New York's senators, Jacob Javits, a Jew, and Robert Kennedy, a Catholic, all spoke. What started out as one ad and one voice of protest turned out to be a bigger success than even Rabbi Schneier could have imagined.

This was the first, but far from the last, protest against Soviet mistreatment of Jews. Ultimately, many Soviet Jews were allowed to leave the country as a result of the protests and world attention focused on the issue.

The Appeal of Conscience Foundation Is Formed

As a result of the overwhelming support of the Appeal of Conscience protest meeting, particularly by the Christian community, Rabbi Schneier was moved to continue his efforts not just for the Soviet Jewish issue but to stand up against other injustices as well. He was concerned about religious freedom in the Soviet Union and elsewhere. He was also concerned about human rights worldwide. In 1965, The Appeal of Conscience Foundation was incorporated. The first chairman of the organization was former U.S. Senator Kenneth Keeting. Rabbi Schneier became its president. The organization started as a Protestant, Catholic, and Jewish organization, with Methodist minister Harold Bosley and Jesuit priest Thurston Davis as vice presidents. Shortly thereafter, the group expanded to include Muslims and later Russian Orthodox and other religions.

In December of 1965, Rabbi Schneier made his first trip to Moscow, and thus began a long and continuing relationship with the Russian Orthodox church, the Jewish community, and the then-leaders of the Soviet

Union. To this day, he maintains excellent relations with leaders of Russia. Since that first trip, he has made 62 trips during 35 years, many times to bring a delegation to act as official observers at elections.

Separate from their activities in Russia, The Appeal of Conscience Foundation has been active in peace talks throughout the world, including Eastern Europe and Northern Ireland. The Appeal of Conscience Foundation has grown over the years to become a leading organization not only on behalf of religious freedom and human rights but also on world peace. It is a religious coalition, but is also a group of business leaders promoting tolerance and pluralism. The idea is simply that the best hope for the future is peace, security, and shared prosperity.

As president of The Appeal of Conscience Foundation, at one point Rabbi Schneier found himself in the middle of negotiating an agreement between the United States and Spain. Major conflict was expected. Fifteen Protestant ministers were planning a hunger strike because Spain was a predominantly Catholic country that was going to require registration of non-Catholics. Finally, with the Rabbi's help, Spain was convinced not to take this action. At that time, the U.S. Ambassador to Spain was Angie Duke. He told Rabbi Schneier that he was so impressed with the foundation's work that after he retired as ambassador he wanted to join its board of directors.

Ambassador Duke not only joined the board, but, after the death of Senator Keeting, he took over as chairman. He also became Rabbi Schneier's closest personal friend.

The Rabbi-Diplomat

Through his commitment to freedom, Rabbi Schneier not only found himself shuttling twice a year to Moscow, but traveling around the world to meet world leaders. He is often able to go places and do things that government officials cannot, speaking about religious freedom, human rights, and tolerance. He works quietly behind the scenes helping accomplish goals. He is clearly proud to be an American, but he is also someone who is accepted where official American representatives are not.

Three weeks after Gorbachev rose to power in Russia, one of the first Americans he met with was Rabbi Schneier. In their private meetings, Gorbachev requested U.S. financial help to buy food for his people.

"He knew about my relationship with George Bush and James Baker, and he said that he trusted me to ask for immediate funding of $200 million," Rabbi Schneier recalled.

Rabbi Schneier left Moscow on a Wednesday night and on Thursday called for a meeting with Baker and later with the President.

When I was with Rabbi Schneier recently in his office, he was packing his bags and preparing to leave to meet President Kostunica, the then new Serbian leader who had taken over from Milosevic. While Kostunica could not receive a senior-ranking American, as Serbian anti-American feelings were strong and it would compromise his new position of power, receiving Rabbi Schneier in many ways was the next best thing. This is a man who is often pulled in many directions. Though constantly in demand, he finds the time to make journeys of world importance as well as to acknowledge the smile of a first-grader in the halls of the Park East Day School. He's equally at home with a president and a child.

Rabbi Schneier has represented The Appeal of Conscience Foundation and American interests in his meetings with world leaders from China to Russia to Czechoslovakia to Serbia. He has been on missions for President Ronald Reagan to El Salvador, for President Gerald Ford to Romania, for President Bill Clinton to China, and for President Jimmy Carter to Hungary.

Always maintaining his own agenda, Rabbi Schneier has served presidents of both parties and numerous Secretaries of State. He serves them officially, but he serves them even more effectively unofficially as an entrepreneur in the true sense of the word. He is a creative, focused visionary, and has built relationships that help further his goals for a more peaceful, freer, and prosperous world through tolerance. On January 8, 2001, he was awarded the Presidential Citizens Medal by President Clinton for his efforts in overcoming the forces of hatred and intolerance, and his encouraging of interfaith dialogue and intercultural understanding.

An Unusual Tribute for an Unusual Man

The year 2000 represented a real milestone for Rabbi Schneier: He celebrated his 70th birthday. This is certainly a time for celebration for anyone, but in Rabbi Schneier's case, the birthday was a very special one indeed.

More than 750 people gathered together in early June at New York's Waldorf-Astoria Hotel to honor a man who had touched their lives and made a difference to literally millions of people all over the world. A commemorative album was created to include the hundreds of birthday greetings that the rabbi received, as well as a photographic history of Rabbi Schneier's life and good deeds. President Clinton served as the honorary chairman of the birthday committee. The co-chairs were Vice President Gore and Rabbi Israel Meir Lav, the chief rabbi of Israel, along with a list of luminaries including New York Mayor Guiliani, Henry Kissinger, Representative Tom Lantos, Ambassador Ron Lauder, Senator Moynihan, and Elie Wiesel. More than 100 others helped to plan the events honoring the rabbi that day.

Although I had come to know a lot about the rabbi following our dinner in Vienna during negotiations over the Kosovo crisis, holding his commemorative album in my hands and perusing the many tributes that were bound inside made me realize that I was in the presence of an amazing and influential man. Throughout his long life, he has been a leader, showing others the way to freedom, building strong links between leaders of the world's religions, and building an enduring home for the Park East Synagogue. Throughout the Cold War and through the first difficult post-Communist decade, he has, through The Appeal of Conscience Foundation, been a flame of hope in the search for religious, political, and economic harmony.

One quote in particular struck me as I looked at the album. In 1965, as he was beginning his lifelong mission to the Park East congregation, he said, "Anything worthwhile in life is not easily attainable." I couldn't agree more. Rabbi Schneier exhibits many of the traits that I consider a must for successful entrepreneurs. Pursuing his visions of what he wanted to achieve for the Park East Synagogue led to a wonderful school for children that continues its mission today. A one-day protest against the persecution of Soviet Jews turned into The Appeal of Conscience Foundation, which has provided a forum for religious leaders all over the world to speak out in a unified voice against violence. Rabbi Schneier's acute sense of opportunity enabled him to grow from the leader of a New York City synagogue to an entrepreneurial leader of an organization recognized worldwide for building bridges to peace.

PART THREE

DISCOVER THE
ENTREPRENEUR IN YOU

Chapter 14

30 TRAITS OF SUCCESSFUL ENTREPRENEURS

When thinking about the traits of "successful" entrepreneurs, it is important to first consider success. Success, for this purpose, is effectiveness in reaching entrepreneurial goals. Success is accomplishing things. In the for-profit area, it would at least in part be measured by financial results. But whatever the area or measuring stick, being successful is accomplishing entrepreneurial goals. This is the kind of success that is greatly determined by the traits described in this chapter.

The entrepreneurs in this book and many others I know share a number, though not all, of these common traits. Many of these traits overlap and reinforce one another. While the individuals in this book differ greatly in their backgrounds, nationalities, ages, personalities, and numerous other aspects, it is nevertheless striking how frequently they share these characteristics.

1. Successful entrepreneurs are natural, charismatic leaders.

Recently, I was sitting in Bernie Rapoport's office at his insurance company. His door was open, and, from time to time, he would see people walking by in the hallway and call out for them to come in. Others simply knocked on the door and came in for other reasons. Each of the people to whom he introduced me, from the president of the company to secretaries and staff from the mailroom, seemed to have a unique rapport with Bernie. He would joke with them, talk to them about business, and ask about personal family things. He knew about them, and they knew about him. There was a sense of respect and clarity that Bernie was in charge, not because of threat or position, but because of the charismatic leadership of someone who inspires others to follow.

Switch the scene to Belgrade and Gerry Hargitai's speech before 3,500 Serbians who listened with tears in their eyes as Gerry described his escape from communism and the building of California Fitness. They were responding to his sincerity and his charisma. Gerry is somebody that people want to follow.

Successful entrepreneurs instill a sense of confidence, direction, focus, and energy.

2. Successful entrepreneurs are passionate about what they do.

Every entrepreneur in this book is absolutely passionate about what he or she does. When you talk to Katharine Wittmann, her passion is obvious. One by one, she wore her opponents down and ultimately won her challenging battles to regain her family business.

When you talk to Ambassador Richard Schifter, he instantly leaps into an inspiring soliloquy of the future. He can talk about a grand plan for the crime center or for facilitating cross-border trade. His charged words paint vivid pictures.

Gerry Hargitai is completely passionate about the latest health supplements he sells and how they can change your life. At a recent dinner with Gerry and his wife, somehow we got onto the subject of my own vitamin regimen. You would have thought I had committed a horrible sin. Gerry became completely agitated: "Oh no, no, you can't take that vitamin without food!" I couldn't believe how important all of these things were to him.

Few can listen to Doraja Eberle talk about Farmers Helping Farmers for more than a few minutes without tearing up. She is fully committed to making a difference in a very troubled place at a very troubled time. Her passion is contagious.

Successful entrepreneurs overflow with enthusiasm, excitement, and desire.

3. Successful entrepreneurs have vision and goals.

Every entrepreneur in this book has a sense of where he or she wants to go. Their road to getting there may have changed many times, but the end goal was always in sight.

For Doraja, it is to help as many victims of the war as possible. For Gerry, it is to build the largest and best sales force possible. For Dick Schifter, it is to make a major difference for people in Southeast Europe. For Katharine Wittmann, it was to get back her family dairy and rebuild its success. Clear visions and goals are significant contributions to entrepreneurial success.

4. Successful entrepreneurs think out of the box.

Dick Schifter was thinking out of the box when he selected Turkish and Greek business leaders to co-chair a business advisory committee. But it was this kind of idea that made the program succeed.

Back in Michigan when I bought Knob on the Lake, people told me I was crazy. But I believed strongly that the creative spark of the "lemony" marketing strategy and immense hours of hard work would make the project fun, exciting, and successful. Creativity and the American system are an explosive combination. Consumers love exciting, new ideas.

Similarly, when we came up with new, creative financial structures for our limited partnerships, we excelled. From the first partnership through several hundred, each evolved with the newest thinking to take advantage of tax laws in the most legally responsible yet creatively structured manner possible. Whether it's financial engineering or marketing concepts, entrepreneurs are rewarded for creativity.

Success in business, as in life, requires creative "outside the box" thinking.

5. Successful entrepreneurs work hard and hopefully smart.

Hard work pays off. For Albert Black, it was mowing lawns, and for Steve Mariotti, it was selling Avon. When I was young and trying to save money, it was simply a matter of how many hours I could work and how little I could eat while I was saving. I remember working as a dishwasher for 75 cents an hour and paying 25 cents for mashed potatoes and gravy as my sole meal of the day—all so that I could save money to invest later.

Those early days were far from the only time I worked hard. Throughout most of my company's growth years, I worked exceptionally long hours, as did most of the entrepreneurs in this book. At the same time, today I am more concerned with "working smart," which is also a critical component of success. Had I been working a little smarter in 1984 and 1985, I might have seen that the economics were turning sour and inflation had turned to deflation. We were headed for trouble, but I was too busy to see it. I was in the wrong business at the wrong time. Hopefully, experience and maturity have enabled me to work a little smarter today and see things more clearly while they are happening.

Successful entrepreneurs learn to rethink what they've seen done before so that they can improve their opportunities and attain their goals.

6. Successful entrepreneurs are survivors.

For Rabbi Arthur Schneier, Ambassador Richard Schifter, Katharine Wittmann, and Gerry Hargitai, survival literally meant fleeing tyranny. This kind of survival leaves scars, but also builds drive, perspective, and skills.

For Albert Black and Bernard Rapoport, surviving childhood poverty built a base for entrepreneurship. For me, surviving epilepsy and the effects of Phenobarbital eventually helped me as an entrepreneur.

Most entrepreneurs struggle to survive early in their careers. As Bernie Rapoport said, "The first five years of my business, if the regulators had looked closely at my insurance company, we were broke." Over time, Bernie's company became not only financially solvent but also hugely successful. Bernie is not alone in experiencing early stage financial stresses. Most entrepreneurs I know go through an initial and sometimes lengthy period of barely surviving, and, having done so, are better prepared to respond to the next stage of their business's development.

7. Successful entrepreneurs are trying to prove themselves.

If they were willing to face the facts, many entrepreneurs would realize that some fundamental past trauma or difficulty proved to be the catalyst for their entrepreneurial efforts. For me, it was a generally difficult childhood. Steve Mariotti had to overcome the fear, frustration, and outrage of an assault.

If you really get to know them, most entrepreneurs have something somewhere in their past that makes them want to prove themselves to someone. They may be proving themselves to their parents or maybe to the world around them. These motivators are not always the healthiest. In some cases, they are personal demons that are tough to banish even with success. In any event, time, maturity, and a greater perspective may help the entrepreneur achieve dual goals: being a successful entrepreneur and ultimately realizing that you don't have to prove anything to anyone.

8. Successful entrepreneurs are focused.

Doraja Eberle loves people who quickly realize that she has no time for frivolous actions in her life. Doraja is intensely focused on Farmers Helping Farmers. Her energy and effort is directed there and toward her family, with little time left for other things.

Albert Black's focus is on his business, being a leader, and helping the greater Dallas community. He has little time or attention for anything outside of those areas. Entrepreneurs rarely make good golfers. Their entrepreneurial direction leaves them with little time for hobbies.

Successful entrepreneurs are determined to focus on the key elements of their plans and direct their efforts towards those goals.

9. Successful entrepreneurs are optimists.

To entrepreneurs, the glass is generally not half full, but overflowing.

Often, ambassadors are focused on seemingly impossible political situations and discuss all of the reasons why something can't change or won't work. Dick Schifter, on the other hand, always seems to be optimistically searching for new solutions and focusing on positive change. Some people see trucks lined up for 12 hours to get to a customs depot where it takes a bribe to cross the border. They see only the virtually "unsolvable" economic problems of the former Communist region that will take generations to change. Dick Schifter sees obstacles that can be overcome and improvements that can be made. Dick, unlike many ambassadors, but like most entrepreneurs, has an optimistic answer for every cynic on virtually any given issue.

Entrepreneurs take risks in part because they don't view risks the same way others might. They focus on a positive result and, therefore, discount the risk.

10. Successful entrepreneurs are realists when they need to be.

If entrepreneurs are as optimistic as I've described, how can they know when to put the brakes on and change direction? The answer is that a successful entrepreneur can be both optimistic and realistic. In the early planning for energy efficiency projects in Romania, Dick Schifter often talked about how he was going to get lenders on board. But when finally confronted with the reality that prospective lenders wouldn't make loans with the rates, terms, or collateral he had in mind, he quickly accepted reality and moved on to a new solution. Realism caused him to move from one solution to another without losing forward motion.

This realist approach enables successful entrepreneurs to rethink their plans when needed in order to attain the ultimate—and bigger—goals they set for themselves.

11. Successful entrepreneurs are creative problem solvers.

Life for entrepreneurs is like a series of hurdles in a long competition. While the entrepreneur may envision a goal, getting there is never simple. One problem after another arises, and things always go differently than planned.

Katharine Wittmann's decade-long battle to regain her family dairy would have defeated anyone less tenacious. Time after time, Katharine would win a small battle, only to find another huge, unexpected problem to solve. She finally succeeded in the end by showing that her failure would result in the loss of an important source of jobs in a tiny Slovakian town. The town fathers wouldn't let that happen. There are always unique solutions to every problem, and entrepreneurs know how to dig and find those solutions.

12. Successful entrepreneurs are often insecure.

Many entrepreneurs I know have basic insecurities. In my case, I felt insecure because, when I was a child, my family and those around me let me know that I wasn't good at many things. My plan was to prove them all wrong.

Similarly, Kenny Blatt was insecure about his relationship with his father. He felt he had to prove his worth. Other entrepreneurs I know also have experienced significant feelings of insecurity despite their successes.

Insecurity, properly refocused, can be a powerful motivator. It also can be a humbling neutralizer. It can make the entrepreneur more sensitive, creative, and innovative. The motivation that may grow out of insecurity can be a powerful force for growth.

13. Successful entrepreneurs never give up.

When Dick Schifter wanted to start SECI, no one could stand in his way. He had to convince the President of the United States and then a number of other countries. He did what seemed impossible because he did not give up.

When I believe I'm right, I don't give up. In Texas in the mid-1980s, I was in a fight for economic survival. I battled the government lawyers and vowed not to let them put me out of business. When less-determined people told me there was no chance, I never, never, never gave up!

Dogged persistence against the odds can stimulate the successful entrepreneur's creativity, flexibility, and business skills.

14. Successful entrepreneurs know when to be flexible.

Flexibility in this context is the ability and willingness to embrace change. It means seeing an opportunity where others might see only a wrong turn. When Kenny Blatt was working on developing feature films in Malaysia and was approached by an old family friend who needed him in Romania, he didn't hesitate to change his plans. He decided that he wanted to see what else the world had to offer. This was a new path, and it led him to establish Romania's first outdoor advertising company.

Steve Mariotti was able to see another way to reach the underprivileged kids in his New York City classroom. He succeeded in part by being flexible and embracing change. He adapted the curriculum to the interests of the students. In the process, he founded an important and enduring nonprofit foundation that helps many people. Flexibility is a state of mind. It means being open to possibilities and being willing to change. It can enable an entrepreneur to turn a good idea into a great one.

15. Successful entrepreneurs are motivators.

Entrepreneurs' unwavering beliefs in the ideas that drive them is often a motivator in itself. The fervor that the entrepreneur exhibits is contagious. This is an unconscious and very effective form of motivation. Motivation is a key ingredient to success because an entrepreneur cannot succeed alone. Success is usually the result of teamwork.

Doraja Eberle motivates simply by being herself. Her great belief in the good that Farmers Helping Farmers does in the world infects her every word. Total strangers offer to help her.

Similarly, Gerry Hargitai motivates people by being himself without pretense. Entrepreneurs are often in a position of selling themselves as a way to motivate others. That motivation in turn helps others contribute to the overall success of the venture.

16. Successful entrepreneurs are on a mission.

It is often said that the easiest person to sell something to is a good salesman. Similarly, if you're a good motivator, for better or worse, you're easily motivated. Knowing your mission and motivation towards it is often what helps an entrepreneur develop leadership style. The mission may be Kenny Blatt's desire to bring Western-style services to Romania. Or it may be Rabbi Schneier's desire to spread peace and tolerance to hot spots of conflict. Or it may be Trevor Cornwell's desire to build the best Internet air charter reservation system. Whatever the specifics, entrepreneurs are highly motivated to accomplish their missions.

Successful entrepreneurs are often relentless in their pursuit of their mission. It's their dream. But the mission can create havoc in the rest of their lives. If there is any one reason why many entrepreneurs are young, it's this: It's much easier when you're young to devote 24 hours a day, seven days a week to making a dream come true.

17. Successful entrepreneurs can "pull the trigger."

A willingness to make decisions and take action is critical to an entrepreneur's success. Making tough decisions even without complete information is a mark of a successful entrepreneur. Entrepreneur Harris Turner, who leads the team developing the RetrieveIt concept, said to me once, "Perfect is the enemy of done." The willingness to make decisions is the ability to take the risk that the decision may be wrong.

The entrepreneurs in this book make the big decisions: Go to market, make the investment, close the deal, and walk away. That each in his field knew when the moment of "pulling the trigger" had arrived was critical to success, to change, and to survival.

18. Successful entrepreneurs are angry, frustrated, and hungry for control.

Steve Mariotti and I were discussing the traits of successful entrepreneurs one day, and the first trait he immediately thought of was, "Entrepreneurs have anger."

I thought that was only me!

A short time later, I was with a cousin of mine who is an entrepreneur. When I described this conversation to him, his wife was nearby and immediately jumped on the anger part. Then he agreed and added that anger leads entrepreneurs to be "frustrated and hungry for control."

While I didn't ask my fellow entrepreneurs in this book to share the experiences they may have had with anger, I will acknowledge my own. My anger probably stems from my frustrating childhood, but it is often directed at people or events around me. Anger leads back to frustration, and, as my cousin suggested, this frustration leads to the desire to ultimately control my environment. Entrepreneurs are often known as "control freaks."

As I've grown older, I've tried to mellow and work against my tendencies to be a control freak because it can be unfair and hurtful to others. But as far as getting frustrated goes, my wife might suggest I haven't mellowed. Many years ago, we went to the Fort Worth Stock Show. It's an annual event that packs in people. Kathy and the kids wandered off, or maybe they would say I did. I spent the next hour looking for them and, once reunited, you could say I displayed anger and frustration traits.

Kathy, in an effort to bring perspective to the moment, saw a vendor that sold dog tags like people used to wear around their neck in the military. She had one printed out for me that said, "If lost or found frustrated, call Kathy Hall" and it listed our phone number. Later, for Christmas or a birthday, she had a similar but more permanent one made in gold. When we moved to Austria, she had a new one made in German!

Anger, frustration, and a hunger for control, tempered by an ability to place perspective on the moment, can be useful forces in an entrepreneur's life.

19. Successful entrepreneurs are introspective.

"The best conversations I've ever had in my life are with entrepreneurs," Steve Mariotti says. I agree. Most entrepreneurs don't pull punches, especially when it comes to talking about themselves. They are their own toughest critics. You can have some great "what's life all about" conversations with entrepreneurs.

Albert Black and I love to get together just to talk about the world's problems. With Gerry Hargitai, it's the same thing. Similarly, I relish conversations with Bernie Rapoport.

Where many people seem to have emotional shields around them, entrepreneurs often have little, if any. While sometimes politically incorrect or not terribly diplomatic, entrepreneurs think about themselves and the world in an intellectually honest manner and are not afraid to share their views.

20. Successful entrepreneurs rely heavily on intuition.

Successful entrepreneurs often rely on their gut instincts. Instead of processing a situation in a rational or organized manner, entrepreneurs often rely on a "sense of the situation," taking in information others might miss.

Gerry Hargitai "sensed" that Eastern Europeans didn't like the idea of selling. The concept was foreign to the Communist approach to distributing goods. But, intuitively, he knew that Eastern Europeans were very relationship oriented. To succeed in setting up a large sales organization, his intuition guided him to approach sales differently. In fact, Gerry does not even use the word "sell." He structured ways people could "help their friends" improve their health by buying California Fitness products. It's just icing on the cake, he explains, that you also get paid for helping your friends.

Intuition is an amazing thing. It involves the subconscious assimilation of current and past data resulting in an instant gut feeling. While I try not to be sexist, it seems to me that women simply are better at using intuition than guys. My wife Kathy, for instance, often has a better gut feeling about people than I do. On first impression, she senses certain situations very clearly. She is not alone. Patricia Meadows, senior vice president at Hall, is someone I often rely on for these kinds of gut feelings about situations. Valerie Reber, a long-time Hall Financial veteran, and a number of other women in my Hall Financial family, simply prove the point that women somehow get it when it comes to intuition.

Whether male or female, entrepreneurs understand that intuitive decisions can and are a necessary part of entrepreneurship.

21. Successful entrepreneurs are emotional and sensitive.

Entrepreneurs appear tough because of their determination, focus, and passion. But the reality is that most entrepreneurs are marshmallows at their core. They are soft, emotional, sensitive people who are easily hurt.

The positive to this emotional side is that they are often better in tune with other people's feelings. Entrepreneurs are willing to listen and learn.

22. Successful entrepreneurs use a win-win approach.

Entrepreneurs spend a lot of time negotiating transactions with others. Actually when you think about it, life itself is a series of negotiations in give and take. In this regard, people often speak of how they "got the advantage of" or "pulled one over on" the other guy. During the time I spent in Central and Eastern Europe, I saw that the prevailing view of entrepreneurs was that when they won, someone lost. In the United States, many people also hold that view.

The reality is that transactions in which one side wins and the other side loses are outmoded, counterproductive, and belittling to both sides. Successful entrepreneurs creatively think about both sides of the transaction and structure deals, where possible, so that everyone wins. The key is to avoid the zero-sum solution. Our efforts should result in more for everyone, not all for some and none for others. Katharine Wittmann had an innate sense for a win-win solution when she convinced the local authorities that closing down her dairy would reflect badly on them. Allowing her ownership of the dairy meant hundreds of workers would remain on the job, and the government officials could get credit for doing something good for the community. She helped to create a larger pie for everyone with a win-win solution.

Entrepreneurs look for the win-win approach to whatever problem arises and want to see others succeed, as well as themselves.

23. Successful entrepreneurs respond best to challenges.

Entrepreneurs are mountain climbers. They like to take on tall peaks that other people shy away from because they like to figure out how to get to the top. Sometimes to a fault, they make challenges a critical piece of their life's work. The danger is that there is always a new mountain and a new challenge. Always looking for mountains to climb rather than enjoying the peace that can come from just being in the present can be unhealthy.

For me, the challenges of turning around a failing property, structuring a complex financial transaction, or building a different and better office park are all challenges that I hope bring out the best in me. Challenge to me has always meant making quantum leaps. Building bigger buildings with more bells and whistles is like climbing a new mountain. I've always thrived on a challenge. Show me an easy, workable business deal and I get bored.

24. Successful entrepreneurs have a "killer instinct."

We know them; we can see them. Some people are just get along, go along people, and others are just "killers." Obviously, I don't mean it literally. You don't have to be an entrepreneur to fit into this category, but the vast majority of successful entrepreneurs I know do have killer instincts.

In my early days in business, I used to make this one of my prime considerations for hiring. The whole idea is some people walk by a piece of paper on the ground and don't pick it up. Maybe they don't see it; maybe they don't care. Someone who is involved and engaged walks by the piece of paper, stops, and picks it up. These are people who are vibrant, full of life, energized, and ready to take on any given situation with aggressiveness and vigor. These are the people in life who get things done.

25. Successful entrepreneurs fill vacuums.

As Steve Mariotti explains to his young students, "Why compete and do what everyone else is doing?" Instead, find a niche that is your own special area, your own product or service that is needed. Filling a vacuum is a key to successful entrepreneurship.

26. Successful entrepreneurs rely heavily on relationships and personal credibility.

Steve Mariotti is an expert at relationships and credibility. He has attracted a number of opinion makers to his board of directors including Jack Kemp, John Whitehead, and David Dinkins. Steve is a skilled networker. He will try to help one person who then helps another person, in the process creating a network of contacts, relationships, and people who ultimately provide help and credibility to his organization.

When Dick Schifter needed to make sure an important foreign policy problem didn't escalate, it was his trusted relationship with the Deputy Chief of Mission of the Soviet Embassy in Washington that made the difference. When he needed to get European support for starting the Southeastern European Cooperative Initiative, it was his established personal relationships with German, French, Austrian, Italian, and other officials that made the difference.

Recently, a former business partner and friend of mine recommended me to a friend of his, whom I only knew casually, as a potential partner for a $2 billion acquisition. The individual with the transaction contacted me, and we are currently in discussions. The transaction may or may not work out, but it appears to be an exciting business deal that came my way only because of a favorable past relationship. Maintaining and nurturing relationships provides entrepreneurs untold personal as well as professional opportunities.

27. Successful entrepreneurs don't accept failure, only setbacks.

You are never a real failure until you allow yourself to be one. Just like defining success is complex, defining failure is also complex. If you own buildings that lose money and ultimately have lenders foreclose on them, does this mean you're a failure? Certainly in some sense you failed at a portion of your business plan. But in the larger sense, failure is a matter of perception. If you feel like a failure, you are. Staying in the game is the key to not being a failure.

If Katharine Wittmann had accepted the answers of government officials who slammed doors in her face and told her she would not get restitution, she would have left town, gone back to Canada, and been a failure. Because she never saw herself as a failure, she ultimately succeeded.

Not accepting failure is what ultimately leads to success. Successful entrepreneurs simply don't allow setbacks to be the end.

28. Successful entrepreneurs can visualize and dream about their plans.

Almost every night when I go to sleep, my thoughts turn to visualizing the success I want to occur on whichever venture is most in flux and important to me at that time. When I awaken suddenly from a deep sleep, I have often dreamt of new ideas and plans. I don't always recall the visions or my dreams, but the point is that my subconscious and my sleep time are part of the process that later helps form my "gut feeling" for things. Visualization about the issues of the day and the goals one wants to achieve brings new answers and energies.

29. Successful entrepreneurs are "stress carriers" who handle pressure well.

Stress can be carried and converted to positive energy and passion, or it can negatively consume your efforts. Life is full of stress. Entrepreneurs by their activities create stress. Half jokingly, people I work with say I am a "stress giver." For the others in this book and for me, putting stress into perspective—not being overwhelmed, but instead being energized to succeed—is a critical trait. Time, experience, and relative values can all be useful to put stressful events into perspective so that you can quickly move to productive, reality-based solutions rather than wallow in the difficulties at hand.

30. Successful entrepreneurs are responsible.

Much of the psychological makeup of business entrepreneurs is similar to that of white-collar crooks. Both are clever, tend to cut corners and red tape, and generally operate out of the mainstream of society. One can argue that entrepreneurial success may be better in a non-level playing field and that my ideas are simply naïve. But I strongly believe that longer-term entrepreneurial success depends on and is defined by society.

Even in my short lifetime, society's definition of accepted behavior seems to be gravitating toward a greater sense of "responsibility" and realization of interdependence within communities. Entrepreneurs who flourish over the long term will do so not with a selfish quid pro quo on every transaction, but with a broader concern for fairness and their fellow man being ultimately rewarded. Sometimes the good acts go unnoticed, but in the broader sense, caring for others and doing what is right, not what is easy, pays off.

Chapter 15

Seven Secrets About Entrepreneurs

The lives of the people in this book teach us a great deal about entrepreneurs. They prove you can make money and make a difference. They show that entrepreneurs are complex people interested in far more than just money. Their successes show that win-win strategies work, and their stories show that none of this is easy. They prove that nice people working hard over time can finish first, and that the roadmap to success is not simple and always changes over time. These individuals have had entrepreneurial inclinations take hold at a wide range of ages.

Through the entrepreneurs in this book, I have tried to dispell commonly believed myths and describe traits of successful entrepreneurs. But there are some facts of entrepreneurship or "secrets" not often discussed that can help you to better understand entrepreneurs, and even why they are sometimes not successful.

Secret # 1: Entrepreneurs aren't always the healthiest, most well-balanced creatures around.

Creative, passionate, high-energy folks often aren't the best spouses or parents. They are not "normal" people. The same ingredients that cause someone to put in the needed work to move mountains and make the impossible possible often make for unhappy people. Initially, breathing life into an entrepreneurial venture demands an intensity that shifts the scales of life, putting almost anything other than that dream a distant second.

Despite the initial motivations, which sometimes can be extreme and even unhealthy, most entrepreneurs mellow and mature. The killer instinct can grow more moderate after an entrepreneur begins to achieve some goals. The wisdom that comes with maturity and experience can lead to a fuller, healthier personal life.

Secret # 2: You've got to know when to hold them and know when to fold them.

In the wee hours of one morning before turning to work on this book, I was reading through various papers on my desk. One was a copy of a memo from Don Braun. Don was writing to the founder of one of the technology companies in which we were small investors. Don had been serving on the board of this company. The memo to the entrepreneur contained what Don saw as five "reality points" that needed quick consideration.

In short, Don brought reality crashing down by pointing out the weaknesses in that company's position that it was failing to address. This brought home to me a lot of thoughts about experiences I've had and what business I'm really in today.

If someone were to ask me the biggest single reason entrepreneurs fail, I would have to say lack of focus and clinging too long to unrealistic ideas. Put another way, to succeed you have to blend a lot of the traits discussed in Chapter 14 like a carefully run chemistry experiment. To be an entrepreneur, you have to start out very self-assured, optimistic, and with a vision. However, to be a successful entrepreneur, you have to survive. Survival usually means adjustments to the business plan. It also means careful refocusing and knowing when to drop the optimist's full-speed-ahead approach to be a realist.

My team at Hall Financial and I often play the role of mentor: counseling and guiding young, enthusiastic, aggressive entrepreneurs. We have worked with dozens over the last few years. Almost always, they start out extremely sure of themselves. Many entrepreneurs are a little cocky in the beginning. They have passion and a commitment to an idea.

Only time and getting beaten up tends to bring them down to earth. But tough experiences test us and teach real lessons. Many of the traits of successful entrepreneurs, especially during challenging times, are conflicting. The resolution of that conflict is often a secret to success.

The secret is in balancing the conflicting traits within the narrow scope of workable bounds. There is no perfect formula that can apply to every situation. Different situations require different skills, and success is dictated by being able to respond accordingly. The key is to hone an instinctual sense of conflict resolution between these various traits.

Secret # 3: It's only the one or two (usually simple) ideas that matter.

So often we make things overcomplicated. People tend to think of business situations as a series of important decisions. The secret is keeping it simple. It's only one or two, usually simple, ideas that really matter. Certainly management is critical, but if the main ideas don't work, the whole concept is doomed.

To succeed you need to find the right formula. In Bernie Rapoport's case, he was running a good but typical insurance company until he came up with one great idea: to focus on specializing and selling insurance to union members. Everyone in his company (including himself) was a union member. They looked like, acted like, talked like, and thought like union members, from start to finish. Because of that one idea and the concentration in that area, his company succeeded big time.

Albert Black's idea that he was not in the supply business but in the logistics business changed his company from what would have been a dinosaur into a fast-growing, highly profitable firm. As a logistics company, the value-added service that On-Target supplies is knowing what a company needs, where, and when. This provides a whole new level of customer service.

The point of each of these examples and for virtually every one of the entrepreneurs in this book is that one simple idea well executed makes the difference.

Secret # 4: Don't underestimate luck and timing.

Sitting around one day in 1975 a friend of mine, Marty Rom, stopped by just to talk. The subject turned to racquetball, a national craze in the United States at the time. Marty and I decided to fantasize about a perfect company for this great business. We made a list of 75 corporations to approach with partnership propositions to start a chain of racquetball clubs. Topping our list was Time, Inc., because we thought Time's *Sports Illustrated* would make a great name to associate with our clubs.

Marty had the idea that he could sell the concept to big partners. For putting the partnership together, he would get 10 percent of the company. I was to put together the investors, manage the clubs, and put in my own money for my piece of ownership. Unbelievably, Marty picked up the phone and got a lunch meeting for the next week with the son of Time's founder Henry Luce. Within 90 days, we had a million dollars of Time's money and the exclusive legal rights to the name: *Sports Illustrated* Court Clubs. Within six months, I had an offer to buy out our position for $5 million more than our investment, which we dismissed immediately.

Though being a partner with Time was a great experience, this fairy tale doesn't have a happy ending. We had caught the crest of a wave of racquetball popularity that quickly eroded, and a year and a half into the venture, we were drowning. Our investors had put up $14 million to become the largest chain of racquetball clubs in the country, and I didn't want them to lose a penny. Between the investors' money and debt, we had built 18 racquetball clubs in different parts of the United States and had dreams of doing 100 more. Unfortunately though, they never made money. I put in money and voluntarily paid off corporate loans to ensure investors wouldn't lose. Though it sounds like throwing good money after bad, I always had been dedicated to keeping my investors happy. They had made their investments relying heavily on me, and I knew that saving them from loss was the right thing to do. In the end, on an after-tax basis, most of the investors broke even or made a little money. While I ended up missing the $5 million opportunity and losing several million dollars as well, I learned that luck and timing are critical to success.

Yes, success depends in great part on luck and timing. While I like to talk about honesty and working smart and hard as being American virtues, the fact is they are not enough. All you can hope to do is put yourself in the best position to take advantage of what comes your way. The markets are bigger than any of us. One player cannot control what drives market changes in any respective industry. Few can come close to predicting the direction of businesses and markets with any consistent degree of success.

Luck comes and goes, and knowing when and how to cash in and take advantage of it is a critical component of success. Sometimes that knowledge comes from experience, critical judgment, or good sense, but often it's just plain luck. I am the first to admit that luck has played an important part in my career. It was a combination of risk taking, hard work, and smart work that led me to purchase, at what turned out to be a good time, both St. Paul Place and Harwood Center, two high-rise office buildings in downtown Dallas. We managed the buildings well and worked hard to implement ideas to improve the return on the properties. At the same time, all of that paled in comparison to our good fortune in selling these buildings a few years after purchase at what turned out to be the top of the market. Did we know it was the top of the market? Of course not. We thought it was a good time to sell, but we actually experienced seller's remorse at the time. When the deal finally closed, we made about $50 million. Luck and lucky timing is without a doubt a significant factor in many American success stories.

Secret # 5: Boredom and believing your own press are the entrepreneur's devils.

My biggest mistakes in business (of which there have been many) have come when I am bored or suffering from delusions created by too much positive press. Perhaps the corollary to Secret # 3 that only one or two ideas matter is that when you put too many other ideas on the plate just for stimulation, the chances of failure increase. This often happens in one of two times: when you're bored or feeling invincible.

I can't tell you the number of entrepreneurs, including me, who, when bored, speculate in stock commodities or other investments in which we don't belong. Similarly, after a string of articles in newspapers proclaiming what a wunderkind I was, it was all too easy to believe it and overexpand at the wrong time. The tendency of entrepreneurs to feel infallible while desiring constant action can be dangerous. It's important for entrepreneurs to understand that it's okay and even good to have time on the sideline. It's important to keep perspective, to look at the big picture, and to hedge your bets. Outside forces are always bigger than any of us might think.

Secret # 6: Being honest and fair pays off.

I've always believed that trying to do things to the best of my ability while treating others fairly is the right thing to do. That's not to say that I didn't drive hard and even make enemies. I did. I've made many mistakes and in some cases regret past actions. At the same time, I've tried to treat people fairly and honestly. Several times over the course of my career, taking advantage of people would have been the easy thing to do, but it was never my way.

Lots of times, I have had legal documents in front of me that didn't represent the negotiated deal. Often significant, better deals can occur in the fine print without the other side realizing it. My position is that this is wrong. If my lawyer does it by accident, or if the other side's lawyer hurts his client, I point it out to all parties, get it fixed, and move on. If my lawyer tries to pull something over on the other side and I find out, first I point it out to the other side and apologize, and then I fire my lawyer. Life is too short to play the wrong way.

Bribery is not a way of life in the United States, although there are exceptions. In a few regional markets where my company tried to do business, people put out their hands for bribes. Usually we chose to avoid doing business in those areas. In those cases where we went ahead with our projects, we never paid bribes. Sometimes, we ended up making far more code enforcement repairs in our buildings than we would have had to perform if we'd simply paid off an inspector. My questions have always been, "Where do you start and stop with bribery?" and "Where do you start and stop with right and wrong?" To me these issues always have been clearly defined.

Adhering to a consistent view of openness and honesty is not always easy in business, politics, or personal life. But I've always found that honesty and directness pay dividends in the long run.

Many people I knew and did business with in the early 1980s in Dallas during the real estate, banking, and savings and loan crisis ended up in jail. They weren't out-and-out crooks who had large bank accounts full of stolen money. They were simply people who did what "everyone else was doing," cutting some corners no one ever thought would matter. Later, the savings and loan debacle ensnared those people and their bad decisions in unexpected ways.

In the United States, just as anywhere else in the world, people get greedy. Attempts are made to take advantage of positions of weakness. These greedy types often try to get the edge on a deal by renegotiating and tying up transactions for months. Indeed, as a seller, I've been the victim of buyers who play these games. While someone might benefit in such a transaction, I believe that being honorable has been far more beneficial than engaging in delay tactics and dirty dealings ever could have been.

Secret # 7: Positive cash flow is an entrepreneurial law of nature.

Being true to cash needs with careful cash-flow budgeting and monitoring is critical to being a successful entrepreneur. As sure as Newton showed the law of gravity with an apple falling from a tree, entrepreneurs over and over prove that positive cash flow is a critical law of success.

When we first invested in Skyjet, we knew it was losing money and needed more investment. Later, after our investment, we saw on the wall in the office a bank statement showing a balance of $1.56 before our investment. Skyjet is the exception in that we invested in the nick of time. Profit is nice, but you can't eat it. Developing new technology or growing fast are both great, but they don't keep the doors open. If you run out of money, the best ideas in the world are doomed. When organizations fail, whether for-profit or nonprofit, it's usually because they run out of cash.

In the heyday of dotcoms, the main focus of the investment community was on growth. Many assumed that endless investment capital would get them down the road. When the capital dried up, so did hundreds of companies with great ideas.

Long ago at Hall, we learned to focus on cash flow to the point that we developed a complex weekly cash flow report for all senior management and hold a meeting every week to discuss this report. We put together actual results of all cash transactions for all of our numerous activities for the week and then add them together. We then reforecast future periods. We believe hands-on cash-flow monitoring at any—or better yet *every*—size is critical to success.

Chapter 16

A MESSAGE TO GOVERNMENT OFFICIALS: "MAKE RESPONSIBLE ENTREPRENEURISM A PRIORITY IN SOCIETY"

As the entrepreneurs described in this book illustrate, some people can succeed even in very adverse circumstances. However, laws, regulations, and the attitude of government officials matter a great deal. The environment created by government leadership can help or hinder the number of responsible entrepreneurs in any society. Because responsible entrepreneurs are so highly beneficial, government officials should encourage their development.

A General Message on Encouraging Responsible Entrepreneurs

Responsible entrepreneurs are a hand-in-glove fit for healthy, participatory democracies. Government officials can and should promote leadership to encourage responsible entrepreneurs through a variety of means:

+ Enhance the legal system in such a manner as to allow the least unfairness and red tape in time and cost for dispute resolution.

+ Providing the best possible education (particularly for young people) on the virtues and benefits of creative, innovative risk taking but with a sense of responsibility and ethics.

+ Making the Internet and technology accessible and available to all.

+ Encouraging and celebrating responsible entrepreneurs who make a difference, whether they're for-profit, nonprofit, or in government.

+ Allowing for "second chances," including strong, workable bankruptcy laws.

+ Making responsible entrepreneurism a priority in the society.

A Message to the Government Officials and Leaders in Central and Eastern Europe (CEE)

Setting a good example, and proving that corruption is out and good government is in, are obviously the critical places to start. Soliciting and getting Western help is an important element as well. In addition to these points, encouraging responsible entrepreneurs can make a big difference.

How Do You Encourage Responsible Entrepreneurs?

For a variety of reasons, many entrepreneurs in the CEE do not adhere to the ideals of responsible entrepreneurs. Theft, cronyism, inside deals, payoffs, and other damaging shortcuts characterize much of the early post-Communist business development. As a result, many people in these societies regard entrepreneurs as robber barons and worse. Some of this attitude is a holdover from Communist dogma on the evils of capitalism, but it is also a reasonable reaction to today's reality.

The increasingly negative view of capitalism many people hold makes it even more important to foster the growth of responsible entrepreneurs. This will not be easy. First, people must acknowledge the problem. Then programs should be created like those described below. It will take time, perhaps a generation or more. It will take leadership. It will take courage. But responsible entrepreneurs can flourish in the emerging democracies and transition economies of the CEE. They will make a big difference.

The Keys to Encouraging Responsible Entrepreneurs

◇ Exposure to and discussion about the concept.

◇ Media exposure and support of the concept.

◇ Positive international and local role models for truly responsible entrepreneurism.

◇ A fair and level playing field enforced by the rule of law.

◇ An end to bribery, accompanied by pay increases for police and bureaucrats to achieve fair compensation and honest law enforcement systems.

◇ A fair, working judicial system.

◇ A system of fair bankruptcy laws that encourage second chances while protecting creditors rights.

◇ A liquid and accessible financial system.

◇ Entrepreneurial education, available at many levels but emphasizing youth.

◇ Leaders from all sectors who are willing to talk about the benefits of responsible entrepreneurism.

◇ Celebration of real, ethical local success stories.

◇ Citizen support for environments conducive to responsible entrepreneurs.

Create a Major Change in Attitudes

It is vital that respect for entrepreneurs and confidence in free market systems increase dramatically within transition economies. Distrust and cynicism need to give way to an optimistic atmosphere of cooperation. Emphasis on the following opinion makers in the CEE would help:

✦ **A Free Press.**
 The media needs to understand the benefits of responsible entrepreneurism and see the real commitment of government and business leaders to an open, fair, level playing field.

To achieve this, members of the press must be made aware of and welcomed to meetings and dialogue about the process. And, of course, they must be able to write freely about what they learn.

✦ Government Leadership.
Visionary and honest leadership is desperately needed to stop corruption and encourage the growth of more positive attitudes. To the extent that a country has good, honest, charismatic leaders, they can help encourage responsible entrepreneurism and speed up the transition to real free markets. In the best case, good leadership will evolve of its own accord. In the worst case, it may never have a chance. In any case, in the CEE, people need to demand it through requiring the highest standards from their officials.

✦ Business Groups and Business Leaders.
The business community needs to come together for dialogue, and, more importantly, follow through with plans to positively change the business environment. SECI's Business Advisory group is proof that this approach works. It's time for CEE business leaders to prove that they deserve respect and that profit is not a dirty word. The key is to actively support an open, fair, level playing field and show a true concern for the community. These are important dimensions of responsible entrepreneurism.

✦ Educational Institutions.
Universities are vital to change in society. In the United States today, social entrepreneurship programs are a new expanding area of education. This is close to the concept of responsible entrepreneurism and a good direction. Similarly, the American University in Bulgaria has taken a leading role in bringing young people in from Central and Eastern Europe together to learn about democracy and economics. They are hopefully providing positive needed education for the region's future leaders.

Commitment to a Fair, Level Playing Field and a True Concern for the Community

An antidote to corruption and the entitlement mind-set is consistent, honest institutions that together create a fair, level playing field. If people can feel confident that they will do better by dealing with fairness and honesty, then they will do so. That is a far more efficient system in delivering goods and services than one that relies on corruption and graft, which can vary from day to day, and person to person, and more importantly, is wrong. Keys to encouraging a fair, level playing field and honest values include:

+ **Make It Fashionable to Deliver Honest Government.**
  To the extent that politicians really believe that they will get elected and stay elected by delivering honest government, they will do so. A free press and an active democratic system will put increasing pressure on corruption and encourage honest government.

+ **Better Pay to Civil Servants.**
  Honest governments should be honest at all levels. One part of the equation in stopping bribes is ensuring that people working in all levels of government make a fair wage. Many CEE government wage earners receive a substantial part of their income through kickbacks and bribes. This needs to be stopped, but any reform must include pay increases. A combination of fees for services and greater tax revenue collection, rather than bribes, could be the source for financing greater payroll costs. Additionally, governments can utilize fewer people working more productively. Fair salary increases can be made affordable.

+ **Transparency at All Levels.**
  Part of the commitment to honest values is openness, whether in business or government. Through legislation and other initiatives, business and political processes can be opened up. People should see and understand the inner workings of government and business.

+ **Cut Bureaucracy and Red Tape.**
Make it easier for people to take risks and start businesses.

+ **Stiff Penalties and More Enforcement Against Corruption.**
Part of providing for honest values is consistent and serious
enforcement and application of principles. Political speeches
and rhetoric are great, but if there is no enforcement, they
are just bandages on the problem. Enforcement needs to be
consistent, at all levels of government, business, and society,
and people should clearly understand the penalties for wrong-
doing.

+ **Address Regional Problems on a Regional Basis.**
It is easier to enforce an anti-corruption program if those responsible for enforcement are also in the program. If a number of countries in a region start to crack down, piece-by-
piece, on border control and other forms of crime, working
together will prove to be very effective.

Regionalize Business

At a time when global business connections are drawing closer, as
they are in countries like the United States, Canada, and Mexico with
NAFTA, and France, Germany, England, and the balance of Western
Europe with the EU, the CEE countries are moving counter to the trend.
Nationalism in the CEE, illustrated most recently in the former Yugoslavia, results in smaller countries that are less competitive in business. This
is a barrier to developing thriving free markets and arguably makes democratic government more difficult. Border-crossing corruption and infrastructure breakdowns are highly counterproductive. Maintaining high
tariffs that are out of step with the direction of global trade is unworkable
in the long run. Overall, anything that encourages isolationism and na-
tionalistic feelings regarding business, in the guise of protecting sover-
eignty, is in the long run doomed to failure. I am not advocating that
countries need to be large to succeed, but just as large countries have
found, smaller countries need to have strong regional cooperation on trade
and other areas.

The more multinational, multiethnic patterns of productivity are encouraged by government policies, the more stable and peaceful the region will become. Elimination of borders, elimination or reduction of tariffs, establishment of regional stock markets, regional rules and regulations on agriculture and other trade areas are all possible goals. The specifics need to be discussed in an open dialogue among countries of the region, but what follows are some considerations:

✦ **Geography Is Always an Issue.**
Defining what is Central and Eastern Europe is a subject that has no absolute right or wrong answer. I have sat in many a meeting where people have talked about "a plan for the Balkans," and inevitably long discussions ensue about which countries to include. Regional plans for the CEE don't have to be so strictly defined. Every country doesn't have to agree on every plan or proposal. The Schengen Agreement for eliminating border crossings was agreed to by eight of the EU countries, rather than all 15. Only 11 EU countries have agreed to the monetary union at this time. This approach also has been used effectively by SECI. The majority does not rule. Instead, countries participate on an issue-by-issue basis, to the extent that they are agreeable. The critical needs are to encourage cross-border, cross-ethnic, interlocking business ties. This will promote greater prosperity and ultimately regional stability.

✦ **Why Not Simply Have All CEE Countries Join the EU?**
European Union expansion is a possible answer for some countries such as Poland, Hungary, and the Czech Republic, and it may be better for them than joining regional Central and Eastern European economic organizations. At the same time, the EU today is neither ready, nor likely to be any time soon, to absorb all of the CEE. The EU is relatively young and is dealing with its own growth issues. Moreover, the CEE countries generally have far more in common with their direct neighbors than the EU in terms of purchasing power parity, political and economic development, and other areas.

✦ **SECI Proves Regional Cooperation Works.**
In the SECI meetings, heated debates occur, yet great civil cooperation results. Historical enemies Turkey and Greece have jointly shared the chairmanship of the Business Advisory Group of SECI. My firsthand observation of how individuals from these countries can and do work together proves to me that good will can come from well-intentioned people working together for the greater good. SECI, with extremely limited resources, has produced results. With more effort, the CEE governments and business and civic groups have huge opportunities for expanded regional cooperation.

A Message to Western Government Policy Makers
Setting the Agenda for Helping the CEE

More than 10 years after the fall of Communism, progress toward free markets is mixed at best. The problems won't take care of themselves. Democracy and free markets don't work with the flip of a switch. Leadership from the West is needed to help ensure a stable transition.

After World War II, the destruction was physical and easy to see. After decades of the Cold War, while the countries under Soviet control suffered physical depreciation and a lack of up-to-date technology, neither of these presented the most serious problem. The real problem lies in the mind-set of the people born of decades of Communism and passed from generation to generation. Communism has simply sucked the spirit, hope, and optimism out of the people. In its place is a negative, cynical perspective.

The West should export its ideas as well as helping to rebuild infrastructure. One of the most valuable things the United States can export is the idea of the American Dream. The view that a fair and level playing field can provide hope and opportunity to all is something people need to believe. Participating in the democratic process and making sure that government officials uphold ideals of fairness is something that people need to be taught to believe. The view that Western countries will in fact help when leaders attempt to overrun democracy with corruption and violate human rights is something that needs to be made clear.

The West could spend its money more wisely and be more effective in its policy if it were to step back and develop a comprehensive plan for the former Communist countries. A new Marshall Plan of sorts could and should still be considered even a decade after the end of the Cold War. The plan doesn't have to be driven by vast sums of funding, but rather by a comprehensive vision of regional participatory democracy that includes economic opportunity for a broad base of people. Education and acknowledgment of the mind-set problems should be part of the comprehensive plan. Responsible entrepreneurism, while not a cure-all, can be a key cornerstone of any future comprehensive, restorative plan.

Absent a plan, it will take many years longer to realize a stable region. We are likely to have more problems like those in Bosnia and Kosovo. The cost of war is far greater than the cost of peace. It's time to step back and look at the fundamental problems that the Cold War has left for this region and how the West can and should aid the leaders and people in Central and Eastern Europe at this critical time.

Finally, the role of the United States is vital. If we do not more broadly and thoughtfully engage our country now, we truly risk security issues later. Moreover, effective engagement will bring trade benefits and help us avoid the tragic human rights violations that have occurred in Bosnia and Kosovo. Rather than reacting to the problem of the moment, a regional, comprehensive, long-term plan is needed.

A Message to American Government Officials About the Low-Income, Underdeveloped Areas of the United States

Much like the CEE, an entitlement mind-set is a major issue in underdeveloped areas of the United States. Racism and prejudice also act to close off the hope and opportunity that is often assumed to be available to every American.

Great strides have been made in race issues and helping underdeveloped areas, but far more work is left to be done. The Clinton Welfare to Work program was a positive move. Encouraging the growth of independence and a sense of personal empowerment is needed.

How Do We Encourage Responsible Entrepreneurs?

Similar to the CEE, a comprehensive plan is needed to encourage responsible entrepreneurs in underdeveloped areas of the United States. Empowerment and spreading the hope and opportunity of a fair and level playing field are needed. Leadership from the federal level is important, but local leadership is critical as well to ultimately build a sense of commitment and understanding that responsible entrepreneurs can make a positive difference in the lives of people who today are left behind in our society.

Specific programs could include:

+ Expansion of programs like Steve Mariotti's National Foundation for Teaching Entrepreneurship (NFTE). Federal funding, followed by hands-off encouragement of NFTE programs and expansion, could make a positive difference.

+ Access to capital, without extensive red tape, on more favorable terms than in other areas of the United States.

+ Education within these regions about opportunities and providing other tools for people to help themselves.

+ Education outside of these areas that we cannot rest until all of America has access to the American Dream of hope and opportunity.

Chapter 17

A Message to Future Entrepreneurs: "Don't Wait to Be Fired— Discover Your Hidden Entrepreneur Now!"

Is There a "Hidden Entrepreneur" in You?

Certainly everyone isn't inclined to be an entrepreneur. Taking risks requires a certain personality, and most psychiatrists and child development experts believe that personality is primarily innate. You can't be taught to be an entrepreneur, but you can learn about entrepreneurship and learn entrepreneurial skills. Most importantly, you can be encouraged through role models and continued education to explore whether there is a hidden entrepreneur in you!

One of my biggest sources of personal enjoyment has come from helping people develop their entrepreneurial inclinations. There are many potential entrepreneurs who simply are not aware of their abilities.

For me, it was Greenrivers at age 10. For Katharine Wittmann, it was a moment of recognizing that her destiny was to reclaim the family business. For Albert Black, it was a passion to work his way out of public housing projects and to make a difference in helping others succeed. For Doraja Eberle, it was seeing on television the terrible impact the Bosnian War was having on children. For Dick Schifter, it was success through a creative approach to his early legal work with the Native Americans. For Bernard Rapoport, it was finding a creative niche in the insurance business. For Steve Mariotti, it was figuring out how to connect with and teach something useful to the youths that had driven him out of his classroom. People discover the entrepreneur in themselves and start activities at all stages of their lives and for all kinds of reasons.

Many people are entrepreneurs-in-waiting. They may not even think of themselves as entrepreneurs. Indeed, some people in this book probably still don't think of themselves as entrepreneurs, but as creative, innovative risk takers, they are indeed entrepreneurs. Oftentimes, entrepreneurs need something to push them into action. Ironically, it is often something adverse that leads to something positive. It is a fact that entrepreneurship booms in the United States in economic downturns. When people lose jobs, they often start businesses of their own. Necessity is often the mother of invention.

"Now What?"

On one of my visits back from Vienna to Dallas, my longtime, very loyal secretary, Jan Jones, told me that her husband's company had gone out of business and he, like everyone else, had lost his job. To make matters worse, Jan's father also worked at the company, and he, too, was out of a job. The company delivered packages from one area of Dallas to another and to surrounding communities. They also warehoused parts for some companies and delivered upon notification. The firm had gone broke. Jan's husband, Jerome, knew nothing about the business side and had no investment capital. Suddenly he was facing unemployment, and it would be hard to get another job.

Some of Jerome's customers came to him and said that they would continue to do business with him if he started a new company. He had never thought of going into business on his own. Neither had Jan. Jan had saved some money, but to think about risking it was not easy. Jerome and Jan talked about it, and then Jan came and talked to me. Could they? Should they? What if it didn't go well?

With my encouragement, Jan withdrew her savings, and with it, her husband, her father, and she started their own delivery company. I knew at that time that my hopes for Jan's success might lead to having to find a new assistant down the line, but that was secondary to my best wishes for her. A year or so later, after Jan had effectively been working two jobs, she finally came to me and said that the business was so successful that she needed to go work there full time.

I still talk to Jan often. She and Jerome frequently work seven days a week and find themselves filling in when an employee doesn't show up. They now employ many people, including not only Jan's father, but also Jan's mother. In their first year, they grossed over $300,000. It's hard work but they own it. Things are looking even better in their second year. Jan and Jerome have become successful entrepreneurs.

To anyone with an idea percolating, I simply would say: Go for it! Don't dream dreams and then look back years later and talk about what could have been or should have been. Do it now. What is the worst that can happen? If you try, and it doesn't work, you simply need to pick yourself up and start all over. You are never a failure until and unless you declare defeat. So, don't wait to be fired; go for it.

Why Consider Doing Your "Entrepreneur Thing" in the Left-Out Neighborhoods of the United States or Central and Eastern Europe?

For Jan and Jerome, because of the circumstances, Dallas was the only place to do their entrepreneurial thing. But for many others, options might include being an entrepreneur in the formerly Communist countries of Central and Eastern Europe, or a disadvantaged area of the United States. This presents great challenges, but it can also offer many opportunities. Dealing with an uneven playing field adds significant obstacles to success. It's not for everyone. But some reasons to consider the more challenging opportunities of doing business in these challenging areas include the following:

✦ **Because you were born there.**
  For Gerry Hargitai, Katharine Wittmann, Albert Black, and many others, going home and being an entrepreneur where you were born is the right thing to do. For one thing, you can make a difference for your own culture and your own people. There is also simply a sense of belonging. We all need roots, traditions, and a sense of place. Being involved with where you came from is important. As we say in Texas, "You dance with the one who brung ya."

✦ **Because you want to, and you care.**
  Many people do entrepreneurial things solely for reasons other than making money. Doraja Eberle, Dick Schifter, and

Steve Mariotti are examples of people who truly care. We become better, more connected people when we make a difference in places that need our help. For many entrepreneurs of the heart, going to the more challenging environments of Central and Eastern Europe or the disadvantaged areas of our own communities makes sense.

✦ **Because as a young person, it's easier to break into and be part of the action.**
If you want to be a big fish in a little pond, these challenging areas are the places to go. For Petra Groiss, Kenny Blatt, Gavin Susman, and many others, emerging democracies offered a much easier way to break into the big time, gain responsibility, and quickly make a difference. One thing that has been clear to me is that even a decade after Communism, the CEE region has a real shortage of educated talent in a wide range of areas. Entrepreneurs with a Western business orientation have tremendous opportunities to do things in those markets that they could not do competitively in mainstream America, Western Europe, or similar mature markets.

✦ **Because there is less competition for products and ideas.**
These markets are places where people have less and need more. Ideas and efforts that are highly competitive and often have small margins in the free markets of the world still can find great reception and profitability in challenged areas. For Gerry Hargitai, Kenny Blatt, Gavin Susman, Fahim Tobur, and many others who have chosen these markets instead of the West, the relative scarcity of goods and services has meant better margins, at least for now.

✦ **Because you can take advantage of incentives.**
In both Central and Eastern Europe and the left-out neighborhoods of the United States there are some, though I believe not enough, special incentives for business. If you look for them, you can find special loan and investment programs that benefit business in these areas.

Entrepreneurship Education and Organizations Are on the Rise

Entrepreneurship is hot in the United States, and on a growing basis it's getting hot in Europe and throughout the world. The end of the Cold War has been a catalyst. The advent of the Internet is also a catalyst.

With the growth of entrepreneurship, education of potential entrepreneurs has become popular at all levels. More than 1,400 business colleges in the United States teach entrepreneurship, and many organizations such as the Young President's Organization and the International Executive Service Corps provide educational support to entrepreneurial activities. And entrepreneurial outreach programs for the young are, of course, the purpose of Steve Mariotti's NFTE.

Today, entrepreneurs are able to find organizations that support many of the concepts of this book, including the belief that as an entrepreneur you can make money and make a difference. One such organization is the Social Venture Network. This is an organization that was started in 1987 by Ben Cohen, owner of Ben & Jerry's Ice Cream, Anita Roderick from The Body Shop, and others. This group believes that responsible business can and should be part of leading to positive social change. As a recent new member, while completing final changes on this book, I participated in my first Social Venture Network weekend retreat. I found myself unexpectedly moved by the energy, ideas, and inspiration of this group. A real sense of compassion for others, concern for sustainability of the world, and spirituality are traits all combined within the members of this organization that I met. These included for-profit businesspeople as well as many nonprofit businesspeople. It was clear that for many, this network was more like an extended family. Another global resource for responsible business practices is Business for Social Responsibility. This group was started as a result of ideas that came from a Ralph Nader speech to the Social Venture Network. An eight-year-old organization, this group is essentially an alternative Chamber of Commerce. The group actively seeks companies as members that demonstrate respect for the communities in which they operate.

Entrepreneurship, particularly the practice of responsible entrepreneurism, is being spread through education and reinforced through diverse organizations.

Prosperity Works, But We Need Perspective and Responsibility

Ultimately the desire to make money and the desire to make a difference don't necessarily go hand in hand. But for responsible entrepreneurs, they are often interwoven. And as Doraja Eberle, Ambassador Dick Schifter, Rabbi Arthur Schneier, and Steve Mariotti show us, not all entrepreneurs are about making money.

We are at the edge of a tidal wave of responsible entrepreneurism that could lift uninspired and hopeless communities around the world to a profoundly better existence. Knowledge, gained through entrepreneurship programs and role models, can be a powerful tool for helping people discover whether or not they have an entrepreneur in them.

If we can encourage the discovery of new entrepreneurs and the spread of Responsible Entrepreneurism, the world will benefit. Entrepreneurs who act on this concept—whether in the left out neighborhoods of America, Central and Eastern Europe, or anywhere else—can create positive change. Instead of looking back at what is wrong with the world, we should all look to a future with hope and opportunity for what can be. The future belongs to those who take risks and make things happen while caring about their fellow man. You can be an entrepreneur. You can make a difference. It's never too soon or too late.

Catching Responsible Entrepreneurs

The people in this book have great stories to tell, but they are far from the only examples of responsible entrepreneurs I know. Indeed, my bigger problem at the end of this project was eliminating a number of other very interesting stories of people who are doing extraordinary things.

At first, I was frustrated by not having more time and space to keep writing about the actions of other responsible entrepreneurs. However, the purpose of this book was not to be a complete guide to every responsible entrepreneur, but to begin raising the awareness and understanding of entrepreneurs who are making money and making a difference. It's my hope that The Responsible Entrepreneur Web site described in the following paragraph, and continuing efforts to help coordinate responsible entrepreneurs and publicize their good works, will make this an ongoing means of raising awareness and support a new perspective toward entrepreneurship.

J. R. Ewing is the all-too-often image of entrepreneurs. Indeed, negative myths about entrepreneurs are memorable. Catching somebody doing something wrong is a great pastime. How about if we turn the tables and catch people doing right, leading their lives as responsible entrepreneurs. I have set up a Web site—*www.theresponsibleentrepreneur.org*—and ask anyone and everyone who has stories about responsible entrepreneurs to post them on our bulletin board, so that they can be shared with others on the Web site.

Entrepreneurs are doing responsible things all the time. Take, for example, a letter I received recently from stock fund manager Cappy McGarr. After years of dramatic positive returns for his clients, in the last quarter of 2000, his funds suffered a large loss. In response, he voluntarily amended the partnership agreement to take away his right to incentive fees for three years to help investors recover their loss sooner. These are the kind of stories we want posted on the Web site. Let's see if we can make connections between people to further the dialogue about responsible entrepreneurship. With permission, we will also be seeking to publicize stories of responsible entrepreneurs to get the good news out into the market.

Whatever kind of entrepreneur you are—in business, nonprofit, government, religion, or other walks of life—being a creative, innovative risk taker also should include being dedicated to improving your community. Being a responsible entrepreneur leads to greater prosperity for all and makes the world a better place.

Going Forward —
A Challenge to Each of Us

As I prepared to have this book published, I met with public relations consultants, book marketing experts, and, of course, publishers. Eventually, they each would come around to the question: "What's in it for you?" They would then share with me that most people these days are writing books related to business to increase their speech price, or to encourage more people to attend their seminars, or something else that would be of personal financial benefit. I would then explain that it makes me feel good to think that sharing my ideas about responsible entrepreneurism might help make a positive difference. Maybe it's one person at a time, maybe it's a large policy issue, but any positive difference that can come from this book brings me personal joy and great satisfaction.

In my view, being a responsible entrepreneur is not about being "a good guy" or being charitable, but is principally about believing in and adhering to a level playing field, treating others the way you would want to be treated. It means trying not to take advantage of the edge, even when it is easy to do so. All of this is the main core of what responsible entrepreneurs are and should be. In doing so, this is a major contribution to a better world.

As I have said, to be a responsible entrepreneur, one does not have to engage in charitable endeavors. However, there is still a need for charity, and caring about others is certainly consistent with being a responsible entrepreneur. In that light, I have dedicated to use all my proceeds of this book to fund organizations that help support or promote responsible entrepreneurs. People whom I've met in the Social Venture Network and elsewhere also extend their views beyond merely concern for a level playing field to charitable and other activities. But learning from people who have a lot and do some good for others is only one source.

As we look for opportunities to be charitable, we often can look to our own companies and co-workers. Recently, our receptionist at Hall Financial, Beth Cabrera, was reading an article about a tragic story of a little girl who had been locked in a closet for up to four years. She had tremendous medical costs related to physical and emotional damage. Her tragic situation involved an abusive home life that, once discovered, only started what will be a long route to recovery. Beth wanted to do something.

Beth approached Valerie Reber, Jennifer Graham, and Rebecca Davis, and the four of them, all part of the Hall home office, started to take up a collection for someone they had only read about and with whom they had no other involvement. Soon, a number of people at Hall got involved and made a contribution. I found this to be the same spirit that takes responsible entrepreneurs to that greater next level. We at Hall are now learning from Beth, Valerie, Jennifer, and Rebecca and trying to figure out ways to organize an ongoing program to help other people in our community. I am proud to be associated with the fine group of people that makes up the Hall team.

This is taking the responsible side of business or entrepreneurship to another level. Again, while this goes beyond the fair level playing field part of responsible entrepreneurship, I intend to challenge myself and suggest we all challenge ourselves to consider turning one-time efforts at helping others into ongoing programs to benefit society. Often, it is people who have very little who give the most. Shouldn't we all be doing more for less fortunate people?

My wife, Kathy, and I do try in various ways to help others. We do this with out time as well as our financial support. We do this in a variety of ways that we hope make a difference. I am pleased to find the desire to help others within those with whom I work.

Beth, Valerie, Jennifer, and Rebecca challenged me with their idea to help this unfortunate young girl. Consequently, the company did get involved and helped support their efforts. But more than that, I learned from them. In this sense, I challenge all entrepreneurs to learn from their teams and to help support your communities. The more we can act responsibly and care about each other in whatever manner, the better off we will make our societies. And, in that sense, each of us will be the biggest beneficiary.

APPENDIX

American University in Bulgaria
U.S. Office for Development
and University Relations
1725 K Street, NW411
Washington, DC 20006
Phone: 202-955-1400
Fax: 202-955-1402
Web site: www.augb.bg

Appeal of Conscience Foundation
119 W. 57th Street
New York, NY 10019
Phone: 212-535-5800
Fax: 212-628-2513
E-mail:
appealofconscience@msn.com

**The Bernard & Audre
Rapoport Foundation**
5400 Bosque Boulevard, Suite 245
Waco, TX 76710
Phone: 254-741-0510
Fax: 254-741-0092
Web site: www.rapoportfdn.org

Albert C. Black, Jr.
On-Target Supplies and
Logistics, Ltd.
1133 S. Madison Avenue
Dallas, TX 75208
Phone: 214-941-4885
Fax: 214-942-0265
Web site: www.otsl.com

Kenneth M. Blatt
Euromedia S.A.
17, Dimitri Florescu Street
RO-78338
Bucharest, Romania
Phone: 40-1-224-4010
Fax: 40-1-224-2783
Web site:
www.euromediagroup.ro

Kenneth M. Blatt
K-U, Inc.
P. O. Box 774
Absecon, NJ 08201
Phone: 917-297-5735
Fax: 212-580-9516

Patrick Brandt
Skywire Technology
2401 Internet Boulevard,
  Suite 201
Frisco, TX 75034
Phone: 972-377-1110
Fax: 972-377-1109
Web site:
  www.skywiretechnology.com

California Fitness
4 Life Europe BV
Beurs-World Trade Center
  Rotterdam
P.O. Box 30133
3001 DC Rotterdam
The Netherlands
Phone: 31-10-205-2256
Fax: 31-10-205-5343
E-mail:
  info@california-fitness.com
Web site:
  www.california-fitness.com

Trevor Cornwell
Skyjet
1424 16th Street, NW
Washington, DC 20036
Phone: 202-544-3000
Fax: 202-546-6155
E-mail: trevor@skyjet.com
Web site: www.skyjet.com

Doraja Eberle
Farmers Helping Farmers
  (Bauern Helfen Bauern)
A-5082 Grodig bei Salzburg
Protschhofstrasse 12
Phone: 43-6246-73408
Fax: 43-6246-75867
E-mail: bhb@bhb.sbg.at
Web site: www.bhb.sbg.at

Euromedia S.A.
17, Dimitri Florescu Street
RO-78338
Bucharest, Romania
Phone: 40-1-224-4010
Fax: 40-1-224-2783
Web site:
  www.euromediagroup.ro

**Farmers Helping Farmers
(Bauern Helfen Bauern)**
A-5082 Grodig bei Salzburg
Protschhofstrasse 12
Phone: 43-6246-73408
Fax: 43-6246-75867
E-mail: bhb@bhb.sbg.at
Web site: www.bhb.sbg.at

**Friends of Farmers Helping
Farmers USA**
C/O Captec Financial Group,
  Inc.
P.O. Box 544
Ann Arbor, MI 48106

Craig Hall
Hall Financial Group
6801 Gaylord Parkway,
 Suite 100
Frisco, TX 75034
Phone: 972-377-1100
Fax: 972-377-1171
E-mail:
 craighall@hallfinancial.com
Web site:
 www.hallfinancial.com

Hall Financial Group
6801 Gaylord Parkway,
 Suite 100
Frisco, TX 75034
Phone: 972-377-1100
Fax: 972-377-1171
Web site:
 www.hallfinancial.com

Gerry Hargitai
California Fitness
4 Life Europe BV
Beurs-World Trade Center
 Rotterdam
P.O. Box 30133
3001 DC Rotterdam
The Netherlands
Phone: 31-10-205-2256
Fax: 31-10-205-5343
E-mail:
 info@california-fitness.com
Web site:
 www.california-fitness.com

Steve Mariotti
National Foundation for
 Teaching Entrepreneurship
 (NFTE)
120 Wall Street, 29th Floor
New York, NY 10005
Phone: 212-232-3333
Fax: 212-232-2244
E-mail: stevem@nfte.com
Web site: www.nfte.com

**National Foundation for
Teaching Entrepreneurship
(NFTE)**
120 Wall Street, 29th Floor
New York, NY 10005
Phone: 212-232-3333
Fax: 212-232-2244
E-mail: nfte@nfte.com
Web site: www.nfte.com

Cheryl Newman
Skytech Europe, Kft.
H-1132 Budapest
Vaci ut. 22-24
Phone: 36-1-450-0878
Fax: 36-1-450-0879
E-mail: info@skytech.hu
Web site:
 www.skytecheurope.com

**On-Target Supplies and
Logistics, Ltd.**
1133 S. Madison Avenue
Dallas, TX 75208
Phone: 214-941-4885
Fax: 214-942-0265
Web site: www.otsl.com

Bernard Rapoport
P.O. Box 21900
Waco, TX 76702
Phone: 254-776-9523
Fax: 254-776-9526
E-mail:
brapoport@swlwaco.com

Rabbi Arthur Schneier
Appeal of Conscience
Foundation
119 W. 57th Street
New York, NY 10019
Phone: 212-535-5800
Fax: 212-628-2513
E-mail:
appealofconscience.@msn.com

Skyjet
1424 16th Street, NW
Washington, DC 20036
Phone: 202-544-3000
Fax: 202-546-6155
Web site: www.skyjet.com

Skytech Europe, Kft.
H-1132 Budapest
Vaci ut. 22-24
Phone: 36-1-450-0878
Fax: 36-1-450-0879
E-mail: info@skytech.hu
Web site:
www.skytecheurope.com

Skywire Technology, LLC
2401 Internet Boulevard, Suite 201
Frisco, TX 75034
Phone: 972-377-1110
Fax: 972-377-1109
Web site:
www.skywiretechnology.com

Southeast European Cooperative Initiative
SECI-OSCE Hofburg
Heldenplatz 1
A-1600 Vienna
Phone: 43-1-531-37422
Fax: 43-1-531-37420
Web site: www.unece.org/seci

Young Presidents Organization International
451 S. Decker Drive
Irving, TX 75062
Phone: 972-650-4600
E-mail: askypo@ypo.org
Web site: www.ypo.org

World Presidents Organization
110 S. Union Street, Suite 200
Alexandria, VA 22314
Phone: 703-684-4900
Fax: 703-684-4955

— ✦ —

INDEX

ABOUT THE AUTHOR

Craig Hall is living proof that Responsible Entrepreneurs can make money and make a difference. Craig Hall has had a distinguished career as a successful self-made entrepreneur, author, and civic leader. Most recently, he has dedicated efforts to helping former Communist countries in democratization and transformation of their economies to free markets.

Mr. Hall began his current business in 1968 at age 18, with $4,000 he had saved from small entrepreneurial ventures begun at age 10. By age 21, he was a millionaire. In 1986, his company, Hall Financial Group, was the largest private placement investment sponsor in the U.S., having raised over $1 billion in equity. The company was also the second largest multifamily property owner with over 70,000 apartments. The company's worldwide activities today include real estate, venture capital, wine production, software companies, hotels in Europe, and more.

In recent years, Mr. Hall has been very involved in issues related to Central and Eastern Europe. He has been a consultant to the U.S. State Department. He recently became one of the few Americans to obtain a Graduate Degree in International Studies from the Diplomatic Academy in Vienna, where he focused specifically on post-Cold War transition economies.

Mr. Hall is on the Board of Trustees of the American University in Bulgaria. He is also a member of the World President's Organization and the Social Venture Network. In the past, he chaired an 18-month task force to determine how to revitalize Dallas' inner city neighborhoods, served as director of the Dallas Symphony Orchestra, the Enterprise Foundation Advisory Board and the American-Austrian Fulbright Board.

In 1977, Mr. Hall set up a foundation that has, over the years, given funding to a wide range of charitable organizations. In addition, Mr. Hall and his wife recently donated to Vienna a major sculpture by U.S. artist Joel Shapiro that is placed in front of the U.S. Embassy. He is also putting charitable funds and personal efforts behind increasing Responsible Entrepreneurism in the U.S. and Central and Eastern Europe, including funding a regional Fulbright Distinguished Chair Professorship to lecture on the subject.

An avid lifelong art collector, from 1998 to 2001, he specialized in collecting contemporary art from former Communist Central and Eastern European countries. A portion of his collection was loaned to the Jeu de Paume Museum in Paris in 2000 as part of a show on Central and Eastern European art. He also recently developed and provided the art for a sculpture garden in the Dallas area that showcases Texas artists.

— ✦ —

THE RESPONSIBLE ENTREPRENEUR WEB SITE

It is my hope that the Responsible Entrepreneur Web site described below—and continuing efforts to help coordinate responsible entrepreneurs and publicize their good works—will make this an ongoing means of raising awareness and the beginning of a new perspective toward entrepreneurship.

We spend too much time trying to catch somebody doing something wrong. Let's spend some time catching people doing right. Responsible entrepreneurs are people who are doing something right. The Web site—*www.theresponsibleentrepreneur.org*—is dedicated to celebrating responsible entrepreneurs. I would ask that anyone and everyone who has stories about responsible entrepreneurs post them on our bulletin board, so that they can be shared with others on the Web site.

Entrepreneurs are doing responsible things all the time. Yet, many do so in obscurity. Let's change that. On the Web site, we will offer bulletin boards with various discussion topics related to responsible entrepreneurism so people can exchange ideas. The site will also allow entrepreneurs to post stories about the things they are doing in a responsible manner, or, for the shy or modest types, a place where their friends or business associates can post their stories. There will also be links to many sites of relevance to responsible entrepreneurism. The most engaging entrepreneurial stories will be featured on the Web site and with the profiled entrepreneur's permission, we will also be seeking to publicize their stories of responsible entrepreneurship to get the good news out into the market.

Come visit *www.theresponsibleentrepreneur.org* and learn about responsible entrepreneurism, discuss views with others, explore the stories of responsible entrepreneurs who may be in your town or even your neighborhood, and link to important related sites. Let's try to learn together how we can do well for ourselves and do good for others at the same time.